Flight of the Bön Monks

"*Flight of the Bön Monks* is a magnificent achievement on many levels. Cole and Rice have not only preserved a vital piece of neglected history, but they present this enthralling tale—virtually unknown in the West—in the form of a riveting adventure story as thrilling as any Jack London ever wrote. I fell in love with the heroic Bön monks, the luminous religion they risked their lives to save, and the book that recounts their inspiring story."

Sarah Bird, Texas Literary Hall of Fame inductee and author of *Last Dance on the Starlight Pier*

"This book presents the fascinating life stories of three Bön monks, Yongdzin Tenzin Namdak Rinpoche, Samten Karmay, and Sangye Tenzin, who later became the thirty-third abbot of Menri Monstery, the seat of the Bön religion, the oldest religion of Tibet. The book, however, is much more than stories about their courage and resilience while escaping from war-ravaged Tibet. It is also a highly valuable historical record of the survival and development of Bön in exile. Being an old religion with a small number of followers, Bön has been shrouded in mystery, legends, and misunderstanding. In China, Bön was traditionally referred to as the 'black religion' due to the popular belief that its followers covered their heads with black cloth. Fortunately, through careful and meticulous research, the two authors recorded a new chapter of the ancient Bön religion and present it to general readers in a smooth and catching writing style. Reading this book helped me to better understand Bön religion and enriched my knowledge of the Tibetan diaspora. I am grateful to the authors and congratulate them for a book well written and work well done."

Jianglin Li, author of *Tibet in Agony* and *When the Iron Bird Flies*

"With six decades of going on adventures to wild places, I'm often asked if I have a favorite. The answer is easy—it's the remote, high Changthang Plateau. *Flight of the Bön Monks* will take you there."

RICK RIDGEWAY, AUTHOR OF *THE BIG OPEN: ON FOOT ACROSS TIBET'S CHANG TANG*

"*Flight of the Bön Monks* is a riveting tale, skillfully layered with despair, adventure, terror, and hope, but ultimately a story of human triumph. This emotionally powerful book isn't just a chronicle of courage, it is a poignant reminder of why Tibet needs to stay in our collective conscience."

ELIOT PATTISON, AUTHOR OF THE INSPECTOR SHAN SERIES AND THE BONE RATTLER SERIES

"Before Buddhism came to Tibet, the indigenous Bön culture had flourished for millennia, and much of what we know today as Tibetan Vajrayana Buddhism has been directly influenced by that culture. So when the Chinese decided that it was in their best interests to eradicate religion from the Tibetan plateau, the Bön suffered every bit as grievously as the Buddhists. *Flight of the Bön Monks* tells the remarkable story of bravery confronted by darkness; it outlines the escape from Tibet of several of the most senior and important Bön monks and how they have courageously kept their religion alive even though they were so rudely expelled from their native land. A story for our troubled times that needs to be told and needs to be read."

WILL JOHNSON, AUTHOR OF *BREATHING THROUGH THE WHOLE BODY* AND *THE SAILFISH AND THE SACRED MOUNTAIN*

FLIGHT OF THE BÖN MONKS

War, Persecution, and the Salvation of Tibet's Oldest Religion

A Sacred Planet Book

Harvey Rice and Jackie Cole

Destiny Books
Rochester, Vermont

Destiny Books
One Park Street
Rochester, Vermont 05767
www.DestinyBooks.com

Destiny Books is a division of Inner Traditions International

Sacred Planet Books are curated by Richard Grossinger, Inner Traditions editorial board member and cofounder and former publisher of North Atlantic Books. The Sacred Planet collection, published under the umbrella of the Inner Traditions family of imprints, includes works on the themes of consciousness, cosmology, alternative medicine, dreams, climate, permaculture, alchemy, shamanic studies, oracles, astrology, crystals, hyperobjects, locutions, and subtle bodies.

Cataloging-in-Publication Data for this title is available from the Library of Congress

ISBN 978-1-64411-858-0 (print)
ISBN 978-1-64411-859-7 (ebook)

Printed and bound in the United States by Lake Book Manufacturing, LLC.

10 9 8 7 6 5 4 3 2 1

Text design and layout by Kenleigh Manseau
This book was typeset in Garamond Premier Pro with Etna used as display typeface

To send correspondence to the author of this book, mail a first-class letter to the author c/o Inner Traditions • Bear & Company, One Park Street, Rochester, VT 05767, and we will forward the communication, or contact the author directly at **flightofthebonmonks.com**.

This work is dedicated to Yongdzin Tenzin Namdak Rinpoche, Samten Karmay, and the late thirty-third abbot of Menri Monastery, His Holiness Lungtok Tenpai Nyima, known in this book as Sangye Tenzin. They teach us by example how to live our lives.

May all beings benefit.

Contents

THE DALAI LAMA

FOREWORD

This book, *Flight of the Bön Monks*, tells the story of the escape to freedom of three individuals, one of whom was Menri Trizin Sangyé Tenzin, who played key roles in re-establishing the Tibetan Bön tradition in exile.

Despite our sincere efforts at peaceful co-existence, the Chinese authorities in Lhasa were intent on crushing any form of resistance. This led to the Tibetan people's uprising of 1959, which in turn forced me and tens of thousands of Tibetans to escape into exile.

Regardless of the challenges of being uprooted from our homeland, we have been able to establish a firm foundation for the survival of our identity and culture in India, primarily with the generous support and encouragement of the Government of India. As this book explains, the comparatively small Bönpo community in exile is a clear example of this success.

Although I often speak of how Tibetans have kept alive the ancient Indian traditions of study and practice upheld at Nalanda University, the pre-Buddhist Bön tradition adds a distinct Tibetan quality. I am confident that readers will appreciate the efforts that authors Harvey Rice and Jackie Cole have made to shed light on the Tibetan Bönpo religious tradition.

28 April 2023

Prologue

A Deadly Encounter at 15,000 Feet

Fear hastened Tenzin Namdak to the top of a rocky ridge, one of the many that crisscross Tibet's highest plateau. A frigid wind whipped his face as he scanned the treeless, rocky landscape, searching for a glimpse of the Chinese troops who hunted him and his companions. He knew the soldiers would shoot them on sight.

The year was 1960. The Chinese had invaded Tibet a decade earlier and cajoled it into surrender with promises of respect for its religion and culture. Forsaken by the rest of the world, its military severely outmatched, Tibet had grudgingly agreed to allow China to station troops in its capital, Lhasa. But Chinese Communism was incompatible with the deeply religious Tibetan culture. Popular resentment swelled, finally exploding in a violent uprising. In retaliation, the Chinese began a vicious campaign of religious persecution.

Tenzin, thirty-four, one of the most revered lamas of the Bön religion, Tibet's oldest and least-known faith, was among thousands of Tibetans fleeing the country to avoid Chinese reeducation sessions, where they were forced to accuse, beat, and even execute neighbors and family members in a campaign targeting religion and class. Chinese troops were dispatched to seal the borders and hunt Tibetans fleeing to Nepal, India, and Bhutan.

Tenzin hoped to outpace his pursuers as he headed west across Tibet's bleakest and least populated terrain. Strung out along the trail with Tenzin were thirty companions, among them the most learned Bön lamas. Others were monks who had renounced their vows of nonviolence in order to protect the lamas. The lamas and their escorts had traveled hundreds of miles from several different monasteries to Tenzin's small, remote monastery on the Changthang Plateau, a vast and desolate landscape of high plains and mountains thinly populated by nomadic herders. In this time of crisis they looked to Tenzin for direction because of his eminent reputation. They would have lost that leadership had he taken an offer of safe passage from a wealthy merchant making his way to the border, who told stories of Chinese cruelty and brought news that the Dalai Lama had fled the country. The merchant had urged Tenzin to leave with him, but Tenzin would not forsake his fellow monks. Disregarding his own safety, he had resolved to await word from the lamas who, unbeknownst to him, were dodging Chinese patrols as they made their way to him.

Tenzin and the lamas had set out three days earlier, joined by dozens of lay Tibetans and a group of armed rebels. Tenzin divided them into three groups. Each group would travel within sight of the others, allowing the others to flee if one group was attacked. Heading west, they changed direction whenever they spotted the black yak-hair tents of nomads or their flocks of sheep; they knew that fear or Chinese silver could induce the nomads to betray their fellow Tibetans.

The monks carried the few sacred texts and artifacts they had been able to rescue from their monasteries before they were looted by Chinese troops. Tenzin carried the most sacred object: a six-hundred-year-old reliquary containing the ashes of the founder of Bön's premier monastery. The artifacts were mere slivers of a culture under assault by the Chinese. Soldiers were torturing and killing monks, razing temples and destroying texts, statues, and paintings. Tenzin's world was being ripped apart. Escape was the only way to ensure the monks' survival and the survival of Bön itself.

Their only escape route was across the daunting Himalayas that lay south of the vast plateau. In Sanskrit, *Himalaya* means "the abode of snow." The Himalayas would be the final abode for untold numbers of Tibetans as they died from hunger, cold, avalanches, and steep plunges from rocky heights during their long trek to freedom.

Moving as fast as possible, members of Tenzin's party continually cast wary eyes behind them. As the cold blue sky faded toward darkness, the monks made camp in the shadow of a mountain at the edge of a lake, tethering their pack animals and pitching their tents. While the animals were being unloaded, a black donkey reared and snorted, refusing to be handled. Tenzin saw it as a dark portent. As the monks crouched around the campfire, heating water for black tea, the crack of a single bullet rent the air. The men bolted upright in alarm. The shot grew to a fusillade as the Tibetans scattered. Streams of green tracer bullets licked at scurrying figures, pitching them onto the earth. Tenzin ran for his life.

1
Beginnings

Tibet is the highest land mass on Earth, more than two miles above sea level, and spans an area the size of Western Europe. The Tibetan Plateau is one of the most inaccessible terrains in the world, a rugged highland girdled by the highest mountains on the planet. Within the isolating ring of mountains, one million square miles of plateau soar to an average elevation of 15,000 feet.[1]

Tenzin's birthplace, the village of Khyungpo Karu, lay near the eastern boundary of the soaring Tibetan Plateau in the province of Kham. The tiny community sat among hills covered with dense, dark forests on the northern slopes, and meadows sprinkled with small clusters of trees on the sunlit southern slopes.[2]

In the summer, swaths of primulas, edelweiss, and daisies carpeted the meadows like snow. Pika and rabbits darted among the rocks, and Tibetan gazelle and musk deer gamboled on the hillsides. At higher elevations the meadows and forest gave way to rocky inclines, home to blue sheep and the elusive snow leopard.

Kham lay on the mountainous frontier with China, a jealous neighbor that over the centuries had often attempted to dominate Tibet with varying degrees of success. At points in history Tibet did the dominating, as evidenced by a large ethnic Tibetan population on the Chinese side of the border. As Tibetan and Chinese sovereigns performed their centuries-old diplomatic and military dance, neither had threatened to eradicate the other's religions. The ascent of the Chinese Communists would change that unwritten rule.

Khampas, as residents of Kham are called, were governed in principle by the central government in Lhasa, the world's highest capital city at 12,000 feet. At the time of Tenzin's birth, Lhasa was home to the Thirteenth Dalai Lama (1876–1933), the supreme Tibetan Buddhist authority. Lhasa, which translates as "Place of Gods," was the religious as well as political center of Tibet. However, Lhasa lay nearly a thousand miles to the west of its eastern provinces, so remote that Khampas ignored the central government's commands when convenient. In contrast to Lhasa's loose control over its distant provinces, the Dalai Lama's spiritual authority penetrated deeply into the lives of Khampas. Although Tenzin's family and their neighbors were Bönpos, as practitioners of the Bön religion are known, they nevertheless saw the Dalai Lama as the supreme spiritual and temporal authority.

The Dalai Lama was a man of peace, but the Khampas were renowned for their fighting prowess. A Khampa was rarely seen without a sword at his waist and a firearm slung across his back, usually a bolt-action rifle or an ancient muzzleloader with a folding bipod to steady its long barrel. The province was notorious for its bandits and feuds. Khampa men were taught to fight in the incessant clashes between families and tribes, which often flared for rather obscure reasons. This warlike way of life is reflected in a popular maxim:

> A blow on the nose of a hated enemy,
> Is surely more satisfying,
> Than listening to the advice
> Of benevolent parties.[3]

For most boys from Kham, the way of the warrior was a natural inheritance. Not for Tenzin. According to tradition, even as an infant he exuded a remarkable sense of calming peace. Before his birth his mother dreamed of receiving a scripture from a white-robed, white-haired yogi who told her, "This is your Bön destiny. Take good care of it!"[4] Born in the Tibetan Year of the Fire Tiger, 1926, into a family of seminomads, Tenzin was an only child, an oddity in a culture where large families were the norm. Except for the aristocracy, Tibetans at the time of Tenzin's birth had no family names. Monks typically named newborns, often bestowing their own names. Tenzin's birth name was Chime Yungdrung, meaning "eternal life." His name would be prophetically changed to Tenzin Namdak, meaning "pure holder of the teachings," after he took his vows to become a monk.

Like other seminomadic families in the region, some of Tenzin's extended family farmed while others roamed with herds of livestock. The farm relied on the few hardy grains and vegetables—wheat, chiles, mustard, and peas—that could survive the cold weather and short growing season at high altitudes. But their most important crop was barley, a grain so central to Tibetan life that it is part of the national identity. Roasted and ground barley is called *tsampa* and is the most widely eaten food in Tibet. Consumed by Tibetans since before recorded history, this staple food is packed with carbohydrates, protein, fiber, and minerals. Tsampa flour is digested easily and provides quick energy when eaten raw or mixed with water, making it ideal for travelers. Tenzin ate tsampa at nearly every meal, pouring a small amount of salted tea into a wooden bowl, adding yak butter, then tsampa, before mixing it into a paste with his fingers and rolling it into bite-sized balls.

The consumption of tsampa is a common denominator in a vast country where customs, dialects, dress, and religion vary across regions. The term *tsampa eaters* has been used to identify Tibetans and rally them in times of crisis.[5] Tsampa is so integral to Tibetan life that it is woven into both Bön and Buddhist religious practices. Small painted figures are molded from tsampa dough for use in religious rituals, meditation, mantras, and songs. Handfuls of tsampa flour are tossed in the air as offerings to the deities when celebrating almost any joyful occasion, from births to weddings. Lamas hand out tiny balls of sugared tsampa as a blessing on sacred occasions.

Tenzin's father, Drepo Padang, likely used a *dzo,* a cross between a yak and an ox, to plow his fields. The family lived on what the herd animals and a small plot produced, trading any surplus for cloth, wooden and leather goods, and other necessities. The household consisted of Tenzin's mother, Dongza Gachung, his father, his father's sister, and two of his father's four brothers. His father's other two brothers were monks at Tengchen Monastery, near the regional capital of Tengchen. In accordance with Tibetan custom, Tenzin's mother was married to all three brothers in the household. In theory, all three were husbands in every sense, but typically one husband would take precedence. Monogamy was more common, but polyandry allowed poorer families to keep their land from being divided among brothers.

The extended family lived in a typical Tibetan two-story farmhouse of rammed earth and stone, the first floor for livestock and the second for the family. While Tenzin's father worked the farm, another brother, Dachoe Pasang, tended the livestock, following the sheep and yaks as they grazed their way across the rugged landscape. The remaining brother, referred to as "the naughty one," was seldom home and contributed little to the family income.[6] Tenzin's mother and aunt collected dry yak dung for fuel, hauled water, cooked, milked yaks, and spun yarn from balls of yak hair and sheep wool. They tended their small Bön shrine with the customary five offerings: butterlamps, water bowls, flowers, small pieces of cake, and perhaps a bell or conch shell. In most Tibetan homes, Bönpo and Buddhist alike, a portrait of the Dalai Lama hung over the shrine.

When Tenzin was four, his father fell victim to a mysterious malady, probably leprosy, and left the family to shield them from the disease. He spent his final days on pilgrimages to some of the hundreds of sacred sites that dot the Tibetan landscape. His illness left Tenzin's mother alone, emotionally and socially isolated. She had a strong bond with Tenzin's father but lacked connection with her other two husbands, his brothers. She was very young, and at her parents' insistence returned to their home after her favorite husband's death.

Tibetan tradition dictates that when a marriage dissolves, sons live with the family of the father and daughters with the family of the mother. Custom thus decreed that Tenzin remain under the care of his livestock-tending uncle Dachoe, who legally was also his father. Too young to understand, Tenzin cried inconsolably, longing for his mother.

Tenzin's uncle Dachoe, devout but simple and illiterate, was left alone to work the farm, care for the livestock, and provide for his sister and small nephew. Although he strained under the burden, he was always kind to Tenzin. Tending the roving flocks and working the farm at the same time proved impossible though, and the ground soon lay fallow. Food was often scarce, and they sometimes went days without tsampa. "Ah, things were really quite difficult sometimes," Tenzin recalled decades later.

In the mornings Tenzin helped his aunt catch yak calves so they could be fed. The calves would sometimes push Tenzin aside and run away, his impatient aunt shouting at him for his failure. Often, Dachoe put Tenzin in charge of watching over lambs in a small thatched hut. One day Tenzin saw what he thought was a wolf among the lambs. Terrified, he ran, crying and shouting that a wolf was killing the lambs. His shouting attracted the attention of the neighbors' fierce dog, who savagely attacked the running boy. The dog bit into Tenzin's thick woolen coat, tearing it to pieces. A neighbor pulled the dog off the boy before Tenzin was injured. Dachoe arrived and ran to the hut. Much to the boy's chagrin, instead of a wolf he found a harmless fox.

Tenzin longed for his mother. One day, overhearing his aunt and uncle chat, he learned that his mother was living in a nearby town, Tengchen Kha. The next day, forsaking his chores, he set off for Tengchen Kha in the hope of finding her. The farther he walked, the more alone he felt and the more fearful he became. He had never been so far from home on his own. Swallowing his fear, he asked directions from passersby and eventually made it to Tengchen Kha. In such a small community it was easy to find someone who knew his mother and could take him to her. Upon seeing her son, Gachung scooped him into her arms and held him tightly, tears dampening her cheeks. She lamented his tattered clothing and shoes, so worn that his feet were bleeding. She cried as she washed and soothed her son's feet. Nevertheless, the joy of their reunion could not withstand tradition, which dictated that Tenzin return to his uncle, who soon arrived to claim his wayward nephew.

Even without the burden of maintaining the farm, the strain proved too much for Tenzin's uncle and his health deteriorated. When his uncle died, Tenzin lost yet another caregiver. What happened to his aunt is unclear, but according to tradition she would have remained alone on the farm or been supported by a monastery. Within three years, Tenzin had been separated from his mother and lost both his father and his uncle.

The obligation to care for Tenzin, now seven, passed to one of his monk uncles, Talsang Tsultrim. Talsang was the *omze,* or chant leader, at nearby Tengchen Monastery, a red, seven-story building built in 1110 on a mountainside. His uncle Talsang brought him to the monastery, leading him up the wide stone staircase that rose steeply to a portico supported by seven scarlet pillars. The boy gawked in wonder as they passed the glittering statue of the many-armed deity Palpa Phurbu, the figure's body forming the shape of a ceremonial dagger.

Tenzin had few belongings aside from his clothes, making it easy to find a space for him in his uncle's spartan quarters, equipped with a brazier for cooking and a straw-stuffed sleeping mat. "My uncle, the chant leader of the monastery, was very good to me," Tenzin would recall.

> During the daytime he would sit in his square meditation seat and let me sit in there with him to keep warm. He was there day and night, and when the time came to sleep, he would lay me next to

him on a small goatskin. When I woke up in the morning I would find myself some distance from him. I suppose he would carry me there while I was sleeping, but I didn't like being away from him and would start to cry. So he would let me stay next to him again. In the morning, my uncle would give me some tsampa in a bowl. He would give me four sentences of scripture to learn a day, then he would give me the tsampa. When he was performing rituals, he would let me make the *torma* offerings [cakes made of tsampa]. You are supposed to go outside and throw the torma high into the air, but I just tossed them a short distance into the air so that they landed by the door. Then after replacing the plate on the altar, I'd go and collect them up to eat later. He knew what I was doing, but he never said anything. I was always hungry, but I was really very happy. This was a very good time for me.[7]

The monks taught him to read and write, life-changing skills in a country where literacy was rare. He also became more acquainted with the Bön religion, properly known as Yungdrung Bön, translated as "Eternal Bön."

In Tibet, only monks concerned themselves with meditation or knowledge of religious texts. Even so, religion was knit into the everyday life in the form of ceremonies and prayers. Nearly all Tibetans chanted mantras, sacred syllables recited to various deities for blessings, as they went about their daily chores. Every Tibetan had a *mala,* a string of 108 prayer beads similar to a rosary, that they fingered to count the recited mantras. Every morning seven bowls of water were placed on the family altar as an offering to the deities, after which family members prostrated three times before the altar. Wives burned food offerings to appease mischievous spirits that could damage crops with disease and drought. In the evening, as soon as it became dark, wives would prepare tsampa soup—tsampa boiled with cheese and, when available, a few chunks of meat or bone. After eating, the family would recite a mantra before retiring.

Now Tenzin's monk uncles exposed him to the history and philosophical underpinnings of Yungdrung Bön and introduced him to the intricate rituals undertaken only by monks. Bön rituals had been so much a part of his life that he had never given them much thought, but now he realized that the monastery was custodian of a rich history and spiritual knowledge far more profound and broader than he knew.

He learned that Bön was founded around eighteen thousand years ago by Tonpa Shenrab Miwoche, a noble from the ancient kingdom of Zhang Zhung. In Bön literature, Tonpa Shenrab is regarded as a buddha much like Shakyamuni, the founder of Buddhism. Shakyamuni was also known as Siddhartha Gautama, who lived from 566 to 485 BCE. Although centuries apart, their lives had many similarties. Both renounced the world, took monastic vows, and taught a path to enlightenment, or buddhahood. Tenzin was heartened to learn that just like Tonpa Shenrab, Shakyamuni, and other masters, he too could, in his lifetime, become a buddha—an enlightened being—by realizing the state of pure consciousness of wisdom and compassion. According to a Bön saying, "There are as many buddhas as stars in the sky."

The founder of Bön, Tonpa Shenrab, spread Yungdrung Bön throughout Zhang Zhung, thought to have been centered in what is now western Tibet, near Mount Kailash, and extending as far west as Persia. According to Bön texts, he made a single trip to Tibet, then a small country bordering Zhang Zhung, persuading Tibetans to abandon their shamanistic religion of bloody sacrifices for Yungdrung Bön. After Tonpa Shenrab's visit, Bön became the dominant religion in Tibet and remained so until Buddhism shouldered it aside. As Tibet expanded into an empire, Buddhism gained its first foothold when the ousted ruler of Nepal, King Narendradeva, asked the Tibetan king, Songtsen Gampo, for sanctuary in the seventh century. While in Lhasa, Narendradeva employed Nepalese architects and artisans to build Tibet's first Buddhist temple, the Jokhang. Buddhism edged further into the royal court with Songtsen's marriage, for diplomatic purposes, to a Chinese princess. She brought the first statue of Shakyamuni Buddha, which was placed in the Jokhang. As Buddhism increasingly gained favor at court, Songtsen continued annexing territory, extending Tibet far beyond the Tibetan Plateau to include vast areas of China and the remnants of Zhang Zhung.

Although Buddhism was by now the court religion, it was regarded with hostility by the populace. Nevertheless, King Trisong Detsen, the thirty-eighth king of Tibet, declared Buddhism the official religion in the 780s. The king was impressed by Buddhism's rational approach to the world and its powerful political and cultural influence in countries bordering Tibet. Bön lacked such international influence.

The official declaration of Buddhism as the national religion led to the suppression of Bön. Tibetan monarchs who adopted the religion for political reasons often ignored the fundamental Buddhist precepts of compassion and nonviolence and persecuted Bönpos in the eighth and ninth centuries. Buddhist scholars wrote diatribes falsely portraying Bönpos as practicing a savage and bloody religion—misinformation parroted by Western scholars. To avoid inquisition and forced conversion, some Bönpos hid in caves, where they secreted their religious artifacts.

Hidden Bön texts began to be discovered in the tenth century, eventually fueling a resurgence of interest in Yungdrung Bön. Some modern scholars believe Yungdrung Bön evolved out of Buddhism, and some view the two religions as virtually identical. Other scholars believe that Bön consisted of traditional rituals unconnected to any organized religion before Buddhism arrived. Bönpos insist that Yungdrung Bön has been practiced in its current form since its establishment by Tonpa Shenrab some eighteen thousand years ago.

Although many Buddhists disparage Bön, scholars believe Tibetan Buddhism took on its unique character by absorbing certain elements of ancient Bön practices, such as prayer flags, smoke offerings, and fire ceremonies, to adapt to the peculiarities of Tibetan culture. These adaptations made Tibetan Buddhism distinct from the forms of Buddhism practiced in other countries. Bön and Buddhism, as practiced in Tibet, became so similar that it is difficult to know which borrowed from the other. Bönpos believe that Shakyamuni—Siddhartha Gautama, the Indian prince who became the Buddha some 2,500 years ago—was taught by a disciple of the founder of Bön, Tonpa Shenrab.

Ngawang Lobsang Gyatso (1617–1682), known as the "Great Fifth" Dalai Lama, studied Bön, as he did the doctrines of differing Buddhist schools, issuing an edict in 1679 that recognized Bön as an official religion. A copy of the edict is inscribed on a wall in the White Palace, a building in the eastern section of the Potala, the Dalai Lama's thousand-room winter residence that looms over Lhasa from its perch on the side of Red Hill. After the Fifth Dalai Lama's death, persecution resumed, and many Bönpos were forcibly converted to Buddhism. Bön remained stigmatized by many Buddhists until 1977, when the present Fourteenth Dalai Lama reinstated it as an official religion.[8]

It's likely that Tenzin learned much from his uncles about the fraught relations between Bön and Buddhism. Most of his instruction, however, focused on the philosophical foundations of Bön. His monk uncle taught Tenzin that desire, anger, and ignorance of the mind's true nature cause unhappiness and suffering, that our current situation results from our previous actions, and only our actions can change our situation for the better. To avoid the suffering that causes unhappiness and realize enlightenment, true peace must be discovered within each practitioner. Such a discovery is done through meditation and purifying negative thoughts caused by the five poisons: anger, desire, ignorance, jealousy, and pride. As Bön teacher Geshe Nyima Dakpa Rinpoche puts it, "We can be like a lotus flower, which is beautiful even though it is growing in the mud. Its beauty is never affected by its surroundings. . . . By applying the teachings to our everyday practice, we are not affected by the poisons of this world."[9]

Decades later, long after he acquired the titles Yongdzin, "teacher," and Rinpoche, "precious one," Tenzin would give his core instruction:

> Your own mind is the root of both happiness and suffering; knowing how to train it in the positive way, that is the basis for happiness. Merely following the passions of your mind, that is the basis for the ocean of miseries and sufferings. Thus, if you know how to choose the right way, you are an excellent person.[10]

In Yungdrung Bön, like Tibetan Buddhism, there is no worship of a supreme being who controls the universe or grants enlightenment. Bön founder Tonpa Shenrab is considered a teacher, not a god. Like Buddhism, Bön has a pantheon of deities who offer support in daily life and in the pursuit of enlightenment. These deities serve as spiritual guides. Envisioning deities during meditation assists the practitioner in achieving understanding and enlightenment. For example, one of the deities most revered by Bönpos is the goddess Sherab Chamma, the "Wisdom Loving Mother." Sherab Chamma is considered the mother of all enlightened ones and the source of all love, wisdom, and compassion. Bönpos pray to her to help overcome the problems of everyday life, such as infertility, personal conflicts, illness, and untimely death. Tenzin and his family chanted the Sherab Chamma mantra every day.

Tenzin was also taught to recognize the reality of impermanence, a fundamental Bön doctrine. Everything changes; everyone dies. The terminal illness of his father and the death of his herder uncle were harsh lessons in impermanence. Tenzin was consoled by the knowledge that they would reincarnate. According to Bön doctrine, all unenlightened sentient beings, animal and human, are reborn after death. The cycle of rebirth connects all living creatures, and one form of being may be reincarnated as another, depending on its actions, or karma. Everyone has reincarnated so many times that all sentient beings are interconnected. This interconnectedness makes Bönpos averse to killing other sentient beings, as they could be killing a relative, even their mother. Escaping the cycle of death, rebirth, and the suffering that goes along with it can be done only by realizing enlightenment. Devout Bönpos would never swat a pestering fly or step on a cockroach, but their aversion to killing did not make them strict vegetarians. The slaughter and butchering of animals was left to the poor who could not make a living through other means and who often belonged to a reviled class, the *ragyabpa*. Ragyabpa were sometimes called "body breakers" because they also performed sky burials: dismembering corpses and leaving them to be devoured by Himalayan griffon and lammergeier vultures. Sky burial was a practical way to dispose of bodies, which Tibetans considered nothing more than empty vessels, in a terrain where the ground often was too hard or rocky for graves, and timber too scarce and too valuable for cremation fires.

Tenzin's religious education at the monastery was interrupted in 1935 when he was nine by the death of his monk uncle, Talsang. With the remaining two uncles on his paternal side unwilling or incapable of caring for him, he was reunited with his mother. He lived with her for about a year before moving in with his maternal grandfather, Dongdo Buga, in the nearby village of Khyungpo Tengchen. His mother remarried and moved in with her new husband in another village. Tenzin, uncomfortable with his mother's new husband, seldom saw her.

His new life with his maternal grandparents opened a fresh phase in Tenzin's education. Tenzin's grandfather, Dongdo Buga, was a well-known and highly regarded painter, the patriarch of an artist family. Tenzin's mother, her two sisters, and three brothers were descendants of the senior Dongdo, Dongdo Buga's father and one of Tibet's most esteemed painters. His fame gave his family aristocratic status and allowed his lineage to carry his name. The family was renowned for its painting acumen. According to tradition, one of Tibet's most revered holy men deemed paintings of divinities by Dongdo's family lineage so perfect that they did not need the typical consecration required of other such paintings. Dongdo senior was famous for his paintings on the walls inside the prestigious Yungdrungling Monastery in central

Tibet that he produced in the nineteenth century. Tenzin was expected to take up the family trade and learn the art of painting, a skill that would help him throughout life and gave him the opportunity to study at one of the most revered Bön monasteries.[11] Although his painting abilities would unlock doors, he would need courage and determination to force them open.

2
An Artist Becomes a Monk

When Tenzin turned eleven, his maternal uncle Tshering Yangphel helped him master the skills he needed before being allowed to apply his first brushstroke on the walls of a monastery or shrine. Hour after hour he practiced, drawing figures in proper proportions, using a stylus on an oiled black wooden board smeared with ashes to give it a white surface. The room was cold and his hands became so dry that they sometimes bled.

A year later he joined sixty artists at the Yungdrung Palri Monastery (not to be confused with Yungdrungling Monastery) in the village of Gogum, Kham, where Tshering had been commissioned to paint frescoes. To prepare the uneven surface of the mud walls, Tenzin learned to mix a blend of chopped straw, partially sieved clay, and a slurry of cow dung. He flung the mixture onto the walls, then smoothed it with his hands. After it dried, he repeated the process at least twice. Next came a layer of river sand, small pebbles, and yellow clay; another layer of fine sand, yellow clay, and a greenish-brown clay; a fourth layer of light beige clay; and a final layer of fine white clay mixed with animal glue and *chang,* Tibetan beer made from barley. Once dry, the surface was painstakingly polished to a glasslike smoothness.

Once the surface was prepared, the artists turned to making rich colors drawn from elements of the Tibetan landscape to infuse into their paint. Tenzin learned to create richly hued blues and greens by washing and scrubbing azurite and malachite that came from copper mines in central Tibet, then grinding them in water. He made deep vermillion with red crystals of cinnabar, a mercury-bearing mineral from China. Black was made from soot or charcoal; white from chalk, lime, bone, or bone ash; an intense yellow from trisulfide of arsenic, sometimes found in hotsprings; and a more subdued yellow from limonite. The colors prepared, he learned to diagram his paintings in charcoal before filling in the lines with the vivid hues.

Tshering also taught Tenzin how to create *thankas,* religious images painted on cotton or silk that can be hung or rolled up for storage or transport. He taught him how to stretch cloth on a wooden frame and coat its surface with a mixture of animal wax and calcite powder before painting the intricate figures of various deities.

After three years of apprenticeship, Tenzin was deemed competent enough to be included in a group of sixty-one artists invited to paint the walls of a new temple. At thirteen he was the youngest artist and eager to assist in such an important project. His uncle Tshering was in charge and, unimpressed by Tenzin's level of artistry, assigned him a dark corner of the temple where his painting would be least open to public view. The treatment by his uncle contrasted sharply with the high regard others showed Tenzin. Most of his elders considered him precocious at everything he attempted. His uncle seemed to think otherwise and would try to block Tenzin's advancement whenever he could.

One day as Tenzin mixed pigments in warm animal glue in preparation for applying them to a wall, the monastery's abbot, Zopa Gyaltshen Rinpoche, entered the temple. He watched Tenzin paint awhile before declaring, "This child is special. He will be of benefit to our teaching."[1] The abbot's pronouncement was significant because Zopa Rinpoche was regarded as a great master, respected for his depth of knowledge. Every day thereafter Zopa Rinpoche would arrive at the monastery as Tenzin and his uncle were preparing to paint. As Tenzin worked, the abbot sprinkled him with blessing water before reading the biographies of great Bön spiritual leaders of the past and regaling him with colorful stories of his travels to India and other countries. The boy absorbed the stories with fascination. "These stories were so interesting and so inspiring that sometimes I would lose my concentration on my work and drop my paints everywhere," Tenzin said.[2] The stories kindled a yearning within Tenzin to become a holy man, wander distant lands and seek enlightenment. He would later credit Zopa Rinpoche with inspiring him to devote his life to religion.

Tenzin began reading deeply from Bön texts. At age fifteen he went alone on a pilgrimage to visit remote places where Bön masters had isolated themselves in meditation. He meditated in caves and by the sides of lakes and rivers as had Bön masters before him, entering into a mental state of clarity, devoid of emotion and desire.

That same year, 1939, the Year of the Earth Rabbit, a monk arrived in Khyungpo Tengchen from distant Yungdrungling Monastery, the most prestigious abbey in the Bön religion after Menri Monastery. The monk, Mongyal Nyerpa, was visiting his hometown, but he had an important mission to accomplish as well. He had recently overseen the construction of a new hundred-pillar temple at Yungdrungling Monastery. The walls of the new temple needed to be adorned with symbols, illustrations of the deities, and portraits of renowned masters. Monastery officials wanted the work done by the best Bönpo painters in Tibet. The monk knew that the best painters were in his hometown. His mission was to hire from the Dongdo family of artists. A hundred years earlier, the patriarch of the family, Dongdo himself, had painted the original Yungdrungling temple, and so it was only fitting that his descendents should paint the new one. The family agreed to a contract, and Tenzin's uncle, Tshering, was placed in charge of organizing a crew of seven painters. Tenzin longed to travel to Yungdrungling and escape the monotony of life in Tengchen, but his uncle told him that he was too young and inexperienced. "Why on earth should you come?" Tshering asked. "You don't know how to paint."[3] Defying his uncle, Tenzin went directly to the Yungdrungling monk who had contracted the Dongdo family. Tenzin's charisma and persuasion proved irresistible, and the monk agreed to hire him. By defying his uncle, Tenzin was defying tradition. This was a direct challenge to an elder. As Tenzin's elder, Uncle Tshering felt a familial right and obligation to oversee Tenzin. From his uncle's perspective Tenzin was flouting his rightful authority.

Miffed at being outmaneuvered, Uncle Tshering took the unusual step of appealing to Tenzin's mother, convincing her that at fifteen Tenzin was too young to go. Tenzin learned of his mother's decision from his uncle, but the boy would not be swayed. As reports of her son's intransigence filtered back to her, she realized the flimsiness of her authority and began to worry that he would run away. She finally decided that it was better for him to go with the other painters from his village than leave on his own. Over the objections of her brother, Tenzin's uncle, his mother finally gave her permission. Because Tenzin had been hired directly by the contracting monk there was nothing Uncle Tshering could do to expel him, so he grudgingly accepted Tenzin and began making preparations for the trip.

Tenzin and the seven other painters, their belongings loaded on several yaks and a single horse, traveled along narrow mountain trails, through alpine meadows ablaze with wildflowers and past snow-fed lakes of shimmering turquoise. The journey took more than a month, as they climbed through rugged mountain passes cloaked in year-round snow, passing within sight of Namcha Barwa, at 24,900 feet one of the world's highest mountains. Finally they descended to the valley of the Yarlung Tsangpo, the longest river in Tibet, and followed it upriver until they reached Yungdrungling Monastery, its new gilt-roofed temple gleaming amid a cluster of monastic buildings about 130 miles west of Lhasa, near the north bank of the river.

After being shown their accommodations and settling in, they got to work preparing the walls. First they coated and smoothed the surfaces before layering them in a deep, vibrant red and drawing intricate designs to be painted in bold shades of gold, green, red, and yellow. In the assembly hall, the artists depicted scenes from the life of a great holy man, Nangzhig Dawa Gyaltsen, on the wall behind the abbot's throne. On the other walls they illustrated Bön deities.

One morning the painters found the door to their quarters locked from the outside. They heard shouting and gunshots. A violent takeover of the monastery was underway, led by four monks who had become wealthy traders on the side. The monks had borrowed money from the monastery to capitalize their venture. Their business flourished and they owned a hundred yaks to carry grain to trade for wool and butter. The monk merchants were angered when Mongyal Nyerpa, the monk who had hired Tenzin, confronted them about their failure to repay the loan. The monastery needed the money to complete the new temple. They refused to repay the loan, and savagely beat Mongyal Nyerpa and other monk officials. They locked down the entire monastery and mounted four machine guns atop key buildings in the monastery complex.

That evening, Tenzin and the other painters broke open the locked door and found the bloody, beaten monks. The painters brought the injured monks to their rooms. Tenzin and his cousin stood guard at their doors to protect them. Tenzin's cousin was armed with a small sword, and Tenzin with a pile of rocks. Mongyal Nyerpa died from his injuries the next day. During the takeover of the monastery, the merchant monks killed the abbot and the head teacher and appointed their own supporters to replace them. Only then did the merchant monks allow some semblance of monastic life to continue.

Horrified by these shocking events, the painters debated whether they should continue their work. They finally decided that Mongyal Nyerpa would have wanted them to complete the temple paintings, and so they continued. The merchant monks persisted in terrorizing the monastery for several months before a complaint reached the government in Lhasa. The merchants' reign ended after government troops arrived at Yungdrungling, arrested the four miscreant monks, and took them in shackles to Lhasa.[4]

For the next two years the painters labored in the temple at Yungdrungling, completing their work in 1942, the Year of the Water Horse. The painting completed, gold and copper reliquaries containing the remains of monastery abbots were moved into the temple, and gleaming statues of deities placed in niches along the walls. The painters began packing for the return to Tengchen—all but Tenzin, who surprised his uncle by telling him he wanted to remain at Yungdrungling and become a monk. As far as his uncle was concerned, Tenzin's declaration was yet another irritation from a pretentious boy with exaggerated goals that far outstripped his station in life. Sometimes shouting, he argued that Tenzin's mother would be opposed to him living so far away from the family. "I'm not leaving you with anything," Tshering said. "You will die here." Tenzin was unmoved. "I don't care," he replied. "I'm not going." Eventually Tshering realized the futility of his opposition.[5] Other than physically subduing the boy and carrying him home against his will, there was nothing he could do. Under pressure from the other artists to begin the journey home, he finally yielded to Tenzin's unbending will. Along with the other artists Tenzin's uncle departed for home. Before leaving, his uncle showed he cared about Tenzin despite their differences by leaving him a box of tea to sell.

Tenzin remained at Yungdrungling, studying in preparation for taking his vows. In the 1940s, entering a Tibetan monastery to become a monk was a simple process. There were no entry requirements, and nearly all comers were accepted. Once vows were taken, monks were seldom expelled except in extreme situations: for example, murder or breaking the vow of celibacy. Nor was devotion to religious study enforced. Only those truly interested in pursuing such studies, like Tenzin, applied themselves.[6] Others engaged in secular pursuits such as monastery administration, gardening, or trading, like the monks who had seized Yungdrungling.

Tenzin dove into his monastic studies. He relished academic life, delighting in the Bön texts. After a year of study he climbed the path up nearby Mount Shari Phowa to Menri Monastery, Bön's most prestigious institution, and took his vows at age seventeen. He entered a small chapel and prostrated three times before the two highest-ranking monks. The abbot, who normally administered the vows to new monks, was away. The monks began chanting a prayer. As they chanted, one grabbed a tuft of Tenzin's hair, cut a lock, and placed it in a small dish. He added a pinch of tsampa and tossed the mixture in the air to symbolize cutting ties with the world outside the monastery. The monk then poured blessed water into Tenzin's left hand and over his head to cleanse him. Tenzin made the bodhisattva commitment to strive for the enlightenment of all sentient beings. He took his monastic vows, including promises to abstain from killing any living being, lying, stealing, using alcohol or drugs, and sex. The monks gave him his spiritual name, Tenzin Namdak, replacing his birth name.

After taking his vows, Tenzin took a break from his studies at Yungdrungling for a year-long pilgrimage to monasteries in Nepal with two other monks. One of his companions was Sherab Tsultrim, who would become a lifelong friend and assistant. The monks carried tsampa with them, but for the most part relied on the hospitality of monasteries along their route for food and shelter.

On his return journey, Tenzin visited sacred Mount Kailash in western Tibet, near the Nepal-India border, the source of four of the longest rivers in Asia: the Indus, the Brahmaputra (which in Tibet is known as the Yarlung Tsangpo), the Kamali, and the Sutlej. The 22,000-foot mountain juts high above the wrinkled landscape, a lonely giant far removed from peaks of similar stature, its summit swathed in white. Kailash is a sacred site for Bön as well as Buddhist, Jain, and Hindu practitioners. Pilgrims from all four religions have journeyed to Kailash since at least the twelfth century. The history of Mount Kailash is so obscured by time that scholars speculate it could have been a spiritual icon for long-forgotten civilizations. The four religions traditionally regard Kailash as the center and birthplace of the world. Bönpos believe that the mountain is the seat of all spiritual power and the home of the sky goddess, queen of existence and protector of Bön, Sipe Gyalmo. Bön founder Tonpa Shenrab is said to have descended from the center of an eight-petaled crystal lotus growing on the summit.

Tenzin and his companions joined scores of other pilgrims circling the base of Mount Kailash to increase their spiritual merit. The thirty-two-mile journey around the base of the mountain is sometimes done in a single day by fit pilgrims, but it is more often done in three days. A single circumambulation, or *kora,* is said to cleanse the sins of a lifetime, and 108 koras guarantee enlightenment.

They began their kora at about 15,000 feet of elevation near the village of Darchen, where merchants hawked prayer flags and incense to pilgrims. They walked along a well-worn path marked by rock cairns and past caves used as meditation retreats by masters. They saw green and brown sandstone ridges, vertical walls of rock soaring above the valley, and waded knee-deep through a river. Along the way they passed dozens of sacred sites and rocks carved with sacred letters. They passed natural formations that resembled mythical objects, like a rock in the shape of a saddle that supposedly was used by a legendary queen. At the highest point in their circuit, the 18,470-foot Dolma Pass, they shouted, "*Ki ki so so lha ghyal lo!*" or "Victory to the gods!" Then they strung a line of prayer flags, adding them to the mass of weathered prayer flags dancing in the wind placed by other pilgrims over the years. They intended to complete as many koras as possible, but a snowstorm enveloped Kailash as they approached the Dolma Pass on their third kora. Hurricane-force winds piled huge snowdrifts on the pass, causing Tenzin and his companions to lose their way. They sheltered under a rocky outcrop to wait out the storm. The toes on Tenzin's right foot became frostbitten, and Sherab Tsultrim became snow-blind. Despite their pain and discomfort, they resumed their circumambulation as soon as conditions allowed. Sherab Tsultrim had to be led down to Darchen to recover, while Tenzin completed three more koras.

As the Bönpos walked counterclockwise around Kailash, they encountered Jains walking the same direction, and Buddhists and Hindus walking clockwise, as their traditions dictated. The most devoted and resolute pilgrims made the circuit by performing continuous prostrations. They would kneel, prostrate full-length, make a mark with their fingers, stand up, and take a step to the mark and make the next prostration. Circling the mountain in this fashion takes about four weeks, often with the same snowy, windy, and icy conditions that Tenzin encountered.

His pilgrimage complete, Tenzin returned to Yungdrungling, which he found much diminished since the coup by the merchant monks. The number of monks had fallen from about two hundred to thirty. Tenzin studied there about a year before deciding to go to one of the most inhospitable corners of Tibet.

3

Four Years in a Cave

Nineteen-year-old Tenzin's merry eyes peered from a round, jovial face. His engaging smile disguised a granite determination matched only by his voracious appetite for learning. While other monks slept, Tenzin read by candlelight, devouring the entire Bön canon, 180 texts attributed to Bön founder Tonpa Shenrab. His passion for learning depended on his own efforts even though he was a monk at one of Bön's most revered monasteries.

Each novice monk at Yungdrungling was assigned an elder monk who served as an advisor but did not give formal instruction. Tenzin's advisor, an aged monk named Gyalchok, recognized his pupil's exceptional abilities. Here was a student worthy of studying under one of the greatest masters of his time, Gangru Tsultrim Gyaltshen Rinpoche. Tenzin eagerly embraced the idea, but Gyalchok made it clear that it would take more than enthusiasm to convince Gangru Rinpoche to accept him as a student. There were a few problems, the first being that Gangru Rinpoche lived in a cave hundreds of miles away, at the edge of remote Lake Jurutso, on the harsh Changthang Plateau. Getting there would mean a long trek across a notoriously inhospitable landscape. Moreover, Gangru Rinpoche had refused to take on students since retiring after eighteen years at Yungdrungling and retreating to his cave. In seeking the solitude of a cave, Gangru Rinpoche was following a tradition common to holy men in Eastern religions. A cave provides the isolation conducive to meditation that can lead to the realization of the pure mind, and thus enlightenment. Gangru Rinpoche had refused all entreaties from students in the eight years since retiring to the cave, and it seemed ludicrous that he would change his mind for this headstrong young monk.

Tenzin knew that rejection likely awaited him at the end of the long and difficult journey he would need to make to find Gangru Rinpoche. As he pondered the problem, he was approached by a monk who had overseen construction of a small village temple in the Lake Namtso region near Gangru Rinpoche's cave. At more than 740 square miles, Lake Namtso is the largest lake in Tibet. Devout pilgrims would cross the ice during winter for a spiritual retreat on one of the lake's three uninhabited islands, with enough provisions to last through the short summer. They would remain on the islands after the ice melted, unable to leave until the lake froze again. The Chinese government would ban the practice.

Northwest of Lake Namtso, close to the new village temple, lay Gangru Rinpoche's cave, on the shore of the much smaller Lake Jurutso. The monk, aware that Tenzin was a member of the famed Dongdo family, asked him to paint religious scenes on the walls of the new temple. Tenzin refused, as he wanted to concentrate on his studies, but the monk kept perstering him until it finally occurred to Tenzin that this might be a way to become a student of Gangru Rinpoche. He struck a deal with the monk: he would paint the temple if the monk would help him convince Gangru Rinpoche to take him on as a student. Tenzin and the monk thus began the long journey to the temple near Gangru Rinpoche's cave.

Lake Jurutso is one of thousands of lakes strewn across the Changthang Plateau, the highest and least inhabited part of Tibet. The lakes break up vast plains crisscrossed by lofty mountain chains and provide waypoints for travelers in a landscape so immense it threatens to swallow them. Over thousands of years the lakes have also served as destinations for holy men and women seeking spiritual solitude. Thousands of meditation caves dot the Tibetan landscape, but those by the sacred lakes offer an added layer of spirituality. The caves ranged from elaborately hewn rooms with stupas, or holy monuments, erected inside, to mere holes in the mountainside. Between Yungdrungling Monastery and Lake Jurutso lay three hundred miles of harsh and desolate terrain. Tenzin and the monk headed north, following a river valley that sliced through the wide jumble of mountains along the edge of the Changthang Plateau. They followed the valley through a pass that opened onto the high plateau, a wide gravel and sand plain where storm-force winds swept in every afternoon, forcing them to seek refuge behind boulders or in ravines. Summer lasted only a few weeks on the Changthang, and the temperature could drop to forty below zero in winter.

They trudged across vast plains and slogged over mountains, exchanging leather slippers for boots with knee-high wool uppers sewn to leather soles. The two walked for days at a time without seeing another person. At night they were shielded from the cold by their heavy wool *chubas,* the traditional Tibetan garment that reaches to the ground and is tied at the waist with a cloth belt. The chuba lacks pockets, but the fold above the belt creates ample space for personal belongings. Here Tenzin kept a bag of tsampa. The chuba sleeves extend several inches beyond the ends of the fingers to protect the hands. The wearer can lie on the ground and curl up inside, converting the chuba into a sleeping bag.

The two monks walked for nearly three weeks before arriving at the small temple that served the sparse nomadic population. Tenzin set to work during the first days of summer, painting images of seated deities and borders of stylized designs in bold reds, blues, yellows, and greens. Occasionally he would remind the monk who had accompanied him of their bargain, only to be told that the time was not yet ripe for a visit to the master. This went on for nearly a year until finally Tenzin decided he needed to act on his own. He had become acquainted with a villager who took food to Gangru Rinpoche's cave, and the man agreed to allow Tenzin to accompany him. They walked until they reached a low ridge on a headland jutting into a lake. This was Lake Jurutso, overlooked by sacred Mount Ponse. Tibetans believe the mountain and the lake are spiritually joined, like husband and wife. The mountain disappeared from sight as they walked behind the ridge on the far side of the headland. They followed a path worn by sheep and goats along the shore of the mirror-smooth lake, the azure sky reflected in its shimmering surface. Marmots poked their heads from holes among the rocks, and a white-tailed eagle floated high on the wind. Near the end of the promontory Tenzin spotted the cave, its entrance blending into the ridge so well that it would have been difficult to find had it not been for the lines of prayer flags fluttering in the wind.

He stepped onto a short stone stairway leading to two stone terraces built in tiers. He paused for a moment on the first terrace that formed a patio overlooking the lake. Tenzin could see small niches in the rock face that contained the ashes of ceremonial fires burned daily as offerings to the enlightened beings for blessings and good weather. Paintings of single calligraphic letters representing sacred sounds adorned the rock face near the cave entrance. He walked up the ten steps to the next terrace, where knee-high stone walls enclosed a smaller patio. On the other side of the patio he saw a projection over the edge of the terrace, a slot in the overhang that served as a privy. Glass windows and a door had been installed with stone and mortar in the cave openings.

Tenzin raised his hand to knock, then paused. His heart fluttered, doubts crowded his thoughts. Had he walked hundreds of miles for nothing? Perhaps the naysayers were right, and he was on a foolhardy mission. He pushed aside those thoughts. It was far too late to waver. He knocked. After a few long moments, the door opened, revealing an elderly man in frayed monk robes. Tenzin sank to the ground in full prostration, then rose to introduce and offer himself as a student. Gangru Rinpoche made it clear in a kind way that he was not interested. Unable to disguise his disappointment, Tenzin openly wept. He bowed in acknowledgment and retreated to the temple near Lake Namtso. He keenly felt the rejection, but decided that it was a setback, not failure. Tenzin resolved to follow an old Tibetan adage about persistence: knock three times at the master's door. In this case the proverb would prove literal.

After a few days, Tenzin returned to the cave with nomads who brought food to Gangru Rinpoche. This time he pleaded, explaining how serious he was about his studies. "No, no, no," Gangru Rinpoche told him. "If I wanted to teach I would have stayed at Yungdrungling and taught many, but because I want to dedicate the rest of my life to practice I don't want to accept anybody."[1] Disappointment again brought Tenzin to tears. Again he returned to the temple, determined to persist. He waited a few more days before returning alone to the cave for his third attempt. This time he was rewarded for his persistence. Gangru Rinpoche, impressed by Tenzin's perseverance and desire for knowledge, agreed to become his mentor in return for Tenzin painting images of sixteen goddesses on small cards to be used in rituals. By employing Tenzin as a painter, Gangru Rinpoche was skillfully engaging in a benevolent deception to avoid the resentment of the many would-be students he had previously turned away. The master said he would lecture Tenzin while he painted.

Tenzin stepped over the threshold into the two-room cave. The first room he entered was a kitchen and work area about fifteen feet long and eight feet wide, with a natural rock ledge used as a countertop. The corner ceiling was blackened by years of cooking fires. A mud wall contained a second door leading to a slightly smaller sleeping and meditation room. The second room was hung with thankas depicting Bön deities. Against one wall was a mud altar with candles, water bowls, and offerings of tsampa. A mat in the corner was used for meditation and sleeping. Two wooden shelves mortared into the wall held sacred Bön texts wrapped in blue cloth.

With the help of a friend, Tenzin built a small stone hut on the lakeshore near the cave. "It was really a lot of hard work, and I scraped off a lot of skin in the process," Tenzin recalled many years later about how he gathered clay, water, and rocks for the walls. Forming a roof presented a challenge because wood was nonexistent on the Changthang. "To make the roof, we went around to nomad camps looking for the skeletons of horses and other animals and collected up the ribs and filled up the spaces with clay," Tenzin said. "It never rained, so that was not a problem."[2] Nomads would appear occasionally, bearing offerings of tsampa, yak butter, cheese, and meat, gaining spiritual merit by doing so. The food was only for Gangru Rinpoche, and it was too little to share. Tenzin survived by painting images and forming sand mandalas for a small monastery on the other side of the lake in exchange for food.

Both Tenzin and Gangru Rinpoche completed forty-nine-day dark retreats. Shut away from any light inside the stone hut, they encountered a darkness conducive to visions they recognized as self-generated, a part of the Bön mind-training curriculum. While Tenzin was in dark retreat, Gangru Rinpoche sat outside the hut and taught poetry, orally correcting Tenzin's compositions.

Tenzin spent four years at the cave in meditation and study with Gangru Rinpoche, learning grammar, poetry, Sanskrit, cosmology, ritual liturgies, and Bön doctrine. He learned how to build a multicolored sand mandala and how to weave sacred threads onto a star-shaped wooden frame, or *namkha,* used to harmonize the energy of the individual with the universe. The master taught him ritual chants and the nine preliminary practices of Dzogchen, considered a direct path to enlightenment. He performed 900,000 prostrations during his stay.

Gangru Rinpoche advised Tenzin to learn everything rather than choose only the subjects that interested him. If you don't, he said, one day you may find yourself in need of such knowledge and regret limiting your study. "If you end up, you yourself, with white hair, an old man, surrounded by many children or young men, trying to teach them, you don't know,"[3] he told Tenzin. The burden of teaching the younger generation may one day fall to him. Tenzin took his master's advice and strove to learn every ritual and prayer that Gangru Rinpoche could teach him. The wisdom of his master's guidance would become apparent nearly two decades later.

Life at the cave was not all meditation and study. Visitors were frequent, some bringing food for the master, others seeking blessings or a view of the famous holy man. Even local Buddhists would drop by the cave to receive the master's blessings. Tenzin made several long, grueling trips to Lhasa to sell butter he received as payment for his artwork, a nearly 200-mile journey. He used the proceeds to buy religious texts.

Tenzin fell easily into a routine of study, meditation, and practice while absorbing every bit of knowledge he could pry from the master. He felt born to a life of cloistered meditation and could envision no other. His life took an unexpected turn when one of the many visitors brought word that the abbot of Yungdrungling was planning a trip to Tenzin's hometown. The news kindled fond childhood memories of Tenzin's life with his monk uncle at Tengchen Monastery. He decided it was time to return to Kham. His intention was to take up residence in a hermitage there and spend the rest of his life in isolated spiritual practice. He wanted to take Gangru Rinpoche's writings with him, but since he could not take the only existing handwritten manuscripts, he began laboriously copying each volume. Gangru Rinpoche initially made no comment on learning that his pupil intended to return to Kham. As the time for Tenzin's departure drew near, the master finally expressed his opposition. "When you first came here," he said, "I'd been here for eight years and hadn't accepted anyone as a disciple. If you go back home now, everything you have learned will have been wasted. I thought I had found in you someone to whom I could transmit all my knowledge. But if you go now, that will not be possible. You should go to Menri and continue your studies."[4] His mentor explained that his religious education would be incomplete without the rigors of studying for a *geshe* degree, the equivalent of a doctorate of divinity, earned from a reputable monastery. He urged Tenzin to earn his geshe degree at Tibet's premier Bön monastery, Menri.

"Your destiny is not here," the master said.[5] Gangru Rinpoche told Tenzin that one day he would need to know all the teachings in order to defend his religion; that knowledge could only come by studying for a geshe degree.

Tenzin could not refuse his master. He gathered his few belongings and began the walk to Menri, a journey of a few weeks. Tenzin, now twenty-four, arrived at Menri in 1950, the Year of the Iron Tiger, to begin study for his geshe degree.

Unbeknownst to him, his world was about to undergo a violent change.

4
Invasion

As Tenzin studied for his geshe degree at Menri, Chinese leader Mao Tse Tung prepared to invade Tibet, a cataclysmic event that would upend the world's loftiest and most politically isolated country, threatening the existence of Bön.

Chinese governments had coveted Tibetan territory long before Mao. The once-powerful Tibetan empire soundly trounced Chinese armies and annexed Chinese territory, capturing the Chinese capital in 763 CE. As Tibetan power waned due to internal struggles, in 1720 the Manchu Dynasty invaded and made Tibet a protectorate, installing a high official, called an *amban,* in Lhasa to administer Chinese interests. Ambans initially meddled in Tibetan internal affairs, even assassinating the Sixth Dalai Lama's regent, but the Tibetans generally remained in control, and amban influence waned over the years. By the time the British launched a military expedition to Lhasa in 1904, the amban had lost so much authority that he was powerless to negotiate with the British on behalf of the Tibetans. The Qing Dynasty sent an army to reassert its authority in 1910, forcing the Thirteenth Dalai Lama to flee to India. In 1911, a revolution in China swept away the Qing Dynasty, enabling the Tibetans to expel Chinese troops and declare independence in 1912. Meanwhile, as Chinese factions fought for dominance, they agreed on one thing: Tibet was part of China.

There had been no Chinese presence in Tibet since a Tibetan army drove out the last vestige of occupation in 1919. After unifying a fractured China, General Chiang Kai-shek tried to renew China's claim on Tibet in 1928 by stationing garrisons in Amdo and Kham. The garrisons were largely ignored by the populace and in practice exerted little authority. After the Chinese Communists drove Chiang Kai-shek and his Nationalist Chinese Army off the mainland in 1949, their leader, Mao Tse Tung, vowed to "liberate" Tibet despite the Tibetan government's vigorous protestations. Chinese Communist negotiators told their Tibetan counterparts that the only way to avoid an invasion was for Tibet to give China control over Tibetan foreign affairs. Tibet refused.

As Mao marshaled his forces on the Tibetan border, the Tibetan government struggled to find an ally while trying to stall the Chinese through diplomacy. The only powers with sufficient clout in the region that Tibet could look to for material and diplomatic support were India, Britain, and the United States. Britain and India did not recognize Tibet as an independent country, and the United States was allied with Chiang Kai-shek and his Nationalist Chinese Army, which had been thoroughly beaten by the Red Army and driven to the island of Taiwan. Chiang too clung to the view that Tibet was part of China, and U.S. officials were careful not to offend an ally with strong ties to U.S. politicians. U.S. officials offered covert military aid to Tibet, but the Chinese acted before the Tibetan government could reply.

Tibet found its efforts to lure international support for independence further hampered by its own policies. Tibetan conservatives had stymied attempts to make connections with the outside world, fearing that contact with foreigners would dampen the Tibetan people's religious ardor. Clinging to its official policy of isolation from the rest of the world, Tibet never asserted its independence from China in an international forum until the threat of invasion loomed. The policy of isolation was one reason Tibet had few allies in its time of greatest need.

China pointed to Tibet's lack of foreign relations to strengthen its claim that Tibet had always been one of its provinces.

Chinese troops began training for a grueling campaign in a roadless land above the clouds. The invasion that would unravel Tibet was witnessed by Robert Ford, one of only two Englishmen in the country at that time.

A former Royal Air Force sergeant hired in 1948 to train wireless operators in Lhasa, Ford was the first Westerner to become a Tibetan government official. Ford, whose receding hairline belied his age of twenty-six, had sought the job because he thirsted for adventure. He grew up in Burton-on-Trent, in East Staffordshire, England, a brewery town 130 miles north of London, and joined the Royal Air Force at age sixteen.[1] During World War II, Ford was posted to India, where he was assigned to a tedious desk job in Lahore and later Hyderabad. Bored with the endless paperwork, he jumped at a chance for a temporary job as a radio operator for the British mission in Lhasa, where in 1945 he became acquainted with Tibetan officials.

Two years later, the Tibetan government decided it needed to begin using equipment for three radio transmitters sitting in crates, wartime gifts from the U.S. government. Efforts to train Tibetans in their use had failed. Most were illiterate, and those with sufficient education considered radio operation beneath their station. The Tibetan government was loath to hire Europeans, whom officials generally viewed with suspicion and likely to contaminate the country with unwanted ideas. Instead, Tibetan officials decided to recruit Indians, viewed as less foreign than Europeans.

Ford had returned to his mundane duties in India when he received a request from the Tibetan government to help find suitable trainees. He understood the Tibetan attitude toward foreigners, yet he thought he might have a chance at the job because he had been well-received during his short assignment in Lhasa. To his delight, his application was accepted.

Ford spent his first year as a Tibetan government employee in Lhasa, where he assembled Tibet's first radio station and put Radio Lhasa on the air. Aimed primarily at influencing foreign opinion, the station broadcast in Tibetan, English, and Chinese.

Eventually, Tibetan officials decided Ford would be more useful on the border with China. The government ordered Ford to travel to Kham Province to set up a wireless station to monitor the border, where the government feared the Chinese would attack. Without a radio, it could take months for the Lhasa government to receive a message from Kham.

It took Ford two months to ride more than six hundred miles by horseback along primitive trails through Tibet's mountainous landscape, from Lhasa to Chamdo, the seat of government in eastern Tibet, in the bandit-ridden Kham region. Ford led a caravan of twenty riding animals, eighty mules and yaks, ten muleteers, and forty porters, protected by an escort of twelve Tibetan soldiers.

The caravan navigated along river valleys, sometimes lush with trees and plots of barley and wheat, sometimes rocky and barren, sometimes carpeted with a rainbow of wildflowers. Blackneck cranes and ruddy geese preened on the banks of rivers that cut through treeless ginger-colored hills, where a flock of sheep would occasionally appear. Antelope, musk deer, and large stags stared from hillsides or ledges at the snaking pack train.

As his caravan emerged from the long trail, Ford caught sight of Chamdo, a drab settlement of about three thousand people living in mud-and-thatch houses. The settlement was clustered on a triangular peninsula at the convergence of two rivers, the Ngom Chu and the Dza Chu, or West River and East River, which course between mountains with peaks as high as 20,000 feet. At Chamdo, the tributaries join to form one of the world's great rivers, the Mekong. On a mountain slope overlooking the city, an unimpressive earthen monastery housed about two thousand Buddhist monks.

More than 100 miles east of Chamdo, the Upper Yangtze River coursed through jagged mountains to form the de facto border with China. About 250 miles farther east, the closest Chinese road ended at Dartsendo, where Tibetan traders swapped salt and other goods for Chinese tea. The terrain was so rugged that the trail linking the cities zigzagged nearly 500 miles through the mountainous landscape.

Ford and his three Indian assistants set up shop in an abandoned government palace and began monitoring English-language broadcasts from China's official radio station, Xinhua New China Radio. China Radio had begun its English language broadcasts on September 11, 1947, from a cave in the Taihang Mountains, as Mao's Communist troops battled U.S.-supported Chiang Kai-shek's Republic of China forces. After Mao forced Chiang to flee to Taiwan, the radio station moved to the capital and changed its name to Radio Peking. Ford and his Indian assistants monitored the English broadcast and sent commercial and government communications to Lhasa, usually in Morse code, but occasionally by voice.

In January 1950, after five months of daily monitoring, Ford heard the message he had long dreaded crackle through the wireless from the Chinese capital: "The tasks for the Peoples Liberation Army for 1950 are to liberate Taiwan, Hainan, and Tibet."

Upon hearing these words, Ford summoned his assistant, donned his fur-lined blue silk robe and mounted a pony to carry the news to Governor Lhalu Shape. He crossed a wooden bridge spanning the frozen West River to the newly built governor's residence, with its gleaming whitewashed walls of rammed earth. The assistant led Ford's horse through a gate with eighty-foot poles on each side flying red, blue, white, green, and yellow prayer flags.

After Ford was ushered into the residence, Lhalu appeared wearing a yellow robe with a red sash, his plaited hair coiled on his head with a piece of gold jewelry flashing from the top. A gold and turquoise earring hung from his left ear, and a diamond ring gleamed on one of his fingers. Butter tea was served. After the customary formalities, Ford informed the governor about the broadcast.

"They will not come yet," Lhalu said. There were no roads passable by vehicles in all of Tibet nor in the ethnic Tibetan region of the neighboring Chinese province of Sichuan. The Chinese would have to negotiate miles of jagged mountains and deep gorges to get to the Upper Yangtze River.[2]

While Ford and Lhalu mulled the menacing Chinese message, the Chinese were busy overcoming the obstacles posed by the difficult terrain. Within two months, thousands of Chinese troops and some ten thousand laborers were building a road west from the trading center of Dartsendo at the edge of Sichuan Province. West of Dartsendo, the terrain twisted into mountains and canyons impassable for anything but pack animals. As workers chiseled the new road, the Chinese army trained a strike force, acclimating soldiers to high altitudes while accustoming them to live on the Tibetan staple, tsampa, instead of rice.

Soon after that ominous January broadcast, Lhalu ordered Ford to send one of his two radios along with two operators to a garrison at Denkok, about a hundred miles northeast of Chamdo, on the bank of the Upper Yangtze River, to watch for a Chinese advance. Lhalu had correctly foreseen Denkok's strategic value. The city lay on the path the Chinese would take if they intended to encircle and cut off Tibetan forces defending Chamdo. The People's Liberation Army planned a four-pronged attack to trap the Tibetan army, with the northern prong taking Riwoche and coming in behind Chamdo to block the only trail heading west to Lhasa. Two prongs would cross the Upper Yangtze and head straight for Chamdo, and another would block a possible southern escape route.

The radio outpost provoked the first pitched battle between Chinese and Tibetan troops. The Chinese monitored Tibetan radio traffic and quickly learned there was a radio in Denkok that could give the Tibetans advance warning of an attack. In July, Ford received a message from Sonam Puntso, one of the Denkok radio operators. The first taps of Morse code in secret cipher indicated the message was urgent. In midtransmission the operator abruptly abandoned the code, which took more time to send, and tapped out, "The Chinese are here." Then there was silence. There would be no more radio messages from Denkok.

Ford didn't know whether Sonam and the other radio operator, Lobsang, were alive or dead until a week later, when a bedraggled Lobsang appeared at his door. "I looked out of the window in the radio station and there they were, hundreds of them pouring into the courtyard," Lobsang told Ford. "I told Sonam Puntso, who was on the key, but he went on tapping, and that's why he was caught. . . . I hid in a cupboard and they never looked in. Then at night I crept out and ran away."[3]

Ford watched a Tibetan force led by Muja Depon, one the army's best officers, march out of Chamdo with five hundred troops in an effort to retake Denkok.[4] Information provided to Muja by a few Chinese sympathizers among the local Khampas led his force into a Chinese ambush. A Tibetan officer died in the ambush, but Muja rallied his troops and launched a two-prong counterattack that routed the Chinese. When the fighting closed in, Muja summoned two hundred Khampa militia from his reserves. The Khampas excelled at hand-to-hand combat and took no prisoners, much to Muja's annoyance, as he had hoped to pry information from a Chinese soldier. Denkok was back in Tibetan hands, but the vital radio equipment was gone. Lhalu asked Lhasa for a replacement radio and three additional radios for other strategic villages. He also planned an offensive to foil the Chinese military buildup at the border, but Lhasa failed to endorse the plan.

By August, the Chinese had blasted a new road through the mountains, and U.S.- and Russian-made trucks loaded with military supplies were rumbling through Kanze, a trading post between Dartsendo and the border with Tibet. Aten, a Kanze opium dealer who had made a small fortune selling the drug to the Nationalist Chinese, reported on the first prong of the Chinese invasion:

> The first Red soldiers entered Kanze on the night of the second moon in 1950. I was not too impressed. Most of the soldiers were dressed in shabby rags and armed with a motley collection of firearms, which despite their diverse origins were relatively modern. Yet what the Communist army lacked in quality, they seemed to make up for in size. For a week the long columns never ended. I soon discovered the errors of my initial assessment. The Red soldiers were extremely well-disciplined. They were the first Chinese soldiers I had ever seen that did not loot and bully the populace. Instead, the soldiers were courteous to the extreme, and even went out of their way to help local people with their harvests and other chores.[5]

As the Chinese buildup continued, Governor Lhalu was replaced by Ngabo Jigme Norbu. The appointment would turn out to be disastrous for Tibet. Ngabo was a *shappe,* a member of the Kashag, the governing council of Tibet. He was "a tall and stately man, long-jawed and with a dignified but cheerful face."[6] Lhalu had planned a strong defense, but Ngabo believed that opposition to the Chinese was ultimately futile, pointing out that a single Chinese warlord had taken Lhasa in 1910. (The Chinese remained for two years before a Tibetan rebellion forced them back across the border in 1912.) One of his first orders was to dismantle some of the defenses Lhalu had constructed around Chamdo, fearing they would provoke the Chinese. He nevertheless told Ford that he intended to resist a Chinese attack.

Ngabo brought two of the four additional radios Lhalu had requested. Ford urged him to place one in Riwoche, a strategically situated village on the way to the crucial crossroad that the Chinese needed to capture to cut off the Tibetan army's escape route. Ford suggested another radio be placed near the border, but Ngabo argued that no Chinese troops had been seen near the border recently. He decided instead to keep one radio as a spare and send the other back with Lhalu. Now there could be no advance warning of an attack.

Some saw Ngabo's appointment to oversee eastern Tibet as a bad omen. Ngabo was the illegitimate son of a nun from a powerful family. His detractors pointed to a Tibetan prophecy: "When the throne of Tibet is guarded by a person of lower birth, then Tibet would be invaded by China."[7]

Ngabo's appointment came after other bad omens. In 1947, the Nechung Oracle, the official state oracle of Tibet, had predicted that the country would encounter a difficult challenge from the east in the Year of the Iron Tiger, 1950. In 1949, a comet appeared in the skies over Tibet, causing many to recall that Halley's Comet had appeared in 1910, shortly before the Chinese invasion that year. Moreover, the month before Ngabo arrived, an 8.5 magnitude earthquake shook eastern Tibet, killing at least 780 people in the region, collapsing buildings in Chamdo, and changing the course of the longest river in Tibet, the Yarlung Tsangpo.

Ngabo had about 3,500 poorly trained troops of questionable discipline to defend two hundred miles of border. Leading the troops were officers chosen for family connections rather than competence. Many of the soldiers were in their fifties or sixties; others were as young as sixteen. Married soldiers were accompanied by their families, who followed them even when they were deployed for combat. Many officers lacked military training in keeping with the government's policy of avoiding the creation of a professional officer corps that could become politically influential. The troops mostly carried outmoded weaponry, although some of the regulars had been recently equipped with Bren automatic rifles and Sten submachine guns supplied by India.

About 1,500 recently recruited Khampa militia of suspect loyalty bolstered the regular army units. Ngabo and his officials were central Tibetans from U-Tsang Province imposed on an eastern Tibetan community that felt little connection with the central government. The Khampas resented the tax collected by the governor that local chieftains had agreed to in exchange for the government's promise to defend Kham from Chinese incursions. The populace viewed officials in Ngabo's administration as interlopers, in part because the haughty western Tibetans spoke a different dialect and their customs were strange. For example, central Tibetans used a healthy dose of yak butter in their tea, but Khampas drank tea without butter. Cultural differences were amplified by prejudice. Central Tibetans viewed Khampas as uncouth and stupid. Khampas viewed Ngabo and other central Tibetans as carpetbaggers aiming to get rich at the expense of the locals. The Khampas also resented their lack of access to political power as well as demands by government officials that forced them to provide free transport for their trading ventures. Lhalu had recognized the problem and made an effort to address the Khampa grievances, but Ngabo exacerbated tensions with his aloof and formal style.

The Chinese wanted to avoid fighting the Khampas, known for their fierce fighting skills and horsemanship. Chinese officials understood that Khampas were ambivalent about the Lhasa government and that they mainly feared that the Communists would assault their religion and culture. To assuage those fears, Chinese troops were given orders to woo the populace by paying for everything in cash, avoiding local women, and remaining in their camps when not on duty. Their efforts reaped results in the ethnic Tibetan areas of Sichuan on the east side of the Upper Yangtze. Some of the populace were won over, and several influential Tibetans began cooperating with the Chinese army.

Facing the meager Tibetan army on the other side of the Upper Yangtze River was a battle-tested Chinese Communist army of five million. Despite their shabby uniforms and assortment of U.S. and Russian armaments, the troops were dedicated and highly trained. The invasion force consisted of a special unit of about twenty thousand men trained for a lightning-fast, four-pronged thrust intended to capture

Chamdo and trap the Tibetan army. The force received special training in night attacks and high-altitude conditioning, with an emphasis on moving long distances without stopping.

Discipline, training, and numbers gave the Chinese an edge, but one that could be blunted if the Tibetans used defenses afforded by the formidable landscape the Chinese faced after crossing the Upper Yangtze. The difficulty of the terrain confronting the Chinese is reflected in the traditional name for Kham: Chushi Gangdruk, or "Four Rivers Six Ranges," a reference to the six parallel mountain ranges that drain into the deep gorges of the Salween, Mekong, Yangtze, and Yalong rivers, all with headwaters on the Tibetan Plateau.

Chinese troops would cross the Upper Yangtze and head into the Hengduan Range running north and south along the border, with peaks as high as 20,000 feet. The cramped trails they would follow from the Upper Yangtze to their objective wound through steep mountains and deep valleys covered with pine forests and groves of maple, oak, and bamboo. In summer, the clearings bloom with clusters of rhododendrons, lilacs, primroses, and roses,[8] beauty that belied the danger the landscape posed to an invading force. The same rugged terrain and ample cover could enable a small and determined group of defenders to hold off a superior force at narrow passes.

At midnight on October 5, 1950, a platoon from the Chinese 154th regiment of the Southwest Army Corps slipped across the Upper Yangtze River and routed a small Tibetan force protecting the Chokhorgon Monastery without firing a shot.[9] The Chinese platoon was the spearhead of a force of about four thousand men that spent the next five days crossing the river.

The main force attacked on October 7. A garrison of about two hundred vastly outnumbered Tibetans opposed the main crossing at Gamto Druga. The well-dug-in Tibetans inflicted heavy casualties on the invaders but were ultimately forced to retreat with the Chinese in pursuit. Another force of Tibetans blocked one of the Chinese prongs at Denkok for several days, but the Chinese outflanked them with a second river crossing farther north. The Tibetan force withdrew intact.

The main Tibetan force made a stand at a narrow pass that provided a natural defensive position. The Tibetans fought fiercely, but even their geographic advantage could not overcome superior Chinese tactics, training, and weaponry. Unable to withstand the Chinese onslaught, the Tibetans withdrew to a nearby town, where they were reinforced. Believing they had left the Chinese far behind, the retreating Tibetans made camp for the night, not realizing that Chinese troops had given chase without pause, moving through the mountains in the night. The Chinese attacked in darkness, catching the Tibetans unawares. Chinese troops terrorized the Tibetan troops by banging gongs, screaming, and firing artillery. Stunned by the unexpected onslaught, the Tibetans were unable to pull together an organized defense. The Tibetan force dissolved in flight, their families in tow. The debacle opened the road to Chamdo to the invaders. There were no reinforcements to throw into the breach because Ngabo had failed to create a reserve.

With no way to communicate with his forward outposts, Ngabo remained unaware of the Chinese invasion until five days after it began. Word came from Ford, who learned about the invasion while at his post in Chamdo monitoring a broadcast from India. Ngabo immediately used the two-way radio to seek instructions from the government in Lhasa. Ngabo's aide-de-camp, Tshogow, spoke over the wireless radio to an official in Lhasa. To his astonishment and frustration, he was told government officials could not be bothered because they were attending a five-day picnic.

"Shit on their picnic!" Tshogow yelled into the radio. "Though we are blocked here and the nation is threatened, and every minute may make a difference to our fate, you talk about that shit picnic."[10]

The Chinese had routed or bypassed Tibetan garrisons all along the border, and two prongs of the attack were headed toward Chamdo with nothing in their way. A third prong was headed toward the crossroads west of Chamdo. Capturing the crossroads would trap what remained of the Tibetan forces. Ngabo received word on October 16 that Chinese troops had been spotted near Riwoche on the trail to the crossroads. The governor panicked. He asked for permission from Lhasa to surrender and was refused, but did receive permission to retreat. Two days later, displaying cowardice and stunningly flawed judgment, Ngabo rounded up all available horses and fled his post at 7:00 a.m. without bothering to notify Ford, the Khampa militia, or other officials. Only the army received notice. The army followed the governor, trailing behind in a procession of soldiers and camp followers strung along the trail for miles.

Ford awoke that morning to find the city in turmoil. The Khampa militiamen, angered that Ngabo had reneged on his promise to defend the city, were looting government buildings. Ford saddled up and made his way out of the city, avoiding the Khampas who might have killed him in their rage. He rode eight hours to finally catch up with Ngabo at 4:00 p.m.

At 6:00 p.m. Ngabo received confirmation that the Chinese had taken Riwoche. The commander of the city's garrison had panicked when the first shots were fired and fled, leaving his troops to put up an ineffective resistance. The Chinese were racing toward the crossroads. Ngabo crossed the 15,000-foot Lagong Pass at 10:00 p.m. About halfway down the mountain, Ngabo encountered a group of about thirty Tibetan soldiers bringing artillery, rifles, and ammunition from Lhasa. Ignoring his stunned advisors, Ngabo inexplicably ordered the soldiers to toss the ammunition and arms over a cliff and join the flight. Baffled by the order but unwilling to question a superior, the soldiers dutifully but reluctantly shoved their precious cargo over the cliff's edge. Shortly afterward, scouts returned with word that the Chinese were occupying the crossroads. About a hundred Chinese cavalry had traveled fifty miles a day to beat the Tibetans to the crossroads and trap Ngabo and his troops.

Ngabo brushed off pleas that they fight their way out and instead decided to seek sanctuary at a monastery a few hours away, at the head of a heavily forested valley. Within hours of the Tibetans' arrival, Chinese soldiers surrounded the monastery. Ngabo immediately surrendered, and the Tibetans handed their weapons over to the Chinese. A Chinese officer addressed the Tibetan prisoners through an interpreter. "We bring you peace," he said. "We have come to liberate you from the foreign devils. The Chinese and Tibetans are brothers—one people, one race, one nation. We have been separated by foreigners who have sat on your necks and kept you apart from the motherland." He looked at Ford, saying, "You can tell these foreigners by their long noses and round blue eyes and light skins."[11] The Tibetans were puzzled. Ford was the only Westerner that most of the Tibetans had ever seen. The only other Westerner in Tibet was another radio operator in Lhasa, a British subject.

As a camera filmed the scene for propaganda purposes, each Tibetan was given a silver Chinese coin and safe conduct pass and told to go home. Ford was led off to prison in China, where he was held for five years of interrogation and "reeducation," with the constant fear of execution.

Although the way to Lhasa now lay open, the Red Army moved westward only a short distance and stopped. Their intention was to force the Tibetans to the negotiating table without resorting to further force. Mao wanted to avoid fighting in such rugged terrain with impossibly difficult logistics. Only mules could ferry supplies along a supply line that would stretch more than a thousand miles to Lhasa.

The invasion shocked the Tibetan government into again reaching outside its borders for help. Tibet appealed to the international community, but the world's attention was elsewhere. North Korea had invaded South Korea a month after the Chinese crossed the Tibetan border. Tibet's appeals were ignored.

In Lhasa, the military disaster in Kham was greeted with scorn, reflected in street songs naming two of the hapless commanders under Ngabo:

Led by the two faced Derge Se,
(Then) the hopeless commander Karchunga
The Kham government's military regimental headquarters
Is filled with the smell of diarrheic excrement
The great and ferocious commander
Who never set eyes on the enemy,
By a piece of shit
Got frightened and ran away[12]

The Fourteenth Dalai Lama fled to the Indian border but headed back to Lhasa in July 1951 after consulting an oracle. Ngabo gained infamy and changed the course of Tibetan history when he signed a seventeen-point agreement on May 23, 1951, in Bejing, promising Tibetan autonomy and noninterference in religion in exchange for Chinese control of Tibet's foreign relations. Ngabo signed the document without consulting the other members of the Kashag or the Dalai Lama. The young Dalai Lama was faced with a fait accompli. Deciding to make the best of the circumstances, he hoped that by cooperating with China he could avoid bloodshed and form a partnership that would ensure that Tibet's religion and culture would be unaffected by Chinese rule.

The worst was yet to come.

5
Recluse Nation

Tenzin was engrossed in his studies at Menri Monastery when the lead contingent of about six hundred handpicked Chinese troops marched out of Chamdo in July 1951, the Year of the Iron Rabbit, toward Lhasa, slogging across the mountainous landscape with no roads or railroads.

The troops entered a country that at the time was known only through the writings of a few scholars, adventurers, and diplomats. Because there was nothing resembling a road within Tibet's borders, travelers had to endure a grueling trek on narrow trails through the world's highest mountains, only to encounter a government intent on keeping foreigners out. The Buddhist-dominated government feared foreign travelers carried alien ideas that would pollute the minds of Tibetans and weaken their religion.

At that time Tibet was fixed in the popular imagination of the rest of the world by the 1937 movie *Lost Horizon,* based on the book by James Hilton in which an aircraft loaded with European refugees from China crashes in the Himalayas. The refugees stumble into the mystical realm of Shangri-la, hidden among snowy peaks. The movie bore no relation to reality, but aside from a few obscure books by a handful of hardy travelers and scholars it was likely the only information about the distant kingdom in the clouds that most foreigners had ever encountered.

Tibet became even more isolated following the 1950 invasion, or "liberation," as the Chinese called it. The Chinese sealed the borders to outsiders and banned international travel for most Tibetans. Foreigners would be barred from the country until 1978, an opening that came after the relaxation of a travel ban to China following the death of Mao Tse Tung.

After an arduous march, the first Chinese troops arrived in Lhasa and were soon followed by reinforcements. Within six months the Chinese occupation force in Lhasa swelled to eight thousand, but the soldiers nearly starved during the first year because of the difficulty of transporting supplies over the tortuous terrain.

The ancient transportation and communication systems through this imposing landscape slowed news of the invasion to most Tibetans. Word that the Chinese were coming likely took weeks or months to reach Tenzin at Menri Monastery. Tibet would not have an airport until the Chinese built one near Lhasa in 1956. In 1950, horses were the fastest form of transportation, and international trade was carried out with pack animals over long, difficult trails etched into the sides of soaring crags.

The Tibetan government, dominated by Buddhists of the Gelug sect that excluded Bönpos from positions of power, had willfully clung to ancient modes of transportation even as railroads, airports, and automobiles had long since transformed the countries around it. The conservative leadership vigorously rejected change as a threat to its perception of Tibet as a religious country untainted by the materialism of Western culture. This view was put forth in a 1946 letter from the Tibetan government to Chiang Kai-shek: "There are many great nations on this earth who have achieved unprecedented wealth and might, but there is only one nation which is dedicated to the well-being of humanity in the world, and that is the religious land of Tibet, which cherishes a joint spiritual and temporal system."[1] Religion permeated the government, where the Dalai Lama was both spiritual and temporal leader of the nation. Prominent Buddhist monks were equal in rank to members of the aristocracy and held the highest posts in government. Government projects were tied to dates that the monks decided were auspicious, and an oracle was consulted on major national policy questions.

Two strands of modernization began a few years before Tenzin's birth, one within the military and one from progressive administrators. Both would founder in the face of fierce opposition from the politically powerful monasteries in Lhasa. The earliest attempts at modernization were spurred in large part by the threat of Chinese invasion. The Chinese briefly occupied Tibet in 1910, but a revolt drove them out two years later. The Thirteenth Dalai Lama began reforming the army to fend off a renewed Chinese threat in 1913. The Chinese government was trying to reassert its territorial claim by moving troops into the eastern province of Kham. The military reform required to counter the Chinese threat relied on young, aristocratic Tibetan army officers who generally believed a strong military was essential for Tibet to defend itself from China as well as from its monasteries, whose monks sometimes resorted to violence to defend their religious and political views. A particularly egregious example of monk militancy occurred in 1920, when monks from Drepung Monastery urinated and defecated in the Dalai Lama's garden at Norbulingka, the summer palace, to protest the banishment of two monastery officials. They later threatened an assault on Norbulingka. After the army intervened, sixty monks were arrested and flogged before being placed in leg irons and wooden collars.

Tibetan military officers wanted to replace religion and superstition in policymaking with efficiency and merit. They admired Western values, adopting Western dress and military practices, particularly from the British army, where many had been trained. One of the commanders organized polo matches and built tennis courts. Others abandoned the Tibetan custom of long hair and cut it short, English-style.

By 1919 the Tibetan army's improved training and leadership allowed it to oust the Chinese from Kham. The Dalai Lama placed one of his favorites, Tsarong, a progressive member of the ruling Kashag, in charge of military reform. Tsarong tried to expand the military and modernize government administration, immediately arousing the ire of the monasteries, their conservative supporters among the landed aristocracy, and the monk-run government bureaucracy. Most of the government's income was devoted to religious purposes, making military expansion an economic threat to the monasteries. The monasteries also saw the military's embrace of Western culture and technology as an assault on Tibetan religious tradition and customs. Religious conservatives set about convincing the Dalai Lama that the army posed a danger to Tibet.

Tensions between the military and the monasteries escalated in the capital city in 1921, and fear of civil war caused some families to move precious possessions out of the city. The antimilitary faction spread rumors that the army planned a coup, eventually causing the Dalai Lama to view the military as a threat to his rule. He dismissed some of the most influential officers, and the army's influence waned. By the time the Chinese invaded in 1950, most Tibetan troops were ill-trained, and nearly all of their officers incompetent.

Another thwarted potential for modernization and reform began in 1912 with the Thirteenth Dalai Lama's appointment of Kusho Lungshar, a talented government official from an aristocratic family, to escort four Tibetan boys to England for a Western education. While in London, Lungshar learned English and the principles of democratic government, convincing him that Tibet needed modernization. Upon Lungshar's return, the Dalai Lama appointed him to a post with authority over the military and revenue.

The four youths returned from Britain at the completion of their education equipped with the knowledge needed to reshape their country. Lungshar used his office to put their abilities to use. Under their guidance the first telegraph wires were strung to connect Lhasa with the outside world, and work began on a hydroelectric dam that would bring electricity to the capital. The first secular school began its brief life in 1923 with a British instructor teaching thirty sons of the aristocracy. A Sikkimese police officer was hired to form a modern police force in Lhasa. The modernizers wanted to tap Tibet's mineral wealth and brought in a geologist to survey coal and iron ore deposits. Tsarong, meanwhile, wanted Tibet to join the Universal Postal Union, produce a Tibetan-language typewriter in India, and bring in automobiles and motorboats.

These modernization efforts, however, threatened the elites, especially the powerful Buddhist lamas who held sway by virtue of the primacy of religion in every facet of Tibetan life. They struck back at the modernizers, arguing that mining, for instance, would offend the deities who watched over precious minerals. The secular school folded in 1924, a year after opening, under pressure from the lamas.

Lungshar alienated aristocratic families by confiscating their unused land and raising their taxes. He supported the increase in the army's size and its pay, further antagonizing the elites and the lamas. Lungshar's enemies struck a decisive blow just as he was planning to expand his authority in order to institute radical land reform. Police arrested Lungshar in May 1934 on the steps of the Potala, the Dalai Lama's winter palace. Officials issued a trumped-up charge of plotting to kill a high government official, overthrow the government, and replace it with a Communist system.

After a show trial he was sentenced to be blinded. As tradition dictated, the gruesome sentence was carried out by members of the ragyabpa, the only segment of Tibetan society allowed to violate the prohibition against harming sentient beings by butchering animals. Ten days after the trial they used an ancient method to blind Lungshar that involved tightening leather thongs to press a yak knucklebone into each temple. The cruel mutilation had not been used as a form of punishment in decades, and the ragyabpa bungled it horribly. They knew the practice only from stories told them by their parents. An attempt to drug Lungshar failed, and he suffered excruciating pain as the knucklebones pressed into his temples and destroyed his eyes.[3]

For the most part, hopes for the modernization that might have enabled Tibet to resist the Chinese invasion died with Lungshar's eyesight.

6
Best Friends

While Tenzin pored over texts at Menri Monastery, more than 1,500 miles northeast, two teenagers whose destiny would intertwine with Tenzin's got word that the Chinese were advancing. A fourteen-year-old monk, Samten Karmay, first learned of the invasion after returning to the Kyangtsang Monastery, in the far northeastern province of Amdo. He was lifting the saddle from his horse when another monk rushed up to him with news that the Chinese had attacked across the Upper Yangtze River in the neighboring province of Kham, about 200 miles south of their home in the Sharkhog Valley. Samten ran to share the news with his close friend and fellow monk, Sangye Tenzin Jongdong.

The invaders would visit persecution, torture, and debasement on Tibetans, eventually forcing many, including Samten and Sangye, to flee their country. Their flight would lead them to throw in their lot with Tenzin Namdak and a British scholar. Unbeknownst to them at the time, the three Tibetans would one day travel with the scholar to a land so alien that it was beyond their imagination.

Because Tibet's ruling elite triumphed over the modernizers, the world outside of Tibet was as strange and unknown to Samten and Sangye as the surface of the moon. The only newspapers were published in Lhasa, a capital city so remote from their homes that it might as well have been in another country. But even if a copy of a

Lhasa newspaper had reached their valley, locals would have found little information about the world at large within its pages. The only Tibetan newspaper with anything other than religious information or propaganda was the *Tibet Mirror,* published in Kalimpong, India, with a minuscule circulation among Tibetan officials and intelligentsia. Amdo was so remote that the Chinese government traditionally had more influence than the Tibetan government.

Worry that the Chinese had come to assault Tibetan religion and traditions threw many Tibetans into a panic, but the world outside Tibet barely noticed. In the United States of the 1950s, the headlines were dominated by America's war in Korea and Senator Joseph McCarthy's Communist witch hunt. Officials had just moved into the new United Nations building in New York. Television reached 1.5 million homes, and the hit tunes expressed the feel-good sentiments of the day: "If I Knew You Were Comin' I'd've Baked a Cake" and "Good Night, Irene."

People in Samten's remote village of Kitsal knew little about the United States other than it was constantly denounced as imperialist in Chinese Communist propaganda. Kitsal was close to the Chinese border and about twenty-five miles from the Kyangtsang Monastery and village of the same name, where Sangye's family lived. The fifteen wood and stone houses in Samten's village were built close together, high on a mountain slope above terraced fields. The women in most families hauled water from a spring, walking about a forty-five-minute round trip from the village, but Samten's family was wealthy enough to have servants perform the task. Like Samten's family, Sangye's grew wheat in the valley and barley, peas, and potatoes on the hillsides. They herded sheep and kept horses, mules, and pigs in a walled compound guarded by a fierce Tibetan mastiff chained during the day and set loose at night to patrol the grounds. Their most prized animal was the dzo, favored for its endurance and hauling ability. The females, called *dzomo,* provided milk.

Samten's house was stone and boasted a roof of Chinese tile, setting it apart from the smaller wooden houses in the village. Samten's mother, Zinmo, ran the household and a staff of servants, some living with the family and some in the village. The servants were paid with grain and bolts of felt. Most of the animals were kept on the first floor of the house, but sheep, horses, and dzomo were pastured high on the mountain during the day and driven back to the village in the evening, a task usually assigned to children.

Samten and Sangye's families were among the few in their villages wealthy enough to engage in the tea trade. Each winter, Samten's father, Tsega, led about seventy-five dzo to the largest city in the valley, Songpan, a Chinese border city near the edge of the Tibetan Plateau. Tsega drove the dzo through one of the Songpan's seven gates with its distinctive thirty-three-foot-high walls built with large blue bricks made of sticky rice, lime, and Chinese wood oil. Stalls lining the narrow brick streets in the crowded market offered a dizzying assortment of goods, including salt, roast duck, fried yam, fresh produce, traditional wool and brocade, Tibetan boots with oxhide soles and curled toes, saddles and silver-studded harnesses, richly hued blankets, finely crafted daggers, religious statuary, and ceremonial brass bells.

At the market, Samten's father haggled for five-pound bricks of black tea with Chinese merchants. After completing his purchases, he loaded each dzo with as much as ninety pounds of tea. Accompanied by four or five armed herders hired from his village, Tsega led his caravan out of the forest-covered slopes of the valley and into Amdo's wide northern plains. They drove the dzo north on a 260-mile journey to Arig Sogpo, a trading hub in northwestern China ruled by a Mongolian queen.[1]

The caravan was constantly on the lookout for bandits as it wound its way across the plains and through long valleys to Arig Sogpo, where Tsega traded the tea to nomads for wool and salt. The round trip usually took about four months. Back home, Tsega sold the wool and salt to

Chinese traders, who sat in his living room bargaining while drinking Chinese vodka and smoking long pipes of tobacco. After a sale, Samten's father would display stacks of silver Chinese coins to his family.

This lucrative tea trade allowed Samten and Sangye's families to financially support their sons when they entered the local monastery for a prized education. In a country with no private or public schools, monasteries were the single repository of knowledge and literacy. Outside of the monastery, semiliterate and self-styled holy men would inculcate a handful of local children with the rudiments of education, as well as perform rituals for villagers in return for meals. One of these holy men took on Samten as a pupil when he was eight. The holy man's teaching methods relied heavily on shouting abuse and using his staff on his pupils' backsides. After two months of scoldings and beatings, Samten learned to spell his first word, *phyogs,* which means "space." Space was what Samten fervently desired to put between himself and his abusive instructor. He rejoiced when the itinerant old man moved on to another village after a few months.

Already soured on his first taste of schooling, a life of study and contemplation held little attraction for Samten. His parents paid no heed to their son's opinions, insisting that as the oldest son he must enter the monastic life. His mother was set on him becoming a monk to bring prestige to the family and to remove him from the toil and grind of life on the Tibetan Plateau.[2]

Soon after the abusive pedagogue left the village, Samten's parents sent him to Nateng, a small Bön monastery about three miles from his village. Monasteries like Nateng, a cluster of about twenty buildings, were the cultural heart of their tiny rural communities. Here Samten and his family joined in religious festivals, propitiated the local deities to ensure prosperity, and sought medical treatment and advice on all the problems of life.

The villagers willingly supported such monasteries with contributions and by paying monks for the rituals that governed every important aspect of Tibetan life. Monks performed rituals for marriages, deaths, births, and certain birthdays, such as the twenty-fifth, thirtieth, and thirty-seventh, ages that are believed to have problems relating to health or prosperity that can only be cleared through prayer. When illness struck, at least four monks would be called to hang multicolored prayer flags and recite prayers. To increase their good fortune, Tibetans had prayer flags blessed at a monastery in return for a contribution, then placed the flags on top of a hill. Every road and trail had auspicious points where travelers added a rock to a pile for luck or where lines of blue, green, yellow, red, and white prayer flags festooned boulders, bridges, and trees, the wind blowing prayers from the fluttering flags across the earth.

Each Tibetan family had an altar adorned with butterlamps, often displaying a portrait of the Dalai Lama, as well as images of important lamas and protective deities. Every facet of life had a ceremony, prayer, or ritual associated with it. The Tibetan world was filled with spirits that lived in the fields, mountains, and lakes. Families put out pans of milk to appease the water spirits that mischievously caused havoc if they were disturbed or displeased. Other gods were given offerings to coax them into subduing the water spirits, known by their Tibetan name, *lu,* and sometimes by their Sanskrit name, *nagas.*

At Nateng Monastery, Samten learned how to perform the rituals of Bön. The tiny monastery had no formal classes and taught only rituals, so at age ten Samten reluctantly made the twenty-five-mile journey to a larger and more prestigious monastery in Kyangtsang, Sangye's village.

The ride, on horseback, took all day along a rutted trail on the valley floor flanked by stands of pines. Samten passed by several small villages like his own before arriving in the late afternoon at Kyangtsang Monastery on a mountain slope just above a valley green with acres of budding wheat. The monastery had nearly 150 monks going about their duties under a roof of expensive Chinese tile, a sharp contrast with the humble monastery of 15 monks he had left. Above the monastery, the stone houses of the village marched up the steep hillside. Samten went directly to a small house on the monastery grounds. There, his great uncle Hortsun Tenzin Lodro Gyatsho Horwa, whom he called Horwa Aku, or Uncle Horwa, had recently taken up residence as the monastery's head teacher. Horwa Aku's house was among two dozen built by families for sons in the monastery. The houses doubled as a place for family to stay during religious ceremonies and festivals.

Across the valley rose Drag Kar, or White Rock Mountain, one of several mountains in the region believed to contain the spirits of ancestors. The men in the village performed ceremonies and gave offerings of tsampa and sweets to propitiate the mountain spirits and bring good luck. The women made their offerings to the lu, spirits that when not being mischievous are believed to provide water, healthy crops, and other good fortune. Every morning the women of each family, sometimes accompanied by the men, tossed offerings into a fire lit in a ceremonial stone oven.

From his first day at Kyangtsang Monastery Samten was under pressure from his family to perform well in his studies because of Horwa Aku's reputation. Horwa Aku was renowned for studying under several great masters and spending thirteen years meditating and performing rituals alone in a cave. Samten entered the monastery the same year his great uncle introduced an advanced curriculum known as dialectic, a form of teaching that forces monks to defend their reasoning. Horwa Aku and Gangru Rinpoche, Tenzin's teacher at the remote cave, were close friends, and both advocated a broad education that acquainted students with every subject, allowing them to specialize later. Neither could have known that their best students would eventually join and put their deep, comprehensive education to work, saving Bön and proving the wisdom of their academic approach.

On weekends and holidays Samten would return to his village and was usually asked to assist the other children tending the flock. Despite the dangers of harsh weather and the wolves and wild dogs that stalked the sheep, he preferred herding to monastery life. One afternoon as Samten, then eleven, and other children took a break from their herding and gathered for a meal on a grassy slope, one of the children shouted and pointed toward Samten's flock. A wild dog had attacked a ram and they were locked together and rolling down a steep slope, the dog's teeth plunged deep into the ram's neck. The struggling ram and its attacker came to rest at the edge of a stream. Samten rushed to save the ram, his father's prize breeder. The children shouted and threw stones until the dog finally released its grip and raced away, but the ram was dead. Samten ran back to the village and asked his father to return with his rifle. Dogs had dragged the ram away by the time they returned. The child monk sobbed, blaming himself for the loss of the valued ram. His father's cold silence was punishment enough.

Sangye entered the monastery in the same class as Samten. Sangye's house on the monastery grounds was near Samten's, and they struck up an enduring friendship. The two were as different in appearance as they were in manner. Sangye towered above the shorter, slender Samten. Sangye bubbled with life, flashing a ready smile that won friends and disarmed the wary. Samten was friendly and kind but reserved. Despite their differences, Samten and Sangye became inseparable. They often joined the other boys at the monastery at play, wrestling and running. Lacking toys or other amusements, the boys would recite poetry and passages from sacred texts in dramatic style as if they were high lamas. Sangye excelled at this game, holding groups of boys in rapt attention.

Unlike Samten's parents, Sangye's were aghast when he told them he wanted to enter the monastery. His family was one of the wealthiest in the region, and his father wanted his five sons to work on the estate and in his lucrative trading business. For Sangye, the arrival of Horwa Aku and the possibility of studying under a distinguished scholar was an opportunity to be seized. His stubbornness finally wore away his father's opposition.

The two boys were admitted to the first class brought to the monastery by Horwa Aku. The study was grueling. They rose at dawn and studied until evening, taking breaks only for tea and meals. They spent hours memorizing page after page of text. Every few days they would be tested by reciting a text in front of an assembly of monks. The exercise sharpened their memories to a point where they could cite the page number and line of a sentence or paragraph. During the summer they pored over philosophy texts and learned the art of debate. They debated in pairs, one monk sitting on the ground and the other standing. The standing monk would shout his points, smacking the heel of one hand into the palm of the other with each point. A kick of the earth with the left foot accompanied each clap. The seated monk was expected to reply instantaneously by citing a section of text in defense of his theological position. The slightest hesitation drew laughter from other monks. Onlookers joined the questioner in attacking the reasoning of the defending monk.

In the winter the monks rose before dawn to recite mantras, meditate, practice rituals, and memorize texts. They learned calligraphy, logic, poetry, grammar, lexicology, traditional Tibetan medicine, music, ritual dance, art, cosmology, astrology, philosophy, painting, and the architecture of religious buildings. Using fistfuls of colored sand or rice, they patiently laid intricately designed mandalas on the floor. After hours of labor, the multihued work of art would be swept away as a demonstration of the impermanence of all things.

Horwa Aku conceived an innovative approach that combined two traditional curriculums into one. In both the Buddhist and Bön traditions a monk could choose between a meditation degree or a geshe degree. The geshe degree involved intense study and memorization of extensive amounts of text. The meditation degree typically required three years in retreat, usually alone in a remote location, to earn the title *Tokden*. Horwa Aku combined the two methods into a seven-year course, breaking the periods of isolation into mini-retreats. At the end of the course, monks were rewarded with a geshe degree, the equivalent of a doctorate, as well as the tokden title.

One year they practiced dark retreat, shutting themselves up alone in a dark room to meditate for forty-nine days. Isolation from light taught monks calmness, clarity, and that the physical world is a creation of the mind. Placed in a tiny room with no light, their only contact with the outside world was through a set of tiny doors in the wall devised so that food could be retrieved without allowing light in.

The first two weeks of dark retreat were difficult for Samten, who felt an overwhelming desire to escape into the light. The darkness closed in on him, suffocating him as if he were at the bottom of a deep ocean where light never penetrates. He coped by concentrating on an intense program of meditation and prayers laid out for him in advance. A monk was stationed outside the door in case Samten asked for assistance, became ill, or needed to be removed because he couldn't come to terms with the blackness. Occasionally a lama would visit and speak with Samten through the door to check on his well-being.

For some of Samten's classmates, the intense isolation evoked visions and caused them to experience intense religious feelings. In some cases monks reported reaching a profound state of meditation that enabled them to control their body heat so that they sat immobile without a fire or extra clothing during the harsh Tibetan winter. The meditative state was so deep for some that it remained for hours after they were brought into the light. Samten's experience was limited to intense boredom. Eventually he accommodated himself to the darkness but was immensely relieved to be returned to the world of sunlight at the end of the seven weeks.

In another exercise the monks fasted. Their diet was reduced for six weeks to a small amount of fruit each day. Samten never felt at ease with hunger and other deprivations. He dutifully pursued his studies, but he found them arduous and unpleasant. The monks were often confined to the monastery during their studies, giving Samten the feeling that he was being punished.

The dialectic coursework sharpened Sangye and Samten's skills in debate. The meditation courses showed them how to overcome human frailties such as envy, jealousy, anger, hatred, and most of all, desire, both carnal and material. Absent were courses in foreign languages, mathematics, world history, comparative philosophy, or anything that might have been familiar to a student in nearly any other country in the world in the early 1950s.

While Samten slogged through his studies, Sangye seemed to dance through his. Sangye immersed himself in the sacred texts, many of them hundreds of years old, spending hours memorizing them. To read the unbound texts, he sat cross-legged on one of the long, rug-covered wooden benches only inches above the stone floor, along with rows of other monks. Sangye placed the oblong texts on a wooden table that ran the length of the bench. He carefully and reverently untied the red ribbons holding the loose pages of each text between their covers. The top and bottom covers of each unbound book, or *pecha,* were wrapped in red silk. He consumed each page of Tibetan calligraphy, tenderly flipping each foot-long leaf in a pile on the worn table. Tradition has it that the writings originated from oral teachings handed down from master to student over thousands of years.

Sangye's zeal for learning was matched only by his willingness to help others. He learned the art of medicine from two of his three brothers, both trained in Tibetan herbal medicine. He put his medical knowledge to work caring for anyone who sought his help, such as two women who appeared at the monastery after a journey of several days. They wore their traditional dark woolen dresses and multicolored aprons under heavy woolen chubas. The women were shy and spoke a different dialect, but Sangye quickly won their confidence. One of the women had a problem she was reluctant to discuss. Sangye sensed her reluctance and spoke with her privately, prying her complaint from her with gentle questions. He arranged for the women to stay with his family. As is traditional in Tibetan medicine, Sangye examined their urine, took their pulse, and looked at the color and characteristics of their tongues before prescribing herbs and a course of diet, exercise, and meditation. They improved markedly after a few days. He refused payment and sent them on their way with a generous supply of medicinal herbs.

Most of Sangye's time was spent immersed in religious texts. After other monks retired for the night, he stayed up, studying by candlelight. Eventually he came across an ancient text that prophesied that the Norbulingka, the Dalai Lama's summer palace in Lhasa, would become "a sea of blood." Lhasa, the texts predicted, would become an "iron hell."[3] The words of this dire prophecy would flash in his mind a few years later when he stood on the rooftop of Drepung Monastery overlooking Lhasa and watched Chinese artillery pound Norbulingka and the city.

7
Tibet's Harvard

Initially the Chinese invaders were friendly to the Tibetans. The soldiers paid in silver coins for food, pitched in to help peasants harvest crops, and went out of their way to be courteous and helpful. They paid cash to the Tibetans they employed and to Tibetan merchants, boosting the local economy. Yet the Chinese mask of friendship was slipping away as Samten Karmay and Sangye Tenzin were finishing their studies under Horwa Aku.

A year before Samten and Sangye graduated, Mao signaled a change in the Chinese attitude during an exchange with the Dalai Lama. In 1954, the Chinese invited the nineteen-year-old Dalai Lama to Beijing for the inauguration ceremonies for the People's Republic of China's new constitution. The Dalai Lama, determined to work with the Chinese if at all possible, arrived with an entourage of five hundred for several days of celebration. During one of the events, Mao took the young Dalai Lama aside to offer him a bit of fatherly advice. Religion is poison, Mao warned. Outwardly polite, the Dalai Lama inwardly recoiled in horror at the admonition. Everything about the Dalai Lama's life was intertwined with his Buddhist religion. It was religion, not temporal power, that held Tibetans together as a people. Nearly every Tibetan looked on the Dalai Lama as their supreme spiritual leader, Bönpo and Buddhist alike. Mao's remark blasphemed the essence of Tibetan nationality. More disturbingly, his words foreshadowed a broken promise.

After the invasion, Mao had promised to respect Tibetan religion and culture. The Chinese had generally followed Mao's plan of leaving Tibetan traditions undisturbed for a few years after the "liberation," as the Chinese called the invasion. Chinese road-building boosted commerce, and the introduction of the first trucks in the country gave China the appearance of a leader in technology and modernity in the eyes of Tibetans.[1]

As Samten and Sangye focused on finishing their geshe degrees, the Chinese were completing roads to Lhasa that made it easier to transport troops and military supplies and assert Chinese control. The increasing Chinese confidence and power began to erode Mao's stated policy of religious tolerance. Troops began disarming Tibetans in Kham and Amdo in preparation for a forced agrarian collectivization program. In Kham, where every Khampa male carried a rifle and a sword, the confiscations caused an immediate outcry, and local leaders sent a petition of complaint to the Dalai Lama.

A Chinese official with a notepad appeared unexpectedly one day at Samten's family home. The Chinese felt themselves superior to the Tibetans, whom they regarded as backward and ignorant, and their hubris grated on Samten's mother and father. They were not pleased to see the official and were reluctant to answer his personal questions, but they feared failure to cooperate could have terrible consequences.

Uniformed Chinese officials fanned out throughout the Sharkhog Valley to tally the population, the number and type of animals, and the value of each family's property. They were preparing the way for new taxes and coming social reforms. The Chinese began calling the villagers to meetings, usually in the local monastery, where they were harangued about the dangers of religion and the predatory nature of the upper classes.

For hundreds of years, the Amdo and Kham regions of eastern Tibet had shifted between independence or being nominally subject to either the governments in Lhasa or Beijing. They revered the Dalai

Lama but paid little heed to government edicts, whether issued from the Tibetan or Chinese capitals. The appearance of Chinese officials in remote villages throughout Amdo demonstrated that the Chinese would no longer endure the flouting of rules made in faraway capitals. The Chinese Communist Party intended to bend every facet of Tibetan life, including the monasteries, to its will. They would permit no views that conflicted with the official Chinese version of reality. The promise to tolerate religion was merely a delaying tactic to allow the Chinese to strengthen their position. They would strike when they were ready.

Samten and Sangye graduated in 1955, the Year of the Wood Sheep, two years early because of their superior abilities. They were in the first class of monks to earn a geshe degree from their monastery under the new teaching methods introduced by Samten's great uncle, Horwa Aku.

The two young geshes chafed under official restrictions. The desire to escape the unpleasant attentions of nosy Chinese officials combined with ambition and a youthful lust for adventure contributed to Samten and Sangye's decision to leave the Sharkhog Valley.

Before they could leave, Horwa Aku had a challenging assignment for Sangye. He asked him to hike more than 460 miles to a print shop in the city of Drugzur, a perilous trip south through territory roamed by brigands. Even more daunting, Horwa Aku wanted him to return with a copy of the complete Bönpo canon of two hundred volumes printed from wooden blocks. Sangye accepted without hesitation. He made his goodbyes, quickly gathered the pack animals needed, and disappeared down the trail. He reappeared six months later leading mules loaded with texts, including books on rituals and Bön founder Tonpa Shenrab as well as texts for his father's library.

Upon Sangye's return, Horwa Aku approved Sangye and Samten's request to go to Lhasa for advanced study at Tibet's most esteemed monastery. Scholarly monks often took advanced studies at a larger monastery, but most Bön monks went to Bön monasteries in central Tibet.

Samten and Sangye aspired to the Tibetan equivalent of Harvard: the Drepung Monastery in Lhasa.

Drepung was a daring choice not only because of the monastery's academic reputation, but because it was run by the Gelug, the most dominant of Tibet's Buddhist sects. Since many Buddhists regarded Bön as an apostate religion, there was no guarantee that the young monks would be welcome.

Samten and Sangye feared Chinese officials would disapprove of monks making a journey to Lhasa. They felt the slow tightening of Chinese control. Like their neighbors, they had to be careful about what they said and with whom they shared their views. They knew that the Chinese had encouraged neighbors to report anti-socialist behavior. The young monks had learned to avoid any conduct that would arouse the suspicions of Chinese officials. Drawing the wrong kind of attention could lead them to be labeled reactionaries and subjected to public humiliation or worse.

To avoid arousing suspicion, Samten and Sangye decided to let it be known that they were making a pilgrimage to the revered Mount Emei, across the border in China, a six-day walk from the Sharkhog Valley. Bön and Buddhism share much of the same sacred geography, and pilgrims from both religions mingle at the same holy lakes and mountains. The monks reasoned that Chinese officials were likely to view travel to China more favorably. There was little chance for political mischief in a country steeped in Communist ideals. Their true, secret destination in Lhasa, was considered antithetical to Communist aims.

Sangye and Samten joined four other monks on the journey that would start in Songpan and descend from the Tibetan Plateau to the Chinese trading center of Chengdu, near Emei Mountain. They would follow the winding Minjiang River, descending 7,000 feet from the high valley to the plains of China's Sichuan Province as the river cut through the jagged, snow-cloaked Min Mountains. When they left Songpan, they could see Shar Dung Ri, the highest mountain in the chain, soaring more than 18,000 feet. Much to the annoyance of his fellow travelers, Samten rented a rickshaw for a short way because he had never ridden in one. The path was so steep at times that the man pulling the rickshaw found it difficult to keep Samten and the rickshaw from careening down the slope.

When the river finally spilled into the Chengdu Plain, the trail led them past emerald-green rice paddies to the largest city they had ever seen. They entered Chengdu through a gate in the city's thirty-three-foot ancient walls, twenty feet wide at the top. The monks marveled at the bustling markets of Chunxi Road in the ancient hub of Sichuan Province.

From Chengdu they made their way east to Mount Emei, which at 10,000 feet was the highest of China's four sacred Buddhist mountains. A series of stone steps wound up the forested slope to the two-thousand-year-old Puguang Hall, a temple on the Golden Summit.

The Bön monks followed the stone steps skyward for two days to reach the topmost temple. They stopped along the way to rest and admire some of the thirty temples along the path, some small and ornate and others with broad porticos and wide, stone-paved courtyards. Near the top they visited a group of monks from an unfamiliar Chinese Buddhist sect. The Bön monks were horrified to learn that the sect practiced self-mutilation. The appalled Tibetans noted that the Chinese monks all had ritual scars on their shaved heads, and one monk proudly displayed a hand with three fingers missing that he had sacrificed to a Buddhist deity. "I am fine," the monk told the inquisitive Bönpos. "It was not hard to do."

At another temple they encountered a Chinese monk who said he could divine the future using a vase filled with foot-long arrows.[2] Sangye paid him one yuan and asked whether he should make the trip to Lhasa. The soothsayer shook the vase, then emptied it on the temple floor. He took a moment to assess the pattern made by the arrows.

"You can go to Lhasa," the monk told Sangye. "I don't think there will be any problem."

Samten put his yuan on the floor and the monk cast the arrows again. This time the monk shook his head. "No, you can't go to Lhasa."

The Chinese monk saw the look of dismay on Samten's face. "If you want, I can do it again once more to make sure the divination is correct." Samten put down another yuan and the seer again shook the vase. "No, you can't go."

Samten glared at the Chinese monk.

"I can do it again. After three times, if it doesn't work, then you really won't be able to go."

Incensed at the prediction and certain that the seer was trying to coax more money from him, Samten stalked out of the temple.

Unswayed by the augury, the monks headed back to Chengdu to prepare for the long journey to Lhasa. The 1,200-mile journey typically took months of walking over tortuous trails, through rugged mountains and valleys. But the Chinese had dynamited a road through the mountains, shortening the trip to about six weeks by truck. Before the road was built, supply from China was difficult, leaving the Chinese army in Lhasa to compete for scarce food with the populace, fueling inflation and pushing both troops and locals to near starvation at times. The road was no more than a winding track hacked through the mountains, often with forced Tibetan labor, but it was like a superhighway for a country lacking roads wider than a donkey trail. The monks intended to take advantage of the modernity that China was forcing on its conquered province.

One of the monks from a family of wealthy merchants rented a truck and driver to take them to Lhasa. They purchased vegetables and meat for the trip, packing them in bamboo boxes. The monks also set about buying goods they could sell in Lhasa, where their Chinese currency would be worthless. They hired a Chinese merchant who helped them convert their currency into bolts of silk, crates of window glass, boxes of noodles, and packages of *khatas,* the ceremonial scarves that Tibetans offer to lamas and drape around each other's necks in greeting, celebration, and blessing.

Word filtered to them from merchants that their efforts had attracted the attention of local Chinese officials, who had learned of their intentions. The monks grew apprehensive, but the Chinese made no effort to stop them.

The monks felt an urgency to leave Chengdu and were relieved when their hired transport arrived: an olive-drab, four-wheel-drive truck patterned on the International Harvester models, given as part of U.S. military assistance to Russia during World War II and copied by Russia and China. The truck had a short bed, no doors, and headlights mounted on the fenders. The monks sat among their crates in the truck bed, peering through the wooden-slated sideboards. The truck bounced over the rough road, jostling and shaking them as the driver ground through the gears amid the whine of the six-cylinder engine. The unpaved road, barely wide enough for the truck, wound through towering mountains and deep canyons in endless switchbacks. The crude track at times teetered on the edge of steep precipices that plunged out of sight.

A thin layer of earth covering the frozen ground below the road surface often wore through and made traction difficult. On one steep slope the dual rear wheels began spinning, and the truck began sliding backward. Samten sat helpless in the bed of the truck as the frightened monks watched the edge of a cliff inch closer. The driver pushed the gas pedal to the floor and the engine screamed, but he had lost the battle for forward momentum. The driver stomped on the brakes and they locked. The truck kept sliding. He tried to steer it away from the cliff, but control was lost. The looming chasm seemed certain to swallow them before they could jump to safety. A sudden jolt rocked Samten. The truck jerked to a halt with a sound of grinding metal, knocking the monks to the bed of the truck. The driver of another truck heading the same direction had seen their plight and rammed them from behind, keeping them from plunging into the deep gorge.

The monks at first felt relief. Only later did they feel the full horror once they had time to realize how close they had come to plunging to their deaths.

Sometimes the monks would spend the night in a village, but often they would camp on the roadside. They tried to find a relatively flat area to erect a tent, then searched for yak dung to fuel a fire against the penetrating cold. They rose early each morning and built a fire under the engine to unfreeze the oil. Whenever possible they spent the night with a Tibetan family, where they were always warmly received. Tibetan custom calls for households to provide food and lodging to pilgrims, especially monks. Hosting a monk was considered an honor and an act that would earn religious merit for the host. In the morning a warm plate of tsampa and *balep,* a pan-cooked or fried bread, and a hot cup of tea would be ready for each of them.

Exactly where they would spend each night became a source of irritation between the monks and the driver. The monks, who had taken vows to eschew alcohol and sex, were appalled that the driver insisted on stopping where he could procure liquor and female company. The monks favored family homes and monasteries. Finally the monks tired of the constant arguing and hired a new driver.

After six weeks of bumping over the crude highway, they pitched their tents in near total blackness. Lhasa, Tibet's largest city, lay sleeping nearby, but there were no street lights to reveal its presence.

In the morning, Samten stepped out of the tent and rubbed his eyes. He was uncertain as to his exact location and wanted to get his bearings. He gasped at what he saw: An intense golden light from the morning sun radiated from the burnished copper roof of the immense palace that is the Potala, illuminating the grand edifice of the Dalai Lama's winter residence. The reflected sunlight made the mountain appear to glow. The other monks joined him, each standing silently in awe at this mystical effect. Looming over the city from the slope of Marpo Ri, the Red Hill, the gleaming, thirteen-story, thousand-room palace with its towering maroon-accented white walls felt mythic to the rustic monks.

The name *Potala* is derived from the Sanskrit word for a mythic magical mountain in southern India. Unable to articulate his wonder, Samten felt as if he was indeed looking at a magical mountain. The Potala was more than an architectural marvel: it was the physical representation of their religious culture.

From the roof of the Potala boomed the low, mournful bellow of the long ceremonial horns that could be heard fifteen miles away at the edge of the Plain of Lhasa stretching below. Monks in maroon robes with saffron mantles sounded the horns that stretched from ten to twenty feet and rested on supports. From rooftops across the city wisps of smoke rose from morning fires of yak dung as women brewed the morning butter tea.

After brewing their own tea and breakfasting, the monks entered the city of whitewashed, flat-topped houses built of stone with narrow streets crowded with monks, pilgrims, merchants, and Lhasans going about their daily tasks. They passed through a line of pilgrims making the eight-mile ritual circumambulation of the city.

They had come to a city that had changed little over the centuries until the Chinese occupation. They were puzzled by a uniformed man standing on a platform in Shagyari Street making strange hand motions—the city's first traffic policeman. The monks stared in fascination at goods from all over the world in the myriad small shops, from Chinese flashlights to Bing Crosby records—foreign merchandise they had never seen before.

They wandered among the many shops lining the crowded streets where merchants sold bales of stout Tibetan cloth, Chinese silk, and Indian cotton. Another street specialized in jewelry shops displaying necklaces of coral and turquoise or charm boxes of gold filigree. Samten walked down Shagyari Street to the fruit and vegetable market, where red apples were stacked in mounds next to peaches, grapes, barley, peas, cabbages, and three-foot long radishes. Other stalls displayed trays of walnuts, chillies, curry powder, cloves, and nutmeg. He passed the Chai Tsonkang Cafe, where sophisticated Tibetans could sit at a long plastic-topped table and obtain a cup of tea brewed Western-style, without yak butter and salt. The "English tea" was served already poured into cups, then yak milk and sugar were added whether requested or not.[3]

As Samten and Sangye explored the city, they encountered serfs and poverty for the first time. The discovery surprised and saddened them. In Amdo, even the poorest villager survived without begging. They had never seen Tibetan beggars before, but they were everywhere in Lhasa.

They found a room for rent that overlooked a small courtyard with a well at the center. They unloaded their goods, paid the truck driver, and were left in a city stranger to them in many ways than a Chinese city like Chengdu.

The group of rustic monks spoke a Tibetan dialect peculiar to their part of the country. Their efforts to communicate with Lhasans were often greeted with puzzled stares, adding to their difficulties in selling the goods they had hauled with them. Samten and Sangye found that they lacked the ability or desire to haggle. They sold some of their goods only with the assistance of their fellow monks. In the end they were unable to recoup all the money they had spent on their purchases and were stuck with bolts of silk and cases of dried noodles.

The two Amdowa monks spent the first few days of January 1956, the Year of the Fire Monkey, observing the Monlam Chenmo, the Great Prayer Festival, a gathering of some twenty thousand monks from Lhasa's three great Gelug monasteries—Drepung, Sera, and Ganden—as well as from other Gelug monasteries all over Tibet. The streets were crowded with monks in dirty robes. Monks took over administration of the city during Monlam Chenmo but made no attempt to solve the sanitation problem created by the surge of visitors. Visiting monks relieved themselves in the streets, creating unhygienic conditions that repelled Samten and Sangye.

Monlam Chenmo ceremonies took place in the 1,300-year-old Jokhang Temple, one of the holiest destinations for the faithful. On most days scores of pilgrims could be seen prostrating in front of the Jokhang Temple. Pilgrims made clockwise circumambulations, or koras, to gain spiritual merit. Two of the most popular koras were the Barkhor, around the Jokhang through streets filled with stalls, and the longer Lingkor, which circled old Lhasa, the Potala, and Iron Hill.

Samten and Sangye made their way toward the Jokhang in hopes of participating in the ceremonies but were barred by Buddhist monks guarding the entrance to Barkhor square. Only monks affiliated with monasteries in the Lhasa Valley were allowed to enter the square. Each monastery had a reserved space in the Barkhor. The guardian monks turned away all the pilgrims who normally filled the plaza.

Unable to participate in the ceremonies in Lhasa, the two monks made a pilgrimage to the mother monastery of Bön, Menri, about 125 miles west of Lhasa. They paid to ride in the back of a truck that took them most of the way, along a new Chinese-built road linking Lhasa and Shigatse, the second largest city in Tibet. They hiked up a mountain to Menri, passing the rock foundations of the original mother monastery, Yéru Wensakha, destroyed by a titanic flooding of the Yarlung Tsangpo River in the fourteenth century. At Menri they met Tenzin Namdak, now the monastery's *lopon,* or head teacher. The meeting was brief, giving no hint that their lives would intertwine years later in another country in a way that would determine the future of Bön.

The two young monks spent several weeks in meditation and prayer at Menri before moving on to nearby Yungdrungling Monastery, a twenty-six-mile walk to the valley below. As they descended from Menri, they could see a tiny mud-walled building silhouetted on a high ridge overlooking the trail: the Kharnak meditation monastery where Bön monks would isolate themselves in contemplation for months or even years.

It was April by the time Samten and Sangye returned to Lhasa. Drepung Monastery, their destination, sprawled across a slope at the base of 15,000-foot Mount Gephel, more than three miles northwest of the city. Drepung was the queen of Lhasa's three prestigious monasteries, the apex of learning for the Gelug school of Tibetan Buddhism, and center of political as well as spiritual power. The three Gelug monasteries were cities unto themselves, each covering dozens of acres. Drepung housed nearly ten thousand monks, Sera about seven thousand, and Ganden about five thousand. Their size mirrored their political influence. The monasteries were semiautonomous governments within the Tibetan state, with the right to judge monks for all crimes except murder and treason. The monasteries had quasi-military forces that rivaled the Tibetan army. At least 10 percent of monks at each of the three monasteries were known as fighting monks, or *dob-dobs,* trained in the martial arts, giving the monasteries, with over twenty thousand monks in the Lhasa area, an edge over the poorly trained Tibetan army of about 1,500 men.

The great monasteries were enormously wealthy. Their earnings came from vast manorial estates, endowments, offerings from the faithful, and grants from the central government. Drepung supposedly had 185 estates maintained by 20,000 serfs, and 300 pastures supporting flocks and herds watched over by 16,000 nomads. Little of that money was spent on monks, who received a small salary paid in grain and tea. The monastery occasionally provided meals during prayer sessions. Most of the money financed religious ceremonies in which prayers were said for the benefit of all sentient beings. The ceremonies were regarded as essential to the well-being of the nation.

So great was Drepung's reputation as a center of learning that it attracted monks from Mongolia and China as well as other Tibetan Buddhist schools, including Nyingma, Kagyu, and Sakya. But Bönpos were a different matter.

Buddhist and Bön monks wore nearly identical robes, so no one would have known that Samten and Sangye were Bön monks when they first entered the gate to Drepung. But in the monastery's administrative offices they were recognized as Bönpos as soon as they mentioned that they hailed from the Sharkhog Valley, where Bön is the dominant religion.

Samten and Sangye were not the first Bönpos to apply for admission to Drepung. Occasionally Bönpos were accepted, but the numbers were few. At many Buddhist monasteries their request for admission would have been greeted with incredulity and almost certainly rejected. Myths and misperceptions about Bönpos were rampant in the Buddhist community. But this was Drepung, renowned for its scholarship and willingness to accept foreigners and other schools of Buddhism. The two Bönpos were received civilly and assigned to a Mongolian monk, who ushered them into a room decorated with Buddhist thankas.

The Mongolian monk made them tea. They sat on floor cushions with steaming cups in their hands as he began to expound on Buddhist doctrine. The two Bönpos listened silently until finally the Mongolian pointed to a small statue of Je Tsongkhapa, the fifteenth-century Buddhist monk and founder of the Gelug school. "Do you believe in him?"

Samten and Sangye were astonished at the monk's question. Although Bön is a separate religion, Bön monks revered the Buddhist deities and religious leaders as much as their own. They could not imagine a Tibetan who did not. Largely ignorant of the intricacies of the Bön faith and its many similarities with Tibetan Buddhism, the Mongolian monk may not have realized that Bönpos also revered Buddhist figures. He likely believed that he was asking a difficult and challenging question—as if he had asked a Christian whether he believed in the prophecies of Muhammad.

"Yes, we believe in him," the two Bönpos said.

With that answer, the Mongolian accepted them as his students.

As they walked to their assigned room, they realized that Drepung was a city unto itself, with dozens of alleys separating multistoried whitewashed buildings. The monks located their six-story earthen dormitory and climbed five flights of stairs to an apartment with a cramped bedroom and a tiny kitchen with a small wood stove. Monks were segregated by region, and the apartment was in a building reserved for those from Amdo. Here they spent hours each day on their straw-stuffed mattresses studying texts and eating their way through the several cases of Chinese noodles they had been unable to sell.

Though the two Bön monks were elated at being admitted to Drepung, Samten was put off by the lack of upkeep in the warren of passageways that linked the many buildings. The grounds were strewn with litter and unswept, far different from the scrupulously clean monasteries in Amdo.

Drepung opened a new world to the young monks. They met monks from every region of Tibet and from China and Mongolia, contacts that revealed more of the world outside Tibet. Gradually they became fluent in the central Tibetan dialect. The academic tolerance fostered at Drepung allowed them to openly defend their religion in debate, a challenge they relished and took at every opportunity. With admittance came social acceptance and respect.

The day at Drepung began with a prayer meeting in the four-story Tshogchen Dukhang, a 19,375-square-foot assembly hall large enough for five thousand monks. After a final trumpeting call from a conch shell, monks who had assembled on the stone steps outside rushed into the hall to find a seat on one of the padded red cushions placed in rows extending the width of the hall, amid wooden pillars wrapped in red silk. The senior monastery officials, abbots, and incarnate lamas sat in reserved seats in front by the altars.

The first time Samten and Sangye stepped into Tshogchen Dukhang they were awestruck by the lavishness of the decor compared to the small monasteries they knew in Amdo. Brilliantly colored frescoes covered the walls, and banners with sacred vowels painted in calligraphy and long streamers of silk hung from the pillars and ceiling. The monks faced a gilded throne flanked by golden altars lined with enormous butterlamps and offerings of food and drink to the deities. The smell of incense and butterlamps hung in the air.

The monks chanted prayers as proctors armed with canes walked the rows, occasionally thumping one of the wayward preteen students for talking or other mischief. After prayers the monks headed for their classes or to their rooms to study.

Each afternoon students were required to participate in daily debates. Anyone caught playing hooky would be forced to perform onerous cleaning tasks. In Amdo, Samten and Sangye had engaged in similar ritualized debates, with one monk sitting on the ground as his opponent stood and slammed the heel of his hand into the palm of his other hand in a sweeping gesture directed at the seated rival.

Drepung had so many monks that Samten and Sangye found it easy to avoid classes and remain undetected. On some days they skipped the evening debate and had tea with their neighbors, two Bön monks from the same region of Amdo. They drew the curtains so that their truancy would remain undetected. Samten would wend his way through the complex of whitewashed buildings, rising as high as six stories, to a well several hundred yards away to fetch water for tea. One of their monk neighbors, Kesang Dargye, would buy fresh butter from vendors at the entrance to the monastery, and Sangye would stoke a fire in the stove. When Samten and Kesang returned from their missions, Sangye would make butter tea and they would sip and chat for hours. One of their favorite subjects was founding a new monastery when they returned to the Sharkhog Valley. In an imagined distribution of roles that would prove prescient, Samten would be the disciplinarian, Kesang the main teacher, and Sangye the abbot.

The dream of their own monastery led each of them to specialize in a subject that would help them fulfill this vision. Samten began studying Sanskrit, Sangye medicine, and Kesang poetry. There were less than three hundred Bön monasteries in Tibet compared to the thousands of Buddhist monasteries, so it seemed reasonable that they would be able to find an unserved group of Bönpos in need of a monastery.

At Drepung the monks fell into the rhythm of classes, study, ritual, and contemplation until the next annual Monlam Chenmo prayer festival in Lhasa. Attendance was normally required, but because the February weather was balmy and clear, Samten and Sangye obtained permission to remain at the monastery so they could savor the beautiful day. They took the opportunity to do some cleaning, and Sangye noticed that insects had infested a straw-filled cushion. He gathered the straw and descended the five floors to dispose of it. They finished cleaning the room and were drinking tea when Sangye suddenly jumped up and slapped his knees. "Where is my gold?"

Sangye's family had given him three pieces of gold to finance his education, but he had forgotten that he had hidden them in the straw pillow.

"Your gold?"

"Yes, my gold. Where is it?"

"I have no idea where your gold is."

"It was among the straw. Oh no! What did you do?"

They rushed downstairs to the disposal area where Sangye had tossed the straw and frantically searched through the pile of refuse. After a while, Sangye accepted the loss of his savings in a manner characteristic of a monk disdainful of material possessions. "I really don't mind at all," he finally told Samten.

Sangye's family was wealthy and could have easily replaced the gold, but his plea to his family for more financial assistance went unanswered. Sangye was now penniless, but he also was resourceful. A chance encounter with a wealthy family from Lhasa's aristocracy revealed the value of his charisma and mathematical skills. Lhasans at the top of the social and economic pyramid were drawn to Drepung because of its prestige. Sangye's charm and kindness made it easy for him to engage with the monied families who performed their religious duties at the monastery. One such family wanted their son to learn *kartsi,* an Indian-based astrological system used to predict solar and lunar eclipses. Sangye graciously offered to teach him. There was no contract, and payment was never mentioned, but the gangly youth who began showing up at the monk's fifth-floor dormitory always brought a generous quantity of butter, tsampa, meat, and vegetables.

The tempo of life at Drepung was interrupted in mid-1958 by the arrival of Sangye's brother-in-law, Palchenpo, and his teenage son, Khedup. Palchenpo had been fighting the Chinese occupiers for nearly three years in Amdo. His fighters had scored some early victories that kept the Chinese on the defensive by harassing their bases and ambushing supply columns crawling up the narrow mountain roads the army had built. In response, the Chinese had poured in troops, hardened Korean War veterans and Mongolian cavalry trained to operate in the harsh Tibetan landscape. Aircraft harried the guerrillas mercilessly with bombs and machine guns. Many guerrilla bands were wiped out or disintegrated into small groups that had a better chance of slipping away from their pursuers.

The Chinese onslaught forced Palchenpo and other Tibetan fighters west, and at least two thousand were in the capital. The Khampa rebel group known as the Chushi Gangdruk, from the traditional name for Kham, had established a base in the Lhoka area south of Lhasa and devised a plan for fighters to leave the city in small groups to avoid attracting Chinese attention. Palchenpo intended to join the Chushi Gangdruk. He knew that a difficult fight lay ahead, and he wanted his son to be safe. Sangye offered to care for Khedup until he could be reunited with his father.

The turmoil and dissatisfaction with the Chinese occupation was spreading to Lhasa, but it had yet to affect the routines that Sangye and Samten had settled into at Drepung. Part of their routine involved taking their raw barley to be ground at a mill in a small village nearby. Their first trip to the mill opened their eyes to a poverty they found as distasteful as the many beggars in Lhasa.

The two monks approached a few small stone houses clustered near an immense walled compound, where the landlord of the mill village lived. One of the villagers ground the barley for them, then invited them into his house. The floor was littered with trash and the walls were stained. They were offered tea without butter, and their host said that he had never tasted butter. The monks were incredulous. They gave him some butter but still found it hard to believe that he had never tasted something so common to the Tibetan diet.

The monks were taken aback by the uncleanliness and disrepair of the houses and the tattered and unwashed clothes of the inhabitants. They witnessed a deep privation unknown in rural Amdo and Kham provinces. In Amdo, even the poorest families owned a small plot of land and had a few animals. However, in central Tibet, thousands of landless Tibetans labored in poverty as part of a feudal system serving wealthy land-owning families, monasteries, and government agencies.

The encounter with the mill worker revealed to the monks the depth of poverty in Tibetan society—a centuries-old social system that the Chinese aimed to upend.

8
Broken Promises

At Menri Monastery, Tenzin Namdak absorbed himself in study, resolved to master every concept and teaching. His previous study with Gangru Rinpoche at the master's cave gave him an enormous advantage over other students. He focused on honing and deepening his practice of the three paths to enlightenment, Sutra, Tantra, and Dzogchen. Each meditation technique is a method of training the mind in calmness and peace, of taming the discordant thoughts that overwhelm daily life. Tenzin listened to his teachers, read and memorized texts, spent time in contemplation to understand the texts, and then hours in meditation. He continued to perfect the open heart and clear mind that results from such training.

Tenzin learned the teachings so thoroughly that after earning his geshe degree in 1952, the Year of the Water Dragon, at the age of twenty-seven, he was quickly elevated to the position of lopon, or head of instruction, making him one of the top officials in Bön. At his ordination as a novice monk he had taken twenty-five vows governing behavior, including vows of veracity, charity, and nonviolence. But at his enthronement ceremony as lopon, the thirty-first abbot of Menri honored Tenzin by administering a second, higher set of 253 vows that included restrictions on dress, fair treatment of others, and correct conduct.

Soon afterward the abbot departed on a long journey, leaving Tenzin in charge of Menri. As the preeminent Bön monastery, Menri had 250 branch monasteries throughout Tibet as well as in India, China, Bhutan, Sikkim, Nepal, and Mongolia. The 450-year-old Menri Monastery, which translates as "medicine mountain," was built high on Mount Shari Phowa, above the Thobgyal River valley. The Thobgyal nourishes a corridor of lush green that winds through brown, treeless mountains, before joining the Yarlung Tsangpo. According to tradition, Bön founder Tonpa Shenrab left a footprint in a rock on the mountain, saying to a young disciple, "Little boy, in the future your monastery will be here."

The three-story red and ocher monastery made of stone and rammed earth sat high on a steep hill, a lonely building adrift in a sea of steep hills and mountaintops. From the monastery's base gurgled a stream, its waters considered sacred. The stream flowed down the hill past the rooftops of some two dozen dormitory buildings spread haphazardly across the steep slope. Farther down the mountain, water from the stream turned prayer wheels held in the current by a yellow wooden structure. Each turn of a wheel radiated prayers for all sentient beings.

The monastery's largest structure was a recently completed assembly hall with low ceilings and two rooms for reliquaries and other sacred objects. Adorning the walls were murals depicting deities and revered holy men. A life-size silver statue of Bön founder Tonpa Shenrab cast its gaze over the hall, which was filled with gilded copper images of other deities and instruments used in ceremonies such as long brass horns, conch shells, and drums. Above the hall were quarters reserved for Tenzin as head teacher and a scripture study room with hundreds of cloth-wrapped boxes containing sacred texts, each resting in its own wooden slot, giving it the appearance of a wine rack. A separate building contained a shrine to the fierce-looking protection deity Sipe Gyalmo.

Two years after Tenzin assumed the title Lopon, the death of Menri's thirty-first abbot, Nyima Wangyal, created a situation that further enhanced Tenzin's standing. The monastery was abuzz with speculation about who would become its next abbot—and therefore the head of Bön. Tenzin's assistant, Sherab Lodrö, was in the running.

Unlike Tibetan Buddhism, which relies on reincarnation to replace religious leaders, in Bön, succession is determined by Bön protector dieties whose will is made known through an elaborate process. The seemingly endless layers of ceremony involved in choosing a new abbot reflected the importance of the choice. To receive divine guidance, the monks made 100,000 offerings to the protector goddess Sipe Gyalmo; ten monks performed 100,000 *yidam* ceremonies for protector deities and made 100,000 ceremonial *tormas,* red and white cakes made from barley flour.

Eventually the names of qualified candidates were written on pieces of paper that were encased in dough balls made of tsampa and medicinal herbs. The ball chosen would contain the name of the Menri abbot. Each ball was measured and weighed so that all were exactly the same. The balls were placed in a large bowl where they sat for seven days as Tenzin and other prominent monks performed ceremonies to propitiate the protector deities.

During the selection process, Tenzin dreamed that a tall, large black man drew a ceremonial khata from his chuba. The khata seemed to be endlessly long, and it formed a growing pile on the floor as he continued to pull it out. Tenzin believed the vision was a message from Menri's protector deity giving him permission to allow his assistant to become abbot.

On the seventh day the bowl of tsampa balls was gently shaken until two fell out. The other balls were discarded and ceremonies continued for another week. Finally, the bowl was shaken again until one of the balls spun out, hitting Tenzin in the chest: it contained the name of Sherab Lodrö, Tenzin's assistant.

Among the monks participating in the ceremonies was a twelve-year-old boy only recently arrived. The parents of the child monk Tenpa

Woser and his brother had sent them to Menri as a display of religious devotion. Tenzin barely noticed the child monk, who in a few years would risk his life to save the new abbot and his religion.

In late 1956, the Year of the Fire Monkey, the excitement over the naming of a new abbot was overshadowed by troubling news. Several of Tenzin's new students told him that the Chinese were forcing children to attend Chinese schools. One of the most promising students had come to Menri after spending three years in Chinese school, and understood their methods and intentions. He had come to Menri to avoid the Chinese, but they found him and ordered him to attend a Chinese school in Shigatse, the regional capital and Tibet's second largest city. As he left, he gave a private warning to Tenzin. Decades later, Tenzin recalled the warning: "He knew how the Chinese thought and what their long-term plans were, and he knew that things were going to turn bad, because these Chinese were not like those we had known in the past. He advised me to leave while it was still possible to get out of the country because it was not safe. Even if they didn't kill me I would certainly be put in prison. He said he was telling me this in confidence, because if it came to be known that he was saying such things he would be in serious trouble."[1]

This warning was reinforced later that year when Tenzin led a delegation on a three-day journey to Shigatse. The group was tasked with an obligatory appearance at a ceremony to honor the Tenth Panchen Lama, a rival to the Dalai Lama who held the second-highest office in Tibetan Buddhism and who was cooperating closely with the Chinese. The Panchen Lama had been living in China, and every monastery in the region was expected to be part of the spectacle organized to mark his return to Tibet. At Shigatse, the monks joined a formal procession passing in review before the Panchen Lama. Tenzin was disturbed to see the route lined by five thousand Chinese troops, a show of force he viewed as a troubling portent.

Previously, Tenzin had viewed the Chinese as a nuisance. Until 1956, the Communists had generally adhered to their policy of noninterference in religion and culture in U-Tsang, the province covering central Tibet, including Lhasa, Shigatse, and Menri. Such outrages as the wanton destruction of sacred images by Chinese soldiers had occurred sporadically, but there had been no official effort to eradicate religion. Reports of Chinese abuses, especially from Amdo and Kham, at first trickled in, then became a torrent. Each report reminded Tenzin of his former student's warning about the Chinese threat. It became clear to him that the Chinese occupiers were much more than a nuisance—they were a threat to everything he held sacred.

The Chinese did not consider the eastern provinces of Amdo and Kham as part of the Tibet Autonomous Region, located in the southwest of Tibet and officially recognized as such in the infamous seventeen-point agreement negotiated by China in 1951. The agreement had promised Tibetans religious freedom in exchange for Chinese control of their foreign relations. The Chinese considered Amdo and Kham to be outside the scope of the seventeen-point agreement. Nevertheless, Tenzin was unsettled by the vicious assaults on religion and culture in these two eastern provinces. He was horrified to learn that the Chinese had targeted monasteries for persecution. He sympathized with reforms ostensibly aimed at equity and fair treatment of all people, but the Chinese seemed to be using those ideals to cloak injustice by forcefully and often brutally confiscating wealth and distributing it to those with political connections as well as to those of lower status. The Chinese won over the poorest Tibetans by giving them money and position, sometimes appointing beggars as village leaders. They encouraged poor Tibetans to chastise and beat their middle- and upper-class neighbors and take their possessions in public *thamzings,* or "struggle sessions," aimed at shaping public opinion through false accusations, public humiliation, and executions. Attendance at thamzings was mandatory. The rich were made poor and the poor made powerful under Chinese Communist rule.

Tenzin was especially troubled to learn the occupiers indoctrinated children and enlisted them as soldiers in their war of ideology. Children were urged to inform on their parents and to punish them. Newborns were forcibly taken from their mothers and sent to China to be raised as Communists. New stories of abuse arrived with every visitor. Tenzin heard appalling tales, like the one from Rigong, in Amdo, where about five hundred monks from thirty-five monasteries were arrested on the charge of being bandits blocking the road to progress. Tibetans, acting under the threat of death, were joined by Chinese women in the public humiliation of the three highest lamas, yanking their hair, taking their shoes, and forcing them to kneel on gravel. Their tormentors mocked their reputed powers of prophecy, asking them, "Since you are lamas did you not know that you were going to be arrested?" The tormentors shoved the lamas into a pit and forced onlookers to urinate on them. The Chinese soldiers sarcastically told them they were free to use their mystical powers to fly out of the pit. Eventually they were hoisted from the pit, chains placed around their necks, and each given a basket of human waste to carry. Their humiliation complete, guards led the lamas off to prison. The rest of the monks were transported to China.[2]

Equally terrible stories came from Tenzin's homeland, Kham. Some of those stories were documented in a 1960 report to the International Commission of Jurists in Geneva, Switzerland. In the village of Derge, the Chinese arrested a lama and twelve monks. They took the lama to the public square and accused him of exploiting Tibetans and amassing wealth. They harnessed him like a horse, compelled him to eat grass, then invited Tibetan women to sit on his back and ride and beat him.[3]

Also in Kham, villagers in Jueba were called to an assembly near the Phuntsogk Ling Monastery, where about five hundred monks resided. There they witnessed the Chinese try to force an old monk to marry. The monk said he would rather be executed than break his vow of celibacy. He was made to kneel bare-kneed on jagged stones for fifteen minutes and on thorns for an hour. As he kneeled in pain, soldiers and the woman they wanted him to marry slapped him, pulled his ears, and pricked his head with a bayonet. He and ten other monks were handcuffed, manacled, and imprisoned. The next day the old monk was publicly beaten to death.[4]

Children in Jueba were encouraged to torment their parents and criticize them if they clung to their customs and religion rather than embracing Communist doctrine. This indoctrination influenced an eighteen-year-old boy to kick and heap abuse on his father after discovering him with a prayer wheel and a mala. The father struck back and a fight ensued. Three Chinese soldiers stopped the fight, telling a gathering crowd that the youth had every right to beat his father. Under their protection, the youth resumed beating and cursing his father. Overcome by humiliation and despair, the father leaped into a nearby river and drowned.[5]

"There were many cases where monks were disrobed and forced to have intercourse with disrobed nuns, with the Chinese cadre then disdainfully proclaiming that such is the religion of the Tibetans and the so-called vows of chastity," recalled Gompo Tashi Andrugtsang, a prosperous trader who was instrumental in uniting the resistance under the banner of the Chushi Gangdruk. "Then these monks would usually be executed and the nuns given to the Chinese soldiers.[6]

"In many areas very few females escaped being raped, regardless of age, and often they were repeatedly raped before being killed. They were stripped of their clothing in the presence of all, and if the man refused to 'confess' to the charges, the women were raped in front of the man," Gompo Tashi said. "There were always enough Chinese soldiers present who had not been with a woman for a long time and who were more than willing to follow orders and participate. There were even cases of the man being forced to have intercourse with his wife in front of the others, after which he would be executed and his daughters and wife then given to the Chinese soldiers."[7]

Exactly how many Tibetans died in Chinese reprisals is unclear, but it's certain that the numbers are high. Several mass graves dating from

1958 and later have been excavated in recent years, but Chinese officials refuse to acknowledge responsibility, viewing any attempt to discuss the issue as an unwarranted attack on their efforts to modernize Tibet. The Tibetan government-in-exile, in Dharamshala, India, has estimated that 1.2 million Tibetans died over several decades, but some scholars question the estimate because it was based on anecdotes rather than any accepted method of calculation.[8]

The Chinese government told the world that they were bringing social, economic, and political freedom to a Tibetan people governed by an oppressive government controlled by the West. The investigation by the International Commission of Jurists shattered that assertion. Investigators interviewed Chinese and Tibetans to examine the conflicting claims about conditions inside Tibet. The 1960 report by the commission to the secretary general of the United Nations exposed to the world the horrors of Chinese occupation. The commission concluded that the Communists were engaged in "religious genocide." Investigators found that the Chinese were systematically eradicating Tibetan religious practices, killing religious figures and forcibly sending large numbers of children to China for indoctrination. "What the Chinese People's Government was seeking to do by this time, according to their own publications, was to break up the monasteries," the commission said.[9]

Bön is mentioned neither by the commission nor the Chinese. The religion was virtually unknown outside Tibetan cultural regions, and it is doubtful that many Chinese officials understood that Buddhism and Bön, despite many similarities, were two different traditions. The Chinese Communists were opposed to the very idea of religion. They persecuted Buddhist and Bönpo alike.

Chinese documents showed their intention to eradicate Buddhism, and by inference, Bön. "What we need is socialist thinking, and all non-socialist thinking must undergo socialist transformation. The viewpoints of lamas are different from socialist thinking, but they must accept socialist transformation, rid themselves of non-socialist thinking, and establish socialist thinking and viewpoints," reads a Chinese document quoted by the commission.[10]

A Chinese proclamation published in a Tibetan newspaper was more direct: "All the crimes and guilts of the monasteries must be exposed. The masks of the reactionary leaders who pretentiously assumed to be kind are in reality cruel as wolves. They must be exterminated. The masses must be informed through a much more intensified campaign about these crimes."[11]

Eventually, Tibetans struck back at the Chinese. Furious nomads from the Golok region of Amdo began attacking Chinese bases in late 1955. The rebellion quickly spread to Kham. In early 1956, twenty-three clan leaders laid siege to a string of Chinese military bases in Kham in a well-planned campaign. Fighting in Kham and Amdo would continue for at least four more years, with thousands of vanquished Tibetan fighters forced to seek refuge in Lhasa in 1957 and 1958.

The merciless Chinese response included the destruction of monasteries and villages by Tupolev-4 bombers. In any other terrain they would fly thousands of feet above the ground, but in the high altitudes and jagged terrain of the Tibetan Plateau they sometimes flew below mountains where Khampa riflemen perched. Khampas fired at the relatively slow-moving aircraft from high ridges, putting seventeen holes in one.[12] "The Chinese brought in reinforcements and increased their air and ground operations against their unruly Khampa subjects in a punitive campaign, committing the classic acts of a rampaging and vengeful army: torture, barbarous executions, public acts of degradation, forced labor, the seizure of private property, the desecration of monasteries, the deportation of men and boys, and finally taking children from their homes for reeducation in China," former CIA case officer Kenneth Knaus wrote in his book *Orphans of the Cold War*.[13]

The growing Chinese assault on religion, his student's warning, and his own experience at the Panchen Lama's ceremony made it clear to Tenzin that it would only be a matter of time before the Chinese turned their attention to Menri.

As Tenzin worried about the looming threat of the Chinese occupation, he realized that Menri was in financial trouble. Menri was in the hands of a young and inexperienced abbot, Sherab Lodrö, Tenzin's former assistant. Tenzin had a strong personal relationship with Sherab Lodrö and wanted him to succeed. He had given the abbot his best advice, but now it appeared that more than good counsel was needed to shore up the monastery's sinking finances. Tenzin decided he could be of better service raising the needed revenue. The region near Lake Dangra, on the Changthang Plateau, was traditionally a lucrative source of contributions for Menri from nomads rich in livestock, one of the most important sources of Tibetan wealth. But donations had waned in recent years. He decided he could revive the badly needed flow of funds by relocating to Sezhig, a small but important monastery in the Dangra region that had no abbot. Sezhig was considered a Menri satellite, a place where Tenzin's status as a highly regarded lama would make it easier to revive the flagging contributions. He also would be free to practice his religion in peace at the remote northern monastery not yet on the Chinese radar. He hoped to eventually return to Menri and resume his position as head teacher.

Tenzin therefore resigned as lopon over the objections of Sherab Lodrö, staying only long enough to participate in the enthronement of a new head teacher. In 1957, the Tibetan Year of the Fire Bird, he decided to make the long trek north to the Changthang Plateau accompanied by his new assistant, Sherab Tsultrim, and two other monks. In resigning from his position at Menri he was leaving one of the most prestigious positions in Bön.

Tenzin worried that Chinese commissars might try to thwart his plans. The Chinese distrusted the monks and watched them closely. Although the monks at Menri were peaceful, monks in eastern Tibet had encouraged rebellion and often took up arms. To avoid suspicion,

Tenzin let it be known that he was going to a remote monastery far removed from areas of Chinese concern. He gathered some food and a few belongings and sacred objects, which were lashed onto several horses and mules, before setting out on a journey of some two hundred miles north along worn trails.

Just outside the monastery he passed Dragon Rock, believed to be a stone apparition of an open dragon's mouth. Legend has it that an invading Mongol army spared Menri because the building became invisible; the Mongol invaders only saw an illusion of a lake covered in birds and Dragon Rock, which appeared to the Mongols as a huge, fire-breathing dragon.

The monastery dropped from view as they descended the treeless slopes past isolated stone corrals used by nomads to keep sheep and goats during the winter to Ruchen, the highest village in the Thobgyal River valley. Farmers outside the village tilled their fields with iron plows pulled by yaks. Each yak had red flags tied near its head to propitiate the gods. The travelers passed through villages shaded by groves of ancient poplars, some with trunks ten feet in diameter.[14] Once they reached the Yarlung Tsangpo, Tenzin turned east, quickening his steps as he approached Yungdrungling Monastery in anticipation of a warm reunion with old friends. At Yungdrungling, the group spent a few days resting, sharing news, and praying for peace and protection. Tenzin walked through halls covered in the images he had painted as a boy, noticing the rich colors and sacred iconography, casting a critical eye on some of his own brushstrokes. All that artistry would later be obliterated by the Chinese in a frenzy of destruction.

After their brief stay at Yungdrungling, Tenzin and his party followed the river west, then turned north up a wide valley until they came to a pass in the mountains girding the Changthang Plateau. They topped the 17,500-foot pass and entered the loftiest part of the Tibetan Plateau.

The Changthang is one of the least populated areas in Asia and the third least populated region in the world after Antartica and northern

Greenland. The plateau rises to an average altitude of 16,000 feet and stretches nearly a thousand miles, from China's Qinghai Province west across Tibet into northwestern India. A leg of the ancient silk road runs across the plateau, where travelers endure weather so erratic that in an instant a cloudless summer sky can turn into a howling storm. The weather can switch from serene to violent several times during a day. Winds sometimes become so intense they can sweep riders from their horses, making travel nearly impossible at times. Temperatures occasionally drop below freezing even during the summer, which can last as little as three weeks. Immense stretches of sand and gravel, bare of even a blade of grass, fill much of the space between mountains on the Changthang. The barren landscape at times gives way to wide steppes that bloom with wildflowers in the summer and are home to herds of antelope, wild ass, sheep, and yak. The Changthang is dotted with some ten thousand saltwater and freshwater lakes varying in size from tiny to 750 square miles. The rarefied air is so clear that views of ten miles are common, and hundred-mile views can be had from mountain vantage points.

The Changthang is bounded and crisscrossed by mountains that rise more than 20,000 feet. The plateau is separated from the slightly lower, more hospitable central Tibet by the Nyenchen Thanglha and Kangkar Mountains, interconnected ranges that form a thousand-mile barrier running east and west that is 23,000 feet at the highest point.

After crossing the pass, Tenzin's party entered a wide, sandy plain. They passed jumbles of rock that have been described by researchers as the remains of ancient fortresses of the ancient kingdom of Zhang Zhung, which sprawled across the Changthang Plateau when a more hospitable climate made life at such a high altitude more congenial. At its height the kingdom is said to have encompassed the upper part of western Tibet and parts of Nepal, northern India, and Pakistan. Now dryer and colder, the plateau is so inhospitable that it is home only to nomadic herders and the rare farmer.

The last few days of the nearly two-week journey took them through rugged mountain trails. The monastery that came into view at the end of the trail was far less impressive than Menri. A white-plastered, two-story temple and a separate red-plastered building housing monks rose from a flat-topped hill at the base of a treeless mountain. Inside they found frescoes depicting the mountain deities Targo Gegan and Targo Ngomar and the lake goddess Dangra adorning the walls. Although Sezhig Monastery's fifteen monks were only a fraction of the five hundred at Menri, the small monastery was considered large among the tiny monasteries in the Changthang region. It was built next to the ruins of a thirteenth-century Mongolian fortress and was revered both for its collection of sacred relics and for its founding in the same year as Menri, 1405. Sezhig Monastery was considered so central to Tibetan history that the Fifth Dalai Lama recognized it, and his government supported it with a small annual cash contribution.

The monastery sat near Mount Targo, which towers over Lake Dangra, one of the three most sacred lakes for Bönpos. The mountain and lake are one of Bön's sacred dyads, the mountain regarded as the male and the lake the female in a spiritual union. The area was so far from the more hospitable areas of Tibet that it remained free of Chinese troops and officials.

After settling in, Tenzin made good on his promise. In the summer he set out with his assistant, Sherab Tsultrim, two other monks, three mules, and a horse to gather donations of food from Bönpo villages in the region in return for performing rituals of blessing, healing, and protection. He collected donations of cheese and butter from nomads, and barley, turnips, and hay from farmers. When he was not raising funds to support Menri he taught the Sezhig monks.

In the autumn, monks traditionally would go house-to-house, offering to perform rituals in return for contributions of yak butter, cheese, and highly prized *yarsa gunbu,* or cordyceps, a type of fungus that sprouts mushroomlike from the bodies of caterpillars and is valued for its medicinal properties. Although such solicitation was a longstanding tradition, Tenzin was uncomfortable asking for donations from the poor. He felt it wrong to ask something from a family that had nothing, so he halted the practice of door-to-door solicitation. Tenzin accepted donations only from those who could afford to give.

In the winter, Tenzin retreated to a cave and practiced sky gazing, a form of meditation with the eyes open and fixed on the heavens, his mind entering its natural state, clear of all thoughts focusing on pure light. By spring, when he returned to Sezhig to resume his duties, Tibetan grievances seethed in faraway Lhasa. The ripples from the resulting violence would upend life at Sezhig.

9
Iron Hell

For more than two years, refugees had streamed into Lhasa from Kham and Amdo, bringing horror stories of Chinese aircraft bombing monasteries and slaughtering entire villages. Many fleeing Tibetans were armed warriors who had fought Chinese troops. Some of them had fought to avenge the destruction of their homes and the abuse of their families. Others were members of the Kham-based Tibetan resistance group, the Chushi Gangdruk.[1]

Now the populace believed the Chinese were poised to commit the crowning outrage. Chinese generals had asked the Dalai Lama to enter a Chinese military compound in Lhasa alone, unaccompanied by his bodyguards, to attend a dance performance. Word spread that the Dalai Lama would become a prisoner if he accepted the Chinese invitation. It was March 10, 1959, and thousands of Tibetans were streaming toward the Norbulingka complex. The Dalai Lama's 364-room summer palace stood inside a high wall surrounding eighty-six acres of lush gardens and buildings near the Lhasa River. They intended to shield the Dalai Lama with their bodies. Tensions heightened after the Chinese announced over the radio, without consulting the Dalai Lama, that he was scheduled to visit Beijing soon. The announcement sparked rumors that the Chinese intended to abduct the Dalai Lama and imprison him in the Chinese capital.

Tashi Lhakpa Khedrup was one of the Lhasans heading to the Norbulingka. He had never met Tenzin, Samten, or Sangye, but his life would eventually intersect with theirs. Tashi was a dob-dob, a Buddhist monk who had forsaken a life of religious study and instead devoted himself to developing his athletic and fighting prowess. Each of the three great Gelug monasteries in Lhasa had a contingent of dob-dobs, warrior monks who protected the monasteries. Dob-dobs were free of many of the restrictions that bound scholarly monks and, like Tashi, could pursue their own interests without damaging their ties to the monastery. Tashi managed a restaurant in Lhasa owned by a former dob-dob but also kept a room at Sera Monastery.

Tashi heard all of the gossip because the restaurant was a popular gathering spot for all levels of society in Lhasa: everyone from aristocrats to monks came to sample Tashi's dumplings and amuse themselves by playing board games and listening to the restaurant's wireless radio. The head of the rebel group Chushi Gangdruk, Gompo Tashi Andrugtsang, was an occasional customer, and the restaurant owner, Gyalpo Chandzo, was a member of the People's Party, known as the Mimang, the Lhasa resistance organization.[2]

Gyalpo grabbed a Mauser pistol and Tashi borrowed a long sword before joining the crowd at the summer palace.[3] The Chinese occupation of Lhasa in 1950 ignited indignation and resentment among Lhasans that had burned unseen, like a fire deep in a coal mine. The influx of refugees and their horror stories stoked that smoldering anger. Finally, the perceived threat to the Dalai Lama, who embodied the national pride in his person, inflamed the crowds like smoldering coal exposed to oxygen.

Tensions were high, and the city was preparing for war. Tibetans were fortifying key buildings throughout Lhasa, including the Jokhang. Pilgrims prostrated on the paving stones in front of the Jokhang as armed men moved through its hallways lined with alcoves holding statues of Buddha, Tibetan saints, and wrathful deities. Riflemen took up fighting positions on the roof. Bales of wet wool to protect against Chinese bullets were used to fortify strongpoints. Barricades and trenches were going up at the Medical College on Iron Hill and at the Ramagang Ferry, a key crossing on the Lhasa River.[4]

The Chinese, aware of the increasing hostility, had been strengthening their defenses for months. At their encampments they excavated tunnels to connect key defensive positions, dug trenches, strung electrified wire, and built machine-gun nests. They made defensive preparations at administrative buildings and key points in the city, placing machine guns in windows of strategic buildings.

Hostility toward the occupation increased hourly. Chinese civilians were likely to be stabbed if they ventured into the streets. Tibetans walked off their jobs in Chinese homes, businesses, schools, and hospitals.

By the afternoon the crowd around the Norbulingka had swelled to about thirty thousand by some accounts. Leaders in the crowd formed a seventy-member Freedom Committee before the mass streamed to the Potala, where the committee renounced and burned copies of the seventeen-point agreement that China used as an excuse to occupy Tibet.[5] The former Tibetan governor of Chamdo, Ngabo, was regarded by the people as a Tibetan quisling for signing the seventeen-point capitulation accord with China nine years earlier, without the consent of the Dalai Lama or the policy-making Kashag.

Soko Karmay, Samten Karmay's brother, joined the swelling crowd of men and women at the Norbulingka, every one of them resolved to give their life to defend the Dalai Lama. Against modern arms and hardened Chinese troops, a few Khampas had British Enfield bolt-action rifles, but others were armed with ancient muzzle-loading rifles. Old men brought knives, shop owners wielded swords, construction workers brandished picks and shovels, farmers brought axes, and women and youth brought any weapon they could scrounge. Zeal outweighed reason. They dug a trench around the summer palace walls and milled about as they waited, defying the Chinese to come for the Dalai Lama. They stood no chance against the Communist war machine. A contingent of Chinese troops had already taken up positions near the Norbulingka, alarming Tibetan officials. Fearing an imminent attack, officials opened the armory and handed outdated bolt-action rifles, bayonets, and cartridges to volunteers. Soko grabbed a rifle and bayonet.

The crowds outside the Norbulingka dismayed the governing Kashag. The Kashag, the cabinet that made all major policy decisions, met to discuss the growing crisis in a building inside the Norbulingka walls equipped to meet their every need. Servants brought tea, steamed bread, and dishes of cold meat from adjoining kitchens to a long table in a room adorned with Buddha statues and woven thankas hanging from the walls. The ministers badly wanted to avoid a confrontation with the Chinese that could only end in disaster.[6]

The next day, Chinese general Tan Guansan sent the Kashag, by now powerless to control the people, an ultimatum: remove the barricades that were being built throughout the city or be responsible for the consequences. The Kashag tried without success to persuade the leaders of the Freedom Committee to remove the barricades; the resistance leaders argued that if the Chinese wanted to be rid of the barricades it could only mean they wanted a clear path to abduct the Dalai Lama. They pointed out that the Chinese had erected their own barricades.

The Dalai Lama abhorred violence and felt that it was his responsibility to thwart its possibility. He never felt threatened by the Chinese invitation and was willing to attend the dance, but canceled for fear of inciting the crowds that had come to prevent him from keeping his appointment. Upon learning that the Kashag had failed to persuade his people to remove the barricades, the Dalai Lama asked to have all seventy members of the Freedom Committee brought to him. He addressed them in front of the Kashag, asking them to disperse and lay down their weapons. For all his power and the esteem he evinced from his people, even the Dalai Lama could do no more than win one grudging concession. The Freedom Committee would regroup the

Norbulingka defenders at the foot of the Potala, two miles distant. The concession did little to ease tensions. Thousands of Tibetans refused to relocate and remained in place to defend the summer palace.

On March 12, Tibetan defiance took the form of thousands of women marching from the foot of the Potala east to the Barkhor neighborhood surrounding the Jokhang, shouting "Independence now" and, "Go ahead and shoot us" as they passed People's Liberation Army troops along their route. The women jammed the streets in a show of courage in front of Chinese guns.[7]

By now the Kashag was urging the Dalai Lama to slip away to avoid the inevitable violence. He refused. In his autobiography he wrote, "I would indeed have been willing to go [to the Chinese headquarters] and throw myself on the mercy of the Chinese if that would have prevented the massacre of my people, but the people would never have let me do it."[8] Without the Dalai Lama's knowledge, his chamberlain, Phala, had made secret arrangements for an escape on March 17.

Chinese garrison commanders, even though they were convinced that the protesters were part of a plot by the Tibetan government, were under orders from the Communist Party Central Committee to remain on the defensive. They nevertheless made offensive plans as a precaution. Soldiers began plotting firing grids for artillery. On March 16, Kashag member Ngabo, who was now openly collaborating with the Chinese, sent a letter to the Dalai Lama asking him to inform the Chinese general Tan which building he would be in so that it could be left undamaged. The Dalai Lama did not reply. Instead, he penned a deceptive letter to General Tan in an attempt to forestall a Chinese assault: "A few days from now, when there are enough forces that I can trust, I shall make my way to the Military Area Command secretly. When that time comes, I shall first send you a letter."[9]

The following day, as the Dalai Lama sat on a gilded platform before the Kashag, an explosion shook the conference room. A Chinese mortar shell had detonated near the building. A second explosion rocked the building and sent a geyser of dust and rock into the air outside the northern wall.

Silence followed the two explosions. The Tibetans believed the Chinese were sending a warning. In reality, the rounds had been fired in error by a mortar company. Troops were under orders to take no offensive action. The errant rounds, however, convinced the Dalai Lama that violence was imminent and that escape was his only option.

The next day, March 17, Phala's escape plans were put into motion. The Dalai Lama's mother and youngest brother left the palace first, both disguised as male servants. A group of key government officials accompanying the Dalai Lama escaped in the back of a tarp-covered truck. Finally, the Dalai Lama, his chamberlain, the commander of his bodyguard, and a high-ranking monk left through a side entrance in the walls surrounding the Norbulingka. The Dalai Lama was disguised as a soldier and carried a rifle, his spectacles tucked inside his pocket.

As they were leaving a strong wind whipped up a dust storm that enveloped them as they threaded their way through the crowd outside the walls, shortening the range of vision to a few feet and making it difficult for anyone to identify the Dalai Lama as the group made its way toward the Lhasa River. They rejoined the rest of their party at the river and crossed in coracles. On the other side they were greeted by a party of rebel cavalry that would guide them to the Indian border.

The following day, Lhasa was prepared for war. Men with rifles settled into snipers' positions on balconies and rooftops; girls could be seen carrying butcher knives, old men with sharpened sticks, children with rocks, and monks with Molotov cocktails and firearms. The streets were filled with people carrying weapons or hauling their possessions as they fled the city. Others milled about and drank chang, a locally brewed alcoholic beverage. Youths smeared feces on posters of Mao Tse Tung that were plastered across the city. Posters appeared on walls throughout Lhasa taunting the Chinese: "Chinese return to China!" "Tibet belongs to Tibet!" "We will wipe out the Chinese!"

Samten's brother Soko was with the ragtag army of rebellious Tibetans on March 19 awaiting a Chinese assault outside the Norbulingka. He knew there was a chance he might not survive a confrontation with Chinese troops. He decided to visit his brother at the Drepung Monastery, to say goodbye, then return to the trenches the next day. The decision likely saved his life. Taking only a bayonet, he made his way to Drepung.

Sangye Tenzin and Samten Karmay greeted Soko with a cup of tea and they talked until nearly midnight. With them was Khedup, Sangye's fifteen-year-old nephew entrusted to his care by Sangye's rebel brother-in-law. Sangye, his nephew, and the two brothers chatted over tea until they grew weary and went to bed. The sound of explosions and gunfire awoke them about 4:00 a.m. on March 20. Soko and Khedup joined the two monks as they dashed to the roof of the six-story dormitory where they could view the city. Fighting between the rebellious population and Chinese troops had begun.

An exchange of gunfire between Chinese troops and Khampas guarding a ferry crossing launched the Battle of Lhasa. Both sides feared an offensive by the other, but the Tibetans were largely unorganized and had no plans to attack the Chinese. The Chinese had only two understrength regiments, probably no more than 2,500 troops, and feared being overrun. At 3:40 a.m., gunshots fired at the ferry could be heard throughout Lhasa. A Chinese company that had been ordered to take control of the ferry radioed that Khampas had fired on them and they had returned fire. Within minutes, Chinese headquarters received reports that Tibetans were attacking barricaded offices in the city. Believing a full-scale attack was underway, General Tan resolved to take the offensive. Tibetans were fearsome fighters individually, but he was certain that they were too disorganized to cope with coordinated attacks from experienced and well-armed soldiers.[10]

As Lhasa descended into violence, from the rooftop of the monastery Samten and Sangye could see little more than flashes of light accompanying the constant sound of gunfire in the early morning darkness. As the orange light of dawn crept into the valley, they could eventually make out smoke curling skyward from the southern end of the Norbulingka about three miles away near the Lhasa River. The cool, transparent air and the height of Drepung offered a crisp view of the Tibetan capital. Despite the clear view, distance hid the grisly details. The smoke rising from Norbulingka gave evidence of a devastating artillery bombardment that slaughtered the volunteers in their inadequate trenches. A charge by Khampa cavalry turned back a Chinese assault, but the incessant bombardment left bodies stacked in piles. In the city, the streets were filled with animal carcasses. A young boy was shot through the head as he peed against a wall. The streets were filled with running, screaming people.[11]

Before Chinese artillery blasted Norbulingka, Tashi, tired of the inaction and chaos there, returned to Sera Monastery. From the grounds of Sera, about three miles north of Lhasa, at the base of Pubuchok Mountain, he and other dob-dobs could see clouds of dust and smoke rising from explosions at Norbulingka. As they watched, three shells landed nearby in rapid succession, shaking the ground and showering the monastery with dust and stones. The dob-dobs dived into nearby ditches and ravines. No more shells landed, but the bombardment only fueled the warrior monks' anger. As they discussed a course of action, one of the monks began organizing a force to go to the Potala to get weapons from its armory. "Hands up anyone who will come with me," he said. Tashi was one of about four hundred monks, mostly dob-dobs, who set out for the Potala.

To reach the Potala the monks had to pass by the Trapchi Barracks, a fortified Chinese camp. As they neared the barracks, Chinese troops opened fire, forcing the monks to shelter under the banks of a stream that ran nearby. Protected from view by its banks, they followed the streambed past another military post near the Potala. The Chinese fired at occasional flashes of movement, but the monks kept to the cover of the streambed and avoided casualties. The firing drew the attention of a Tibetan army detachment stationed at the Potala, which began firing at the Chinese, distracting them from the monks lying in the streambed waiting for an opportunity to move forward. As they lay there, three Chinese armored cars from the Trapchi Barracks attacked the Potala. A Tibetan army mortar round struck one of the armored cars, which exploded in flames. The other two cars scurried away. Meanwhile, the monks crept to a grove of poplars that shielded them as they made their way to the north gate of the Potala. Tibetan soldiers guarding the gate allowed them in and directed them to the armory, which was on the south side of the Potala, exposed and within range of a Chinese position. The soldiers warned the monks that it would be foolhardy to go there. One of the monks called for volunteers. Every monk raised his hand.

To reach the armory, the monks sprinted down a wide, slippery stone staircase, through a door, then across a courtyard to the armory. The armory was in a white stone tower that offered partial shelter from Chinese view. The monks ran for the armory as the Chinese began firing mortars and machine guns at them. They made it unscathed, then broke open the armory door. The monks took several hundred rifles and dodged Chinese bullets to carry the weapons back to the sheltered areas of the Potala. The ammunition was stored separately, in an even more exposed room near where the rifles were stored. The monks lined up along the stairway and through the courtyard, passing boxes of ammunition along the line as bullets whizzed by and mortar rounds exploded. Several monks were wounded, and a bullet killed a boy from Lhasa who had insisted on joining the monks.

Chinese artillery shells rained on the sacred Potala, Tibet's symbolic heart, killing and wounding many of the women and children sent there for safety. The palace was filled with screaming children and their mothers, and the monks tried to comfort them. There was little they could do. There were no medical supplies, food, or water. Occasionally the bombardment would stop long enough to allow loudspeakers to blare out demands for surrender. The bombardment focused on a tower occupied by Tibetan soldiers overlooking the Chinese position. The shelling reduced the tower to a pile of rock and masonry. The Kindling Monastery next to the Potala went up in flames. Tashi could see monks being shot as they fled the fire. Late in the afternoon he could see shells falling on Sera Monastery.

The monks from Sera fired from the Potala at any Chinese they saw, but otherwise felt powerless. As the fighting died down and darkness approached, Tashi wandered through the thousand rooms of the great Potala. He climbed wooden stairways and walked narrow, dark hallways into cavernous halls and small rooms. He saw shrines dedicated to past Dalai Lamas in one room, and in another he gaped at the cathedral-like space holding the colossal gilded shrine of the Thirteenth Dalai Lama, the predecessor to the current title-holder. Gold and bejeweled bowls, butterlamps, crowns, and other priceless objects lay unattended. Tashi never saw a single Potala official in his wanderings.

Tashi and the other dob-dobs were thirsty and hungry, but the only available water and food were offerings and therefore taboo. They looked longingly at the butter, tsampa, and bowls of water laid on shrines. Finally they reasoned that they would be forgiven because they were fighting for the Dalai Lama. They devoured the offerings.

At nightfall the monks crept back to Sera, again using the streambed for shelter. Chinese troops probed the darkness with searchlights and caught a group of monks in a beam of light. They opened fire. One monk was killed and several wounded. The injured were carried to Sera. The shelling continued intermittently throughout the night. After each explosion the monastery dogs howled and horses in the stable whinnied and stomped in fright.

Exhausted, Tashi fell asleep. He was shaken awake a few hours later and told that he had been chosen to escort the young Sharpa Lama, the most important figure at Sera Monastery, in an attempt to follow the Dalai Lama to India. Tashi and the entire escort, with the exception of Sharpa Lama and two other lamas, exchanged their robes for chubas and rifles. They left while it was still dark, a line of pack mules and horses winding along a back trail in order to avoid the Chinese and reach safety outside Tibet. Tashi would never return to Lhasa.[12]

10
Flight

As explosions and gunfire rocked Lhasa, the head lamas at Drepung Monastery convened the monks in a great hall at noon on March 20, 1959. Samten, Sangye, Soko, and Khedup had been on the dormitory roof all morning, listening to the boom of artillery and watching shell strikes cause puffs of smoke and eruptions of black earth in the city below. They could make out tiny figures among burning buildings in the distance but could not distinguish between Chinese and Tibetans. Their minds buzzed with questions. What happened to the Dalai Lama? What was happening to the people of Lhasa? They hoped for answers in a meeting called by the Drepung lamas. Instead of sharing news about the fighting the lamas told the incredulous monks, all of whom could see smoke and hear gunfire, that nothing was amiss. After the brief, puzzling announcement, the assembly was dismissed. The leaders of the monastery had decided to ignore the destruction and killing engulfing the city, clinging to the unbelievable notion that they could remain aloof from the conflict until they could return to their familiar routines.

A boom that shook the monastery buildings underscored the monks' skepticism. An artillery shell left a smoking crater on the slope in front of the monastery, a clear warning from the Chinese.

Passions ran high among monks. Many monasteries had armories, and even monks who were not fighters were arming themselves and rushing to the city to join the fighting in the streets. Samten and Sangye remained cool-headed, taking into consideration their vows of nonviolence and the reality of the overwhelming Chinese military power. They recoiled at the idea of a group of untrained monks taking on the well-equipped, battle-tested Chinese army. "We thought that it was quite hopeless," Samten said.[1] The two monks pulled Soko aside. Soko wanted to fight and was worried about their mother, Zinmo, who usually could be found selling butter at the Barkhor market in the center of the city. Samten convinced his younger brother that it was futile to join the fight and too dangerous to go into the city. "That, of course, was impossible," Samten said about trying to find his mother amid the carnage. "There was no possibility of going back from Drepung to Norbulingka because of the fighting."[2]

From the rooftop they eventually saw a swarm of figures fleeing Norbulingka toward the Lhasa River. They were unaware that the Dalai Lama had already fled the city. They could tell from their rooftop perch that the fighting was fierce, but they were unaware that Chinese artillery had obliterated the Medical College on Iron Hill. Tibetan soldiers had dragged outdated artillery up the hill and pounded a Chinese base. In response, the Chinese brought in a battery of modern artillery that rained accurate fire on the hilltop. Few defenders survived.

That night, while Chinese and Tibetans battled for control of the city, Samten, his brother Soko, Sangye, and his nephew Khedup decided to slip away. Samten wanted to leave quickly and travel light so they could put as much distance as possible between them and the fighting. He was baffled when he observed Sangye stuffing sacred, silk-wrapped, heavy Bön texts into a leather backpack. Sangye wanted to haul away so many texts that Samten objected, saying the extra weight would make the journey more difficult, but Sangye was determined to save as many as possible. They argued until Samten agreed to carry a few texts and Sangye grudgingly agreed to leave a few behind. Sangye carried many more texts than Samten but never complained about the burden during their long journey.

Joined by three other monks, the group began hiking the steep trail leading up the 18,000-foot mountain behind Drepung. They could see fires burning in the city and bursts of light from explosions, all accompanied by the constant clatter of battle.

The last rebel bastion to fall would be the Jokhang, on March 22, where scores of Tibetans had fled. Chinese shells crashed into the elaborate golden roofs and machine-gun bullets ripped into the throng of Tibetans making a ritual walk around the temple in an attempt to invoke the protection of the deities. Khampas, fortified inside the temple, fired back with their own machine guns. Sword-wielding cavalry sallied from the temple grounds. After a three-hour battle, a Chinese tank smashed through the main gate.

Bodies clogged the streets in the aftermath. An estimated 15,000 men, women, and children died in the fighting. The Chinese imprisoned tens of thousands of Tibetans, including 25,000 monks from the three great monasteries.[3]

As tensions had built over the previous weeks, Samten and Soko had arranged to meet their mother at Yungdrungling Monastery, about a six-day walk west of Lhasa, if the worst happened. The worst had happened, and the brothers hoped they would find their mother waiting for them at the monastery.

Sangye led the group along the steep trail as star shells fired by the Chinese to illuminate the urban battleground below cast an eerie light on the rocky trail. The fleeing monks hoped the Chinese were too focused on putting down the rebellion to worry about their flight, but a nagging fear hastened their pace. They made it to the top of the mountain behind Drepung before daylight, then continued down the other side until they found a hollow where they could rest.

In the morning, another party of monks appeared behind them, higher on the trail. As the morning progressed, others appeared until finally there was a stream of refugees. As Samten watched the numbers swell, he became more and more certain that the decision to flee was the right one. Most were fleeing south, toward the Yarlung Tsangpo, which they could then follow to Bhutan or to Assam Province in India. The little band of Bönpos headed west to rendezvous with Samten's mother.

After brewing morning tea and eating a few handfuls of tsampa, the monks set off for Yungdrungling Monastery. The early chill faded by midmorning, and the monks could feel the heat of the Tibetan sun on their shaven heads. One of the three monks who had joined them, Kesang Dargye, astonished the others by ripping cloth from his sacred robes, an act of desecration that normally would be unthinkable. He draped the cloth fragment over his head as a shield against the harsh rays of the sun. The makeshift hood had the added benefit of keeping his head warm during the cool nights.

After walking all day, they came to a Buddhist monastery. This potentially presented a problem. Normally, traveling monks found food and shelter at monasteries along the trail, but there were no Bönpo monasteries between Lhasa and Yungdrungling. If the Buddhist monasteries refused to offer them hospitality, the Bönpos would suffer through some miserably cold nights with no food. To survive their journey of more than a hundred miles, the Bönpos would have to depend on the hospitality of Gelug monasteries. To avoid being turned away, Samten and Sangye decided to introduce themselves as students at Drepung, the premier Gelug monastery. The robes of Bönpos and Buddhists were nearly identical so they could be sure of a warm greeting, food, and shelter if they merely declined to identify themselves as Bönpos. Fortunately, the several Gelug monasteries along the route proved hospitable. The monks at the monasteries received the news of the conflict in Lhasa with horror and apprehension. They wondered whether the Chinese would begin arresting them as well and debated whether it was best to stay or flee. At every Gelug monastery along their route the travelers revealed themselves to be Bönpos only upon thanking their hosts and departing. At a few such monasteries the revelation instantly chilled the formerly warm relations with their hosts. Religious prejudice sometimes proved stronger than national unity, even in the face of Chinese oppression.

When they reached Yungdrungling, Samten and Soko rushed into the monastery looking for their mother. After searching the monastery grounds the brothers had to accept that she wasn't there. Only then did they report to the abbot, giving him his first news about the uprising in Lhasa. The abbot received the news with astonishment, but he and his monks didn't grasp the urgency of the situation. They considered it something that happened in a faraway place, too removed from them to interfere with their daily routines.

Samten and Soko worried about their mother and watched the trail from Lhasa every day. After a few days they asked the abbot for a divination. The abbot chanted, running his fingers across the beads of his mala as the brothers waited expectantly. The abbot paused before revealing the divination: their mother, Zinmo, would eventually arrive at the monastery. They were cheered by the divination, which strengthened their resolve to wait.

After the fighting ended in Lhasa, Zinmo went straight to Norbulingka to look for her son, Soko. She looked through the piles of bodies, clinging to the hope that he still lived. Failing to find him among the dead, she went to Drepung to find Samten. Women were rarely allowed onto the monastery grounds, and several times she was forcefully ejected from the monastery by stern-faced monks. Certain that her son was inside and determined to see him, Zinmo spent days close to the monastery entrance, hoping to catch her son leaving. One day she was startled to see what she at first thought were monks carrying rifles. Then she realized that the armed men were Chinese soldiers taking monks away for interrogation or imprisonment.

By this time Zinmo feared that both of her sons might be dead or captured and felt overwhelmed with sadness and despair. She felt that if she discovered her sons were dead she would throw herself in the river. Despite her despair, she continued her desperate vigil at the gate until eventually she recognized a monk from her village who knew Samten. He told her that her sons had left the monastery during the fighting, but he didn't know where they had gone. Only then did Zinmo remember the arrangement to meet her sons at Yungdrungling Monastery if they became separated. She immediately struck out for the monastery, accompanied by a cousin who had come with her to Lhasa from Amdo to help her in the butter trade.

Samten and Soko had been at Yungdrungling for six weeks when one day they saw figures in the distance coming along the trail from Lhasa. When the figures came into focus, the brothers dashed from the monastery down the trail to embrace their mother.

Zinmo wept with happiness to see that her two sons were alive, but was uneasy about the complacency she saw at Yungdrungling. She had seen monks being led away at gunpoint from Drepung, the violent retribution exacted by the Chinese soldiers, and the smoldering ruins of the buildings where the monks had resisted. She was certain that eventually soldiers would come to Yungdrungling, and that put her on edge. Every time a dog barked, she rushed outside to see if the Chinese were coming. She urged her sons to flee the country with her. Samten was reluctant to leave Tibet, but his mother was adamant. "What?" she exploded when he objected. "How stupid to stay on!"[4] They were leaving, and Zinmo would tolerate no argument.

Samten and Soko obediently began purchasing supplies for the journey. Zinmo also persuaded Sangye and he joined in their preparations to leave. Before setting off for Nepal, they bought two donkeys to help carry their meager provisions. They were joined by Sangye's nephew, Khedup, and another monk.

Zinmo's worry about the reach of the Chinese caught the attention of some of the monks at the monastery, who began to debate whether they should stay or flee. Most elected to leave, but some, like Kesang Dargye, the monk who had shredded his robes to make a hood, decided to stay. They would later learn that the Chinese forced him to return to Amdo, where he was treated brutally.

It was spring and the weather was fair, making it a good time of year for the six travelers to undertake their long journey. But even in the summer months the Himalayan passes could be mercilessly cold. The travelers shed their robes for the traditional chuba and boots, better suited to the fickle Tibetan weather. Their boots had leather soles with uppers of thick woolen fabric. Unlike Western shoes, each boot was identical and could be worn on either foot.

All agreed that they would cloak their real destination by posing as pilgrims on their way to one of Tibet's innumerable religious sites. They trekked up and down the sides of steep mountains and through deep valleys as they made their way toward the border, visiting the many monasteries along the way. The first travelers they passed stared at the bayonet stuck in Soko's belt. A blade of forged steel carried an air of authority and threat. After seeing their reaction, Soko worried that the bayonet might lead travelers to believe they were bandits or agents of the Chinese or Tibetan governments, so he decided to keep it out of sight thereafter, flashing the threatening blade only if he distrusted the intentions of anyone they met along the trail.

They avoided speaking to people along the way except when necessary, fearing informers who might see an advantage in alerting the Chinese about the strange group of pilgrims. For weeks they labored up and down the creases in the wrinkled Tibetan landscape. Each day they would rise before dawn and walk for several hours before halting for a breakfast of tsampa and tea. They then would walk until midday and make camp before preparing a meal. The brothers and their mother clustered around one fire and Sangye, his nephew, and the other monk around another. They would sleep early and rise in the morning darkness to repeat the routine.

At the top of passes they pushed through deep snow, sometimes for two or three days, before descending again to another valley. The mountains became steeper as they journeyed deeper into the Himalayas. To cross the border into Nepal, they climbed the 15,300-foot Kora Pass, which took two days to the top and two days to descend.

The trip was grueling even for Tibetans raised in such a harsh environment. They were exhausted by the time they halted each day. Rising each morning to another weary day of climbing required effort. Small pains developed in their legs, feet, and backs and became a constant annoyance. Their diet of tsampa and tea was monotonous and inadequate. Yet they trudged on.

No matter how drained they were, no matter how difficult the terrain, Sangye insisted on performing a puja, a ceremony of gratitude, anytime they were offered a good meal at a village or a monastery, at each of the many holy places that dotted the trail, at caves used for meditation, or sometimes even when they encountered an especially scenic vista or resting place. At monasteries and holy places he would undertake a daylong ceremony, his nephew Khedup assisting. Sangye dedicated each puja to Nyame Sherab Gyaltsen, the founder of Menri Monastery. The innumerable stops for pujas annoyed the other members of the party who wanted to push on instead of spending so much time performing ceremonies, but Sangye would not be dissuaded. His companions resigned themselves to the endless stops for prayers. They respected his piousness and could not help but admire his leadership, devotion, and determination.

After crossing the Yarlung Tsangpo in coracles, the party split and headed in different directions. The brothers and their mother wanted to take the fastest and most direct route to Kathmandu. Sangye, Khedup, and the other monk wanted to take a longer route to visit Bön monasteries in Tibet and Nepal.

As Samten, his brother Soka, and their mother, Zinmo, trudged on, their supplies of cheese and dried meat long gone, they ate nothing but tsampa. The steady diet of roasted barley flour without vegetables became tiring and they began to dream of potatoes, cabbage, radishes, carrots, and onions. One day they happened upon potato fields near the trail. They all ran into the rows and began digging up potatoes. They were interrupted by the angry shouts of a farmer. Samten calmed the farmer, explaining they were on a long journey and that they craved vegetables. They were from Amdo, where vegetables were an important part of their diet, he told the farmer, and they would pay any price he named for the potatoes. After hearing their explanation, the farmer became friendly and declined the offer of payment. He told them to take all they could carry. After roasting the potatoes and feasting, they pushed on.

Meanwhile, Sangye, Khedup and the other monk worked their way slowly to the Nepalese district of Mustang, stopping at every monastery along the way to perform ceremonies. It took them two months to travel several hundred miles from Yungdrungling Monastery to the Nepalese border. They wandered through Nepal visiting Bönpo communities and monasteries, Sangye using his medical skills to heal the sick, rich and poor alike, refusing to accept payment from the poor. Eventually he decided it was time to deliver Khedup to his father, who had fled to Kalimpong, in the Indian state of West Bengal, after the collapse of Tibetan resistance. They knew Kalimpong was near the eastern Nepalese border but were uncertain of the route. Their inability to speak any language other than Tibetan made it difficult to get directions. They sought directions by repeating, "Kalimpong, Kalimpong," and passersby would point the way. Eventually they took a train to Kalimpong, where Khedup was reunited with his father,

Palchenpo. Father and son embraced, and the brothers commiserated over the fate of their country. Sangye listened to his brother describe the failure of rebels in southern Tibet and how they surrendered their arms to Indian border guards to gain refuge in India.

After the bittersweet reunion in Kalimpong, Sangye returned to Nepal to begin looking for Samten.

11
Forsaken Vows

Still groggy with sleep, seventeen-year-old Tenpa Woser struggled to rise from his pallet. Someone was pounding on the door of his small apartment below Menri Monastery. Tenpa opened the door to a fellow monk wearing normally forbidden civilian clothes instead of the burgundy robes required by the monastery.

"What are you doing with these plain clothes?" Tenpa asked.[1]

The monk ignored the question, telling Tenpa that the abbot had sent for him.

Tenpa shared his quarters with his older brother, Tenpa Wangal, who was away. The gray stone building was one of about two dozen small apartments scattered on the steep slope in front of the monastery. Tenpa's building contained two apartments, each with a room for sleeping and another for cooking. The monks slept on mattresses filled with yak and goat hair. A three-legged iron stove used for cooking warmed the apartment. The only other objects in their quarters were a box with tsampa, dried meat, and dried cheese, an altar with butterlamps, and an image of Bön founder Tonpa Shenrab Miwoche.

Tenpa Woser's brother, Tenpa Wangal, was the assistant to Menri's former lopon, or head of instruction, Sangye Tenzin Rinpoche (not to be confused with the Sangye who escaped Tibet with Samten Karmay). Tenpa Wangal and Lopon Sangye Tenzin were on a trip to seek financial contributions from the district of Hor, the same district where the brothers had been raised, near the village of Zampon Tsungdo. The brothers were born to a family of nomadic herders of yaks, sheep, goats, and horses, who moved their tents to better grazing grounds as the seasons dictated. At age eleven, Tenpa Woser and his two brothers, sister, and parents made a pilgrimage to sacred Mount Kailash. Only the truly pious made the nearly thousand-mile journey of at least two months from Hor over Tibet's mountainous terrain. They completed a kora, or circuit, of the mountain. The experience was so inspiring that Tenpa's parents decided to send their two oldest sons, Tenpa Woser and Tenpa Wangal, to Menri.

The two brothers had settled into monastic life at Menri when the first Chinese cadres arrived in the valley below the monastery. As in other areas of Tibet, initially the cadres were friendly and handed out silver coins, but by 1959 their hostility toward religion had become increasingly apparent. Chinese soldiers sent to protect the cadres were stationed menacingly near the monasteries. The cadres visited Menri and conducted indoctrination or "struggle sessions," called *thamzings*. The indoctrination sessions became more intense after the Lhasa rebellion was crushed, and now were imposed almost daily.

The Bön monks remained immovable as the Chinese officers screamed at them, calling their religion a myth and their lamas charlatans. The Bönpos were horrified to hear that monks at a nearby Buddhist monastery, urged on by the Chinese cadres, screamed insults and beat the lamas who had taught them and given them spiritual guidance. At Menri the Chinese had given the unyielding monks an ultimatum. The cadres would leave the monastery while they celebrated the coming Chinese New Year for the Year of the Iron Rat, which fell on January 28, 1960. When they returned, the Bön monks must decide whether to take "the black path or the white path."

Sherab Lodrö, Menri's abbot, knew that the "black path" signified refusal by the monks to denounce their lamas and their religion. If they chose the black path, the Chinese would violently coerce them to submit, imprison them, or kill them. Choosing the "white path" of voluntary submission was unthinkable.

The abbot decided to take advantage of the temporary absence of the Chinese cadres and escape with all those willing to go. He asked a group of young monks to renounce their vows of nonviolence so that they would be free to defend the escaping lamas if necessary. They would steal away to join their former head teacher, Tenzin Namdak, who had left two years earlier to raise funds at Sezhig Monastery, north of Menri, on the Changthang Plateau.

The monk who had come to fetch Tenpa left the doorway and headed for the temple. Without hesitation Tenpa followed him up the steep hill to the red-painted monastery. Although Menri is Bön's most revered monastery, it is tiny compared with the vast Drepung in Lhasa. Tenpa entered the *gompa,* an oblong room painted a deep red and hung with richly painted cloth thankas, where monks gathered for ceremonies and teachings. Here he found the abbot huddled with his aides, working out the details of their escape.

Some of the monks had exchanged their robes for chubas and were hustling about making preparations for the journey. Tenpa prostrated before the abbot, Sherab Lodrö. The abbot asked Tenpa whether he wanted to wait for his brother to return or help protect the monastery's highest officials and the sacred relics they would be carrying on what was sure to be a dangerous and arduous journey. The abbot told Tenpa he was under no obligation to join them.

Tenpa considered the likelihood that he would never see his brother again. He thought about abandoning the life he had lived since entering the monastery at age eleven. Like all Tibetans, he had been taught all his life to eschew violence and be kind to all sentient beings. The vows he took upon entering the monastery reinforced his commitment to nonviolence. Now he was being asked by one of the holiest men in Bön to renounce those vows and take up arms. His answer came quickly.

"I will go," he said. His devotion to the abbot and to the Bön tradition outweighed everything. He would not see his brother for another six years.[2]

A monastery official handed him a chuba. The abbot told him to place his monk's robes on the abbot's throne, before the shrine to Nyame Sherab Gyaltsen, who founded Menri in 1405. Tenpa performed three prostrations before the shrine and asked the enlightened ones for permission to renounce his vows. He shed his robe and tossed it on the pile of discarded habits piled so high on the abbot's throne that it was almost hidden. Tenpa donned the chuba and was a monk no more.

More than thirty monks had agreed to relinquish their vows and the robes to protect the two holiest figures at Menri. Although some monasteries kept arsenals, Menri did not. The monks armed themselves with the few weapons they could scrounge from an institution devoted to learning and prayer. Tenpa was told to go to the adjacent temple of Sipe Gyalmo, a blue-skinned, six-armed goddess of exorcism and protection, to fetch a ceremonial sword. He shoved the blade into its wooden, leather-covered scabbard and thrust it under the cloth belt that bound his chuba. Like Tenpa, most of the monks who had surrendered their robes were armed with edged weapons. Only a single firearm could be found, an ancient rifle carried by Tenpa's friend Machen.

The monks who had decided to stay were shaken by the visible change on the faces of those who had decided to leave. The enormity of the undertaking and the sudden realization that they were to be responsible for the life of their abbot had instantly transformed them. Their faces appeared fierce and resolute in a way that sent a chill through the monks who remained.

The prospect of evading or fighting the well-armed, well-trained Chinese army, of possibly dying on some desolate hillside on a journey that would be difficult even in the best of circumstances, held little appeal for the dozens of monks who stayed behind. Most of those who remained at the monastery would have reason to regret their decision.

They would endure harsh interrogation and torture, imprisonment, and forced labor. The Chinese would subject them to a mind-numbing reeducation process. A few would cooperate with the Chinese and spy on their fellow monks.

The fleeing Bönpos rounded up horses and lashed sacks of tsampa onto them. They also loaded the horses with texts and sacred objects to prevent them from falling into the hands of the Chinese. The most revered among the sacred objects was the Nyame Kundung, a six-hundred-year-old reliquary containing the bones and ashes remaining from the cremation of Nyame Sherab Gyaltsen, the founder and first abbot of Menri. The three-foot-tall, fifty-pound silver reliquary is an ornate cylinder sitting on a bell-shaped base encrusted at its bottom with silver lotus blossoms. The Nyame Kundung was stowed in a leather case and entrusted to Machen.

The monks also needed to silence a translator the cadres had left at the monastery. The translator would no doubt hurry to inform the Chinese troops stationed in the valley if he suspected that the monks were preparing to leave. The newly defrocked monks overpowered him and bound his hands with rope. They forced him to join the escape party to make sure their departure remained unknown as long as possible. He would be released only when they had covered enough distance to feel safe about doing so. Within a few hours they were ready, and a group of about thirty-six set out to cross the mountain behind the monastery. They chose the steep, narrow, difficult path that wound up the mountain, avoiding the easy trail to the valley below, past villages where potential informers would be quick to notify the Chinese. With luck, the Chinese wouldn't learn of their departure for several hours or even a day.

They split into three groups about an hour apart, with the lamas in the middle group, allowing them to escape if the lead or trailing party was attacked. By the third day they were on the Changthang Plateau. Unfamiliar with the route, they were forced to risk exposure to informants in order to get directions whenever they encountered a village. Tenpa and Machen were in the lead group, all of them mounted. They constantly scanned the broken, treeless terrain for signs of soldiers. In the morning they came upon a village where locals gave them directions that made them suspicious. The villagers insisted that they must cross a pass through a range of rocky hills. The monks discussed the villagers' advice and most were skeptical, wondering why the villagers were so adamant that they use the pass. Finally, Machen said they didn't have an alternate route and must face whatever lay ahead.

Tenpa and Machen took the lead. After a few miles they could see something suspicious in the distance. Something was moving, disappearing, and then reappearing. They couldn't tell whether it was animal or human. They trotted forward to get a better look. As they strained to identify the dim shapes, bullets began snapping by. Machen returned fire with his muzzleloader before a bullet struck his horse, causing it to rear and crash to the ground. As Machen rolled away from his mount he was shot in the hand.

Two other monks crumpled to the ground, blood pouring from their wounds. Tenpa galloped toward Machen, grabbed his outstretched hand, and pulled him up onto his horse behind the saddle, achieving this despite the heavy relic tucked under Machen's arm with the wounded hand. They galloped away, bullets whizzing after them. The remainder of the dozen monks in the lead group had already scattered.

The middle group with the abbot heard the gunshots and could see fighting in the distance, giving them ample time to hide in a ravine. Tenpa and Machen were the only members of their group to rejoin the abbot at sunset. The rest were never seen again.

After dark they tried to elude the Chinese by taking a difficult and little-used route up a nearby mountain. They climbed for hours up rocky slopes covered with snow before finding a cleft in the rocks to rest until daylight. In the morning, one of the oldest lamas, Kharna Gyaltshab, said that he was too ill to continue and urged the others to go on without him. They were reluctant to leave him, but he was adamant. It was clear that he was dying and that the divine protectors would watch over his final hours. With deep regret, Tenpa and the others left Kharna Gyaltshab with a few supplies for his comfort and resumed their flight.

Kharna Gyaltshab's body was found later by his former teacher, Lopon Sangye Tenzin Rinpoche, the lama to whom Tenpa's brother was an assistant. Lopon Sangye Tenzin was escaping along the same route with another party of monks. They had returned to Menri shortly after the abbot fled and hastened to make their own escape. After making camp one day, they sent a thirteen-year-old boy to find dung to use as fire fuel. Within minutes he came running back to camp, saying a man was sitting nearby in meditation posture on a cushion. Lopon Sangye Tenzin found his student and close friend in the death pose that years of meditation and training prepared him to assume. They removed the cushion and found a nugget of gold, which they believed Kharna Gyaltshab had left for Lopon Sangye Tenzin, somehow knowing that his former teacher would be the one to find his body. Lopon Sangye Tenzin escaped to Nepal via a different route where he eventually reunited with the Menri abbot.

The Menri party survivors exhausted their meager rations of tsampa and walked without eating for the next two days. They spent the second night in a stone and mud corral built by shepherds to contain their flocks. In the morning they saw in the far distance a thin trail of smoke. Objects can be seen at far distances in the clear air of the Changthang, so they knew the camp was miles away. The Bönpos walked toward the smoke until they came within sight of the camp at nightfall. They could see a flock of sheep milling near the camp and indistinct figures appeared to be dressed in traditional Tibetan chubas. The observation eased their fears of encountering Chinese soldiers. They made camp, hoping they would be able to get food and water the next day from the herders.

The stars and the waxing moon illuminated the night as they made a fire to brew tea before collapsing into an exhausted sleep. A noise awakened Tenpa and two of his companions. In the moonlight they could see indistinct shapes about a quarter mile away coming toward them. Behind the shapes they could see dozens of campfires. They realized with alarm that they had made their camp next to a Chinese army encampment. The Tibetans they had seen were captives.

Tenpa awakened the abbot, who sought divine guidance by tossing a handful of bones onto the ground. The omen was bad. They roused the rest of the party and Sherab Lodrö gave each one a blessing pill, known as a *mendrup,* made of an assortment of herbs. They hurriedly loaded the sacred relics and texts onto the pack animals and fled into the night. Tenpa, Gen Singtrug, and Menyag, armed only with swords and knives, remained to slow the Chinese and give the lamas a chance to escape. There was still a lingering doubt about whether the approaching figures were Chinese soldiers or Tibetans. They worried about mistakenly killing a Tibetan. Gen Singtrug, who spoke Chinese, said, "You should wait here and I'll go closer to these persons and speak to them in Chinese. If you hear a reply in Chinese you should be ready to attack them, but if they reply in Tibetan, remain calm."[3]

Gen Singtrug shouted a greeting, "Ni hao," and heard the Chinese greeting shouted back from a group of three soldiers moving ahead of the other troops. Confused by a greeting in their own tongue, the soldiers held their fire until the three Tibetans were on them. Gen Singtrug was in the lead and struck the first soldier on the shoulder with his sword. The blow was deflected by a strap or buckle. Tenpa brought his sword down in long arc before the soldier could react, a fraction of a second before Gen Singtrug struck again. The soldier went down. Menyag stood over one of the other soldiers with a bloody knife. The third fled in terror.

Menyag grabbed the rifle of the soldier he had stabbed and shouted at the others to run. Tenpa hesitated as his companions disappeared into the darkness. It occurred to him that their newly acquired rifle needed ammunition. He tried to cut away a bandolier stuffed with cartridges from one of the bodies. He found it awkward to use the sword to saw through the thick webbing and his hands trembled with fear as other Chinese soldiers rushed toward him, some stopping to fire.

He felt a twinge near his abdomen and instinctively put his hand on the spot. He felt the wet warmth of blood and knew he'd been shot. He began running, his hand clutching the bleeding wound, the sound of gunfire in his ears.

Tenpa reached the Bönpo camp and found it deserted. He would later learn that the Menri lopon and a few others had been captured, but the abbot had managed to elude the Chinese. He trudged on alone, heading north, toward the monastery at Sezhig. The wound was throbbing with pain and he resisted the urge to lie down and curl into a ball. He had to keep moving.

After several hours, the morning sun illuminated the landscape, making it easy for him to pick out two figures in the distance. They had seen him and were moving toward him at a fast pace. He could make out the baggy outlines of their chubas, marking them as Tibetans. Even so, he worried that they might be bandits, and if they weren't bandits that they might betray him to the Chinese. Though he still had his sword, he was too weak from his wound to wield it.

The figures gradually became more distinct, and Tenpa could see that they were armed. His hand tightened on the hilt of his sword. Finally he could see their faces. His face split into a smile of relief and pleasure as he recognized two friends from his party, Machen and Anik. Machen, despite his wounded hand, still carried the sacred reliquary containing the ashes of Nyame Sherab Gyaltsen. Tenpa had doubted his chances of survival, of ever seeing his friends again. Machen and Anik had been sure that Tenpa was dead. Overcome by the moment, the three clasped one another and shouted a prayer of thanks to the protectors. After exchanging accounts of their escape, they continued their flight until Tenpa could walk no more. Concealing themselves in a dry streambed, they collapsed from exhaustion.

In the morning, Machen and Anik pulled Tenpa to his feet, but he was too weak to stand. Each put one of Tenpa's arms over a shoulder, bearing most of his weight despite their own weariness. Tenpa was delirious and insisted that they were heading the wrong direction. They gently told him that he was confused because of his wound. He refused to believe them, but they coaxed him into coming with them. The three walked for another two days without water or food. Tenpa grew weaker and would have been unable to go on, but his friends never wavered. Despite their own hunger, thirst, and waning strength, they half-carried him all day. In the evening they found a sheltered spot among piles of rocks and gently laid him in as comfortable a spot as they could find. The next morning they roused him and again set off in the same manner, each step growing more difficult as their strength ebbed.

Late that second day they came upon a stone hut, a lonely structure on the bleak expanse that housed a family eking out a living by hunting marmots. Tibetan tradition called for the family to treat strangers with kindness and generosity, but this family had little to give. Nevertheless, they could see Tenpa was badly wounded and gave him a small cup of tsampa and some goat's milk. He thanked them for the food and took a finger full of tsampa mixed with milk. A bite of tsampa set off a whirring in his head. A fog seemed to lift, and suddenly he could see the world around him with clarity. He now felt he could walk on his own.

He shared the remaining tsampa and goat's milk with his friends. The family said they could spare no more tsampa but could give them a supply of marmot meat. None of the three had ever tried it. Their hunger abated by the tsampa, they declined the offer. The family understood and told them that if they crossed the next pass they would find a more prosperous family with more food.

The three thanked the family for their kindness. As he stepped out of the hut, Tenpa could see now that his friends had indeed taken him in the right direction. Without his friends, he would have wandered in the wrong direction and likely been swallowed in the vast plateau, his body undiscovered. At the thought, a deep sadness overcame him, a despair that so overwhelmed him he began to sob. He was separated from his brother and the lamas, his teachers, whom he had sworn to protect. "We don't know where they are and so there is no one left, even my brother who I am closest to," he thought. "So now in this situation, I must die."[4]

Tenpa, exhausted emotionally and physically, dragged himself after his companions as they slowly climbed a pass over one of the rocky spines that crisscross the Changthang. As promised, they encountered another stone hut, housing a wealthier family that gave them about four pounds of tsampa and an entire lamb. Their hospitality included a warm spot by the fire and a safe place to sleep.

The group set out the next day. Tenpa's wound was infected, making his every step excruciating. He bore the pain silently, willing himself to put one foot in front of the other. Each day the infection worsened. Walking became increasingly difficult, but with the help of his friends they reached another family dwelling. The head of the household was inquisitive, asking them who they were, where they had come from, and where they were going. The travelers' first instinct was to say nothing. His questions worried the three Bönpos. Perhaps he wanted to rob them. Maybe he would betray them to the Chinese. The treasure Machen carried would be a tempting target. They were willing to give their lives to protect one of Bön's most sacred relics, but protecting it would be difficult because Tenpa was barely able to walk and Machen was unable to use his left hand because of the wound he had received in the first ambush. Only Akin was uninjured.

So they lied, saying that they were pilgrims. Their host looked at them carefully. "No, I don't think you are like that. Yesterday there were two persons who came here who were quite similar to you, saying that days ago their camp was destroyed by the Chinese and all their friends dispersed. They asked that if I see any persons like them, two or three or one, people like this, please tell them to come to Sezhig Monastery. They left a message like that. I think you are one like that."[5]

Tenpa's despair vanished at the possibility that he might rejoin his lamas. All three tried to speak at once, admitting that they were fleeing the Chinese. Their host smiled, then asked what Machen was carrying in the leather case. Learning that it was a sacred Bön reliquary, he asked to see it.

As Machen carefully withdrew the reliquary from its cover, their host's smile broadened. "The Chinese coming is very bad for us generally, but for me one good thing is that I am now able to see this important, precious relic. I am so happy."

At his host's request, Machen placed the reliquary on a table. Then the man disappeared for several hours, leaving his disconcerted guests to be entertained by his wife, his aging parents, and several children. He returned with a sack full of ceremonial objects such as butterlamps and water bowls that he had hidden out of fear the Chinese would confiscate them. He arranged them to form a shrine, then prostrated three times before sitting cross-legged with his eyes closed. He chanted ancient mantras and prayers as he fingered the 108 beads of his mala.

After completing his devotions, their beaming host treated his guests to heaping plates of tsampa, meat, and cheese, all washed down with endless cups of butter tea. After the meal, the three travelers slept soundly on comfortable woolen blankets. Tenpa slept well despite his worsening infection.

As they prepared to leave the next morning, their host remarked on the seriousness of Tenpa's declining condition. The wound was red around its edges, and the redness was spreading outward. Pus seeped from the wound and it stank. Tenpa was feverish and growing weaker, but he was determined to make it to Sezhig Monastery, where he hoped the lamas would be waiting. Their host had no medicine for Tenpa but offered them a yak to carry the reliquary and Tenpa.

They politely refused, explaining that a yak would be difficult to hide if they encountered Chinese troops and slow them down if they had to flee.

They left about midday and walked until evening. Night on the Changthang is illuminated by stars so bright they cause shadows. The starlight made it easy to spot a solitary nomad tent. There they were welcomed with typical Tibetan hospitality and given food. This time they admitted that they were fleeing the Chinese. Their hosts told them that two other men had arrived the previous day with a similar story, saying they had been separated from their lama after an ambush but had found him. The three were camped nearby, a white tent marking the presence of a lama.

Tenpa, Machen, and Akin left as soon as was polite and after a short walk saw the white tent. They would have run to the campsite had it not been for the need to support a flagging Tenpa. At the tent, they joyfully prostrated before Abbot Sherab Lodrö before embracing their friends Gen Singtruk and Menyag. Tenpa was in pain and could not bend to perform a prostration, so he fell to his knees, grateful at being reunited with his lama. "You are alive!" the pleasantly surprised abbot said to Tenpa. "Menyag told me that you were killed by the Chinese soldier."

As Menyag was running away with the rifle he had taken from the soldier, he heard gunshots and looked back to see that Tenpa was not behind him. He was certain that Tenpa had been killed, so his arrival amplified the joy of the reunion.

They learned that the abbot had arrived alone at the nearby nomad camp but had presented himself as an ordinary traveler. The next day Gen Singtruk and Menyag arrived at the camp begging for food. When they saw the abbot, they burst into tears, then fell to the floor and prostrated. Their reaction astonished their hosts. They realized their guest was an important lama. Deeply impressed, the family offered the best of their humble fare.

Eventually, Tenpa asked for a blessing from the abbot for his wound, so painful that it was difficult for him to move. The abbot left him for a moment and returned with a cup of urine, a traditional Tibetan remedy. He instructed Tenpa to take a gulp of the abbot's urine. He raised the cup to his lips without hesitation, ignoring the smell, and swallowed without gagging. The abbot spread the remainder of the warm urine on the wound. Tenpa slept after the treatment. In the morning, the pus began draining, the swelling was temporarily reduced, and the redness had partially receded from his belly and chest. The pain had diminished and he felt better, but the bullet remained. The infection subsided, but would eventually resume its spread.

The abbot and his party broke camp the next day and headed toward Sezhig. Tenpa at times doubted he would survive. Each step shot a bolt of pain through his body. Yet his earlier despair did not return. He walked slowly, his hand to his side, willing each step. To deal with the agony he chanted the mantras and prayers he had committed to memory through long hours of practice during his years at Menri. By concentrating on chanting he hoped to invoke the help of the deities. *So ma ma ra yo za, so ma ma ra yo za,* he chanted, repeating sacred sounds that have meaning only to the deities, in this case the protector Yeshe Walmo. The chanting also kept his mind off the agonizing jolts that came with each step. He tried not to think about the miles that lay ahead.

12
Enter the CIA

Tenzin received disturbing news at Sezhig with the arrival of a jangling caravan of mules and horses laden with goods accompanied by an armed escort. It was late 1959, the Year of the Earth Pig.[1]

The rare arrival of a trading party on the vast, empty plateau was always a pleasant break in the routine of life on the Changthang. The wealthy trader who led the party asked to pay his respects to Tenzin. The trader had been doing business on the Changthang when he received news of the failed Lhasa rebellion, the scale of the killing and the destruction of the city. Upon learning that the Dalai Lama had fled the country, the merchant had decided to follow the Dalai Lama's example. He couldn't leave, however, knowing that a lama of great repute was nearby and would certainly be a target of Chinese retribution. Even though they had never met, the trader felt it was his religious duty to assist Tenzin.

The trader described the carnage in Lhasa and what he knew of the Dalai Lama's escape.[2] He urged Tenzin to flee with him to Nepal. He and his retinue were well equipped with pack animals, supplies, and weapons and could make Tenzin's escape as comfortable and safe as possible for such a journey. But Tenzin could not leave without first knowing whether the abbot of Menri and his friends at the monastery were safe. An emissary from Menri was due to arrive at Sezhig to collect the mother monastery's share of donations, which had increased substantially since Tenzin's arrival. The trader waited for several days but finally told Tenzin he could wait no longer. Each day the danger of capture increased.

Tenzin waited as 1959 faded and turned into 1960, the Year of the Iron Rat. When the emissary from Menri finally arrived, he confirmed the news about the Lhasa revolt, the Dalai Lama's escape, and the flight of many Tibetans from their country, but said nothing to suggest that Chinese pressure on Menri had worsened. Tenzin listened with concern. He was worried about his friends and students at Menri. He was worried about his country.

Several weeks later, Tenzin was alternately alarmed and overjoyed when Menri abbot Sherab Lodrö and a group of disheveled monks stumbled into Sezhig. Two were nursing wounds from Chinese bullets and all wore tattered, dirty clothing. Tenzin listened with dismay as they told him about their clashes with the Chinese and their struggle to survive. Only fifteen of the thirty-six who set out from Menri made it to Sezhig; they would never learn the fate of the missing.

Tenpa Woser was barely able to walk by the time he reached Sezhig. He staggered into the monastery and collapsed. Within minutes of his arrival he was carried to a bed and placed in the care of Shanghee, the only monk at Sezhig with any training in Tibetan medicine. Shanghee immediately prepared to remove the bullet. Monks surrounded the bed and chanted, some sprinkling blessing water and others wafting smoke over him from the smoldering bunches of herbs they held in their hands. Shanghee had no anesthetizing herbs to offer, not even alcohol. He cleaned the wound and began cutting with a small knife as Tenpa passed in and out of consciousness from the pain.[3] The bullet was removed and the infection cut away. The monks bandaged the wound as best they could with strips of torn cloth. Tenpa still bled. He sipped a bit of his own blood with a cupped hand, following the Tibetan belief in the restorative powers of blood. It seemed to ease his pain somewhat. He lay there for days, barely able to move, as the wound slowly healed.

While Tenpa was recovering, Tenzin Namdak began making plans for their escape to Nepal. He listened with sorrow as the abbot of Menri, Sherab Lodrö, told him about their deadly encounters with the Chinese and the missing monks, either captured, killed, or in hiding. He was disturbed to learn that their most sacred relic, the Nyame Kundung, had been hauled into a battle. Machen, one of the young monks to whom the relic had been entrusted, had to fight the Chinese with the relic lashed to his horse. He nearly lost it when his horse was shot. To ensure that the sacred Nyame Kundung would not be lost should they be confronted again by Chinese troops, Tenzin took it into his care, along with several solid gold butterlamps and other sacred objects carried by the Menri monks.

Refugee monks from Menri and other Bön monasteries straggled in to Sezhig with similar stories of flight from Chinese pursuers. The most important figures in the Bön religion were now assembled at Sezhig, but the arrival of Tenpa and the refugees from Menri also meant that the Chinese were likely not far behind.

"Let us leave as soon as possible," Tenzin urged.[4] Preparations began immediately, and monks at Sezhig were given the same option as those at Menri: leave or await the Chinese. Amid the preparations for departure, a group of armed Tibetan resistance fighters arrived. They were led by a powerful tribal leader in the region, Nagtshang Powo, who had taken up arms against the Chinese. Nagtshang Powo bragged to Tenzin that the Americans were going to supply him with weapons that would enable him to protect the monks as well as arm those who had renounced their vows. He asked Tenzin to wait two weeks for the shipment to be air-dropped. As a sign of goodwill, he made an offering of gold and food to the monastery.

The weapons that Nagtshang Powo promised were to be delivered by the U.S. Central Intelligence Agency. The CIA was making arms drops as part of a covert operation to supply and train Tibetan rebels.

The program would last until 1961 and remained secret until the late 1990s. The Cold War was at its height, and the administration of U.S. president Dwight Eisenhower viewed covert action as a means to challenge Communism while avoiding overt military action that could lead to war.

The secret CIA program had begun in 1956, after the intelligence agency decided it needed Tibetans on the ground who could assess the strength of the resistance movement against the Chinese Communists. Agent John Hoskins would be tasked with putting the plan into operation. Hoskins had arrived at the CIA Calcutta station in September, assigned to making contact with Chinese stationed in India. That changed in November 1956 with an urgent cable from CIA headquarters asking him to contact Gyalo Thondup, the second eldest of the Dalai Lama's four brothers. Gyalo had come to the CIA's attention that summer after he distributed a letter he translated into English describing Chinese abuses in Tibet. Gyalo's connections and sophistication made him the perfect choice for helping the CIA find Tibetan recruits.

Foreign governments had long courted the tall, slim Gyalo as a conduit to the Tibetan government. Gyalo was fluent in Chinese, having traveled to China in November 1946 to study at the Central University of Politics in Nanjing. His travel and studies were paid for by General Chiang Kai-shek, whose U.S.-backed army battled Mao Tse Tung's troops for control of China. There were no roads linking Tibet with China at the time, so Gyalo and his entourage traveled seventeen days by horseback to reach India, where he could catch a flight to Nanjing. In Calcutta, the eighteen-year-old Gyalo marveled at the paved roads, railroads, and movie theaters. Whenever he left his room and entered the lobby of the Grand Hotel, the other guests would stare at him. His long, straight black hair had never been cut and hung to his knees. He wore the traditional chuba, and a turquoise-and-gold earring dangled from his ear, Tibetan-style. He soon cut his hair, stopped wearing the earring, and exchanged his chuba for pants, shirt, and coat.[5]

Sporting his new look, Gyalo flew from Calcutta to Nanjing in a U.S.-built C-46 cargo plane sent by the Chinese Nationalist government, then still in power in China. After settling into a three-bedroom house equipped with servants, car, and driver, he became a frequent dinner guest of Chiang Kai-shek, who paid all his expenses and gave him a monthly allowance. His studies at the university revealed a world he barely knew existed. "I had known that Tibet was backward from the time I first set foot in India, and my studies in China only confirmed that judgment," Gyalo would later write in his autobiography.[6]

Two years after his arrival in China, Gyalo married Zhu Dan, the daughter of a Chinese general. She was a university-educated administrator who worked with children and refugees at the Nanjing Baptist Hospital. In January 1949, Gyalo and his wife fled to Hong Kong days before the Communist People's Liberation Army took Nanjing. Seven years later, after sojourns in the United States and Taiwan, he resided in Kalimpong, in India's northeastern state of West Bengal, a thumb of territory squeezed between Tibet to the north, Nepal to the west, Bhutan to the east, and East Pakistan (now Bangladesh) to the south. Here he found himself at the center of intrigue among Indian, British, and U.S. intelligence services as well as diplomatic officials.[7]

CIA agent Hoskins's task was to persuade Gyalo to become a recruiter for the CIA's training program for Tibetan rebels. Hoskins learned that Gyalo would be visiting Darjeeling and that tennis was one of the Tibetan's favorite pastimes. He found a tennis racket and got the next flight to Darjeeling, where he arranged to play in a doubles match with Gyalo. The match began a relationship between the agent and the Dalai Lama's brother that would make Gyalo a key CIA contact. When the agency asked him to recruit candidates for a covert military training program, Gyalo eagerly accepted.

Gyalo's recruitment by the CIA began an operation that would bring false hope to Tibetans and actually made it easier for the Chinese to target Tibetan fighters. The CIA recruitment efforts kindled the illusion that U.S military intervention and aid were possible. "The Americans who negotiated with [Gyalo] in 1956 probably did make promises to back Tibetan independence—promises that were never honored," former CIA agent John Kenneth Knaus wrote in his 1999 book *Orphans of the Cold War: America and the Tibetan Struggle for Survival.*[8]

Many Tibetan CIA recruits would die nurturing that false hope. The Tibetan recruitment and training program was part of a U.S. self-interested policy of doing anything to hinder the Chinese Communists without intervening militarily. The agency never intended to give Tibetan insurgents the military aid needed to support their rebellion against the Chinese, but allowed the Tibetans to believe otherwise. The Dalai Lama would later accuse the United States of using Tibetans to carry out its foreign policy without any regard for Tibet or the consequences to its people.[9]

Gyalo was asked to choose eight candidates for the CIA. They would come from a group of twenty-seven young Khampas who had come to New Delhi in 1957 to meet the Dalai Lama, who was making a pilgrimage to India to celebrate the 2,500th birthday of Shakyamuni Buddha. The young men had been living in exile in Kalimpong, desperate to do something to help their country. They sought a meeting with the Dalai Lama to voice their demand that the Chinese halt a brutal counteroffensive against Khampa rebels, but were disheartened by his request that they have patience. At the time, the Dalai Lama still believed that the Chinese could be convinced to honor their agreement and ensure the religious rights of Tibetans. The crestfallen Khampas followed the Dalai Lama when he moved on to Gaya, in eastern India, the city where tradition has it that the Buddha attained enlightenment. There they bumped into Gyalo, who asked to take their photos.

Gyalo showed the photos to two senior Khampas from the extended family of Gompo Tashi Andrugtsang, the leader of the Kham-based Tibetan resistance, the Chushi Gangdruk. The Khampas helped him choose CIA candidates. Their first choice was Wangdu Gyatotsang, twenty-seven, Gompo Tashi's nephew. Wangdu, the son of a wealthy and influential Kham family from the town of Lithang, had fled to India after the Chinese invasion along with his three brothers. They walked out of Tibet with the family's wealth in gold and silver carried by a train of horses and mules. Wangdu was known for his quick temper. At age seventeen he journeyed to the headquarters of a regional Khampa chief in the village of Menling, where protocol called for all visitors to remove hats, firearms, and horse bells in front of the chief's residence. Wangdu kept his hat on because it was raining, prompting the chief's bodyguard to knock the youth on the head. Without pause Wangdu drew his pistol and shot the guard to death. Only his family connections saved him from punishment.

Wangdu immediately accepted Gyalo's invitation. By this time the CIA had reduced the number of trainees needed for the project from eight to six. Five of the chosen, including Wangdu and his servant, were from Lithang. The sixth was one of Wangdu's friends from the nearby town of Bathang.[10]

A few days later, Gyalo and his cook, Gelung, packed the six recruits into the back of a Jeep and drove about forty-five miles south from Kalimpong toward what was then East Pakistan. (East Pakistan eventually would separate from West Pakistan after a war with India and become Bangladesh in 1971.) Gyalo, whose diplomacy would be compromised if he were arrested illegally crossing the border, dropped Gelung and the six recruits off at a tea plantation about twelve miles from the border. They walked along a trail through the plantation toward East Pakistan, with Gelung as escort and guide. Gelung was the only one who could speak Hindi if they encountered Indian officials and the only one who could read the one compass that would be needed beyond the plantation. They made their way to the Mahananda River, which formed the border between India and East Pakistan. They forded the river and moved inland about 150 feet to a small road. Suddenly three soldiers emerged from the dawn mist. The Khampas were on the verge of panic when Gelung moved toward the soldiers and flicked his flashlight. The soldiers returned the signal. The tension melted as it became clear that the soldiers were part of the plan. The Khampas were surprised to find that one of the soldiers was no soldier at all, but the servant of Thubten Norbu, the Dalai Lama's oldest brother. The servant, Jentzen Thondup, had been drafted by the CIA as an interpreter. The Khampa recruits boarded another Jeep and traveled for an hour to a remote cottage shielded by thick vegetation. There they met a CIA officer for the first time, forty-three-year-old Edward McAllister. McAllister offered them tea and biscuits and they exchanged pleasantries through the interpreter, Jentzen Thondup. Then they were loaded onto a truck for a five-hour drive to a train station. To cloak their mission, they boarded a train surrounded by Pakistani soldiers, giving them the appearance of prisoners. The train stopped somewhere on the outskirts of Dhaka, where they disembarked and were trucked a few miles north to a safe house in Kurmitola, East Pakistan, near an airstrip used by the CIA.

The Khampas, accustomed to chilly high altitudes, suffered mightily in the tropical heat, taking turns cooling off in a shower for the next two days. They finally piled into a truck and were driven to the airstrip, where they saw a large unmarked cargo plane. The aircraft was a C-118 crewed by a U.S. Air Force special operations unit known innocuously as Detachment I of the 322 Troop Carrier Squadron, Medium (Special). The aircraft was pieced together from many different serial-numbered parts, making it untraceable if it crashed. The tail had removable numbers that were sometimes changed multiple times during a mission. The crew entered the cabin through a door separate from the one used by passengers and never knew who they were hauling. The truck pulled up next to the C-118, and the Khampas were hustled aboard, along with interpreter Jantzen Thondup and CIA agent John Reagan.

They were first flown to Okinawa for a physical examination, then on to the U.S. trust territory of Saipan, a twelve-mile-long limestone island in the middle of the Pacific Ocean, where the CIA ran a base for the training of anti-Communist agents and guerrillas. The Khampas joined Chinese Nationalists, Koreans, Lao, Vietnamese, and Thai already being trained at the camp. CIA trainers found the Tibetan names too difficult to pronounce or remember, so they gave each of the Khampas an American name. Wangdu became Walt, Tashi became Dick, Athar became Tom, Tswang Dorje became Sam, Cho Bulu became Dan, and Lhotse became Lou.

Despite the CIA's experience training other nationalities, the Khampas were a challenge because of their lack of formal Western-style education. Like all but a few Tibetans from the elite ruling class, the Khampas were nearly illiterate and had trouble with numbers and concepts like the twenty-four-hour clock. The CIA scrambled to find someone who could teach them enough Tibetan grammar that they would be able to communicate by radio using Morse code. They turned to the only qualified scholar on Tibetan Buddhism in the United States that the agency knew of at the time: Geshe Ngawang Wangyal, a Kalmyk Mongolian teaching Tibetan at Columbia University.

CIA trainers soon learned that what the Khampas lacked in education they made up for in fighting ability. "They were brave, honest, and strong," said case officer Roger McCarthy. "Basically, everything we respect in a man." Another trainer, case officer Harry Mustakos, made the mistake of tossing a short Tibetan sword to Lou during close combat training. Within seconds Mustakos' knife was knocked away, his hand bleeding from a slash as Lou's knife poised for a death thrust. "I learned from that," Mustakos said.[11]

The initial training disappointed the Khampas. They felt an urgency to learn skills they could use against the Chinese so that they could return to the fight as quickly as possible. Instead, the CIA instructors placed a heavy emphasis on teaching them wireless communication, which was vital to gaining the intelligence they wanted. To the Khampas, wireless training seemed pointless. They couldn't kill Chinese with a wireless transmitter. Worse, they were training with antiquated British Enfield rifles and Bren guns, weapons they already had and knew how to use. They wanted to be trained in the use of modern Chinese weapons such as artillery and heavy machine guns, which they had captured but been forced to discard because they didn't know how to use them. After about a month the group met with instructors to demand training with modern weapons. The instructors said they would pass the complaint to their superiors, a reply that failed to satisfy Walt. He refused to continue training and demanded to return to India. Trainee Dan was also Walt's servant and therefore obliged to join him in any dispute. The instructors separated them from the rest of the trainees for much of the training, although they would eventually rejoin the others and participate in one of the first missions. Walt never learned how to operate a radio.[12]

The CIA instructors taught the remaining Khampas how to operate radios and the encoding and decoding of a special Tibetan-language telecode developed during training. They were taught fire-and-movement tactics; ambush, sabotage, and booby-trap techniques; report-writing and spy craft; parachute training; and first aid and basic psychological warfare techniques. McCarthy was impressed by their attention to detail, marksmanship, and the speed with which they learned to read maps.

Once the training was complete, the Khampas were outfitted in traditional Tibetan dress that had to be flown in by diplomatic pouch in preparation for their first mission. They would parachute into Tibet in an operation code-named ST BARNUM, following a U.S.-military convention of using all uppercase for mission code names.[13] The CIA used a two-letter geographical code called a digraph with each mission name. The ST signified that the operation was run by the CIA Directorate of Operations, Far East Division, China.

The Khampas found themselves once again at the Kurmitola airstrip in East Pakistan. This time they boarded a B-17 painted black, stripped of all weapons and national markings and equipped with special mufflers shielding the engine exhaust. The aircraft was crewed by a covert team of Polish and Czech expatriates so that the United States couldn't be linked to the operation if the plane crashed. Tom and Lou were to be dropped near Lhasa to make contact with Gompo Tashi Andrugtsang, the leader of the largest Tibetan resistance group, to assess the state of the resistance, and with Phala, lord chamberlain to the Dalai Lama, for an evaluation of the political situation in the capital. They were to gauge the strength of the Chinese military and its positions. Tom initially refused. "I had agreed to train so that I could kill Chinese. Well, Kham was where the fighting was, not Lhasa. Besides, I didn't know any of the high-ranking officials in Lhasa. What could I do there? Also, I thought of the Lhasa officials as cowards, always doing exactly what the Chinese told them to do. I was afraid that some of the Lhasa officials might betray us to the Communists." He relented once he learned he was to meet with rebel leader Gompo Tashi.[14]

Three others were to be dropped into Kham near Lou's hometown, Mocha Khashar, an area of heavy fighting, to establish contact with the resistance. They were expected to hit the ground ready for battle. Supply bundles would be dropped with each group that included clothing, weapons, ammunition, food, radios, cameras, signal mirrors, binoculars, and first-aid supplies.

Mustakos had taught the Tibetans the sign of the cross and, welcoming all possible blessings, they crossed themselves while they chanted the mantra of Vajrasattva, the bodhisattva of purification, while crossing the brick runway to board the black B-17. Norbu told the Khampas that the full moon made it an auspicious time for their reentry. The bomber lifted off on October 20, 1958, using the Himalayas as a screen to avoid detection by Indian radar, and headed for Lhasa. Unlike the crew, the Tibetans had no need of oxygen masks at high altitude. Most

Tibetans have genetically evolved to use oxygen more efficiently and resist the ill effects of high altitude.

Tom and Lou were to be dropped about forty miles south of Lhasa over a stretch of the Yarlung Tsangpo River with broad sandbars, identified from aerial reconnaissance photos. As the aircraft neared the drop, they moved toward the "joe hole," as the exit port in the floor was called. Tom was connected to the supply bundle by a three-hundred-foot line to make sure the supplies didn't go astray. A signal flashed from the cockpit, and the bundle was pushed out first. Seconds later, Tom disappeared through the joe hole. Lou was right behind, seeing two parachutes blossom beneath him. He followed Tom by steering a parachute specially designed for maneuverability. They landed safely on the banks of the river, unhooking their harnesses and unslinging the 9 mm Sten guns strapped across their chests. They buried the supplies from the bundle, much of it packed in specially sewn vests so that they could be worn for ease of transport. Then they donned Tibetan garb and began their mission.

The B-17 changed course for Kham, where it found skies so overcast that the drop zone could not be identified. The mission was scrubbed for the next full moon. Ten days later, a coded message in badly garbled Tibetan crackled across the radio at CIA headquarters. Because of the Khampas' poor spelling abilities in their own language, their message was at first difficult to decipher. Finally, a CIA agent decided that "it basically says, 'I'm alive.'" That was enough to fill the room with elation. "The entire Far East Division was electrified," said Irving Holober, head of the Tibet Task Force, known in the CIA as ST CIRCUS.[15]

Weather for the second drop became favorable the first week of November, and all four remaining Khampas again clambered aboard. The B-17 arrived over Kham and the signal to jump flashed from the cockpit. As the Khampas lined up next to the joe hole, Dick began to hyperventilate and slumped into unconsciousness. Without hesitation,

Sam followed his supply bundle through the joe hole, followed in rapid succession by Dan and Walt. The three landed safely on a hillside of conifers and quickly stashed their equipment. In the dark they could hear the distant sound of gunfire. Onboard the aircraft, Dick revived and returned to base with the air crew.

The Khampas awoke in the morning to find they had landed about six miles from their drop zone. They walked along a ridgeline until they came upon a Khampa herder tending five ponies. At first suspicious, he eventually agreed to lead them to a nearby guerrilla camp. Walt's older brother turned out to be part of the group, ensuring a warm reception. The next day they retrieved their hidden gear and radioed CIA headquarters.

The successful drops encouraged the CIA to move beyond merely collecting intelligence to full-blown support for the growing rebellion inside Tibet. By Memorial Day 1958, training was moved from Saipan to Camp Hale, a remote camp near Leadville, Colorado, in the high Rocky Mountains, where conditions were similar to those in Tibet. Tibetan recruits were trained at Camp Hale in guerrilla warfare and how to signal for drops of arms and supplies.

From 1958 to 1961 the CIA dropped more than 250 tons of equipment, arms, ammunition, radios, medical supplies, hand-operated printing presses, and other supplies into Tibet. The supplies never met the needs of the rebel group Chushi Gangdruk, which had many more volunteers than the CIA could supply with weapons and ammunition. The lack of modern weapons was one of many problems hindering the resistance movement. Despite the leadership of Gompo Tashi, the real power lay with dozens of tribal leaders. The CIA-trained agents tried to convince the Tibetans to break into small guerrilla bands using the small-unit tactics the CIA had taught them, but doing so went against the Tibetan tradition of relying on large groups and massed cavalry charges. Adopting a tactic that seemed imperative to the Americans made little sense to the Tibetans.

The first CIA drops in 1958 were made south of Lhasa to Chushi Gangdruk rebels, mostly Khampas who had fled Kham to set up a base far from home in a culturally different area that, to them, was almost a foreign country. The CIA hoped that their arms would be distributed to rebels who would form small units that would blend in with the populace and come together for guerrilla attacks. The agency never understood that the Khampas could not blend in with the local population because they dressed differently, had different customs, and spoke a different dialect.

Closer to Kham, where fighters operated on home ground, CIA efforts were hampered by the Tibetan view of war as a family affair and the agency's failure to understand the cultural barriers that made it nearly impossible for Tibetan warriors to adopt modern small-unit tactics. The Tibetans brought their families with them, along with their herds of sheep, goats, horses, and yaks. A gathering of fighters could include thousands of animals. Breaking up into small units operating independently meant leaving their families and herds behind, a concept too foreign to embrace. CIA arms drops attracted huge gatherings of fighters that the Chinese quickly spotted and targeted with bombers. Swarms of Chinese cavalry and ground troops attacked on the heels of the bombings.

One of the last groups of CIA-trained Tibetans to parachute into Tibet could have been linked to Nagtshang Powo, the warlord who offered to escort Tenzin Namdak. In September 1959, nine graduates from the CIA's Camp Hale in Colorado were dropped onto the Changthang Plateau about 250 miles east of Sezhig, near Lake Namtso. Their mission was to convince a local leader, Nagtshang Phurpo, and his four thousand fighters to attack Chinese trucks hauling borax from mines in the area. Nagtshang Powo means "the man from Nagtshang," so it's possible that Nagtshang Powo and Nagtshang Phurpo were the same person.[16] Another possibility is that Nagtshang Powo and Nagtshang Phurpo are so similar that the names were confused or that they are the same name but transcribed differently. What is certain is that Nagtshang Phurpo never received the CIA arms drop. A traitor alerted the Chinese, and they moved quickly to attack the guerrillas before the arms could be dropped. Unaware of the betrayal and Chinese retaliation, the team of CIA-trained Tibetans who were to call in the arms drop were parachuted near Lake Namtso. Nagtshang Phurpo had fled, leaving the CIA-trained Tibetans on their own. They avoided capture during a difficult 350-mile escape to Nepal that took eight weeks.[17] Unknown is whether the CIA made further attempts to drop arms to Nagtshang Phurpo.

Of the forty-nine Tibetans parachuted into Tibet as part of ST BARNUM, thirty-seven were killed, ten survived after arduous treks to India and Nepal (including those dropped near Lake Namtso), one surrendered, and one was captured.[18] The CIA's proxy war with China left many Tibetans feeling betrayed. Among them was one of the Dalai Lama's brothers, Taktse Rinpoche, once a strong supporter of the CIA's program. "What I should say, honestly speaking, they just fooled us. . . . It was for their own information. There was nothing that would be helpful for us."[19]

For Tenzin Namdak at Sezhig, the CIA efforts to arm the resistance would also cause the Chinese to send thousands of troops swarming to the remote Changthang Plateau, magnifying the danger of any escape attempt.

13
Ambush

As Tenzin Namdak waited for the tribal chief Nagtshang Powo, monks prepared supplies to be loaded onto pack animals for the coming journey. Tenzin planned to head west and then turn south to Nepal and cross into the Dolpo region in western Nepal, home to a large population of Bönpos. To get there they had to walk hundreds of miles across the Changthang Plateau and then cross the Himalayas.

Tenzin finally tired of waiting for Nagtshang Powo and set out, leaving word for him to follow. Nagtshang Powo, perhaps prompted to action by Tenzin's departure, followed shortly after, accompanied by hundreds of nomads with an even larger number of yaks and sheep. They set off across a treeless landscape of vast plains broken by mountains, hills, boulders, ravines, and lakes. To make detection more difficult, the mass of refugees split into three groups. The highest ranking lamas and their guards, about thirty, traveled in a central group along with a portion of the nomads. Tenpa Woser, now recovered from his gunshot wound, traveled in another group that led the way. A third group headed by Nagtshang Powo and his warriors brought up the rear. The three groups tried to stay close enough to be able to aid one another if one got into trouble. If one group was discovered by the Chinese, the others would have time to get away.

At night each group camped separately, sending out lookouts to keep watch. On the second day the sound of distant gunfire pierced through the din of baggage slapping against animals and the chatter of tramping refugees. The lamas and their escorts could see a swarm of tiny figures in the hazy distance. A battle was underway. A few hours later, a small group of dispirited rebels caught up with Tenzin's party and told them that Nagtshang Powo's forces were scattered and he was on the run. The Chinese had overwhelmed Nagtshang Powo and his warriors in a short, sharp fight. With few weapons, the monks and refugees were powerless to offer aid. There was nothing to do but quicken the pace and hope that they would not be spotted.

They moved west, crossing one of the numerous mountain chains that run north-south across the Changthang and rise as high as 20,000 feet. As they descended the pass, they could see herds of antelope on the plains below.

Three days and about a hundred miles from their starting point, the ragged train of yaks, donkeys, and horses halted in the afternoon near Muro Ri, a mountain of limestone named after a local diety. Muro Ri rose from a flat, grassy section of the Changthang on the northern shore of Lake Teri Namtso. A salt lake thirty-four miles long and sixteen miles wide, Teri Namtso is one of the largest of the thousands of freshwater and saltwater lakes the dot the Changthang.

It was late afternoon when they chose a campsite on one of the relatively flat areas of the plateau at the base of the northern side of Muro Ri. Tenpa Woser and his group camped about three miles west. They could easily see the other groups in air so clear that it made distances deceptive. They unloaded their pack animals, hobbled them, and left them to graze. A black donkey with Tenzin's party was so unsettled that its owners had trouble unlashing the gear on its back. Tenzin took this as a bad omen.[1] They pitched their yak-hide tents among the pale green clumps of white sage, one of the hardy forms of vegetation able to survive at 15,000 feet in the fierce, cold winds that scour the rock-strewn, uneven plain. The temperature dropped into the low teens. Fires were built so they could begin brewing black

Chinese tea and mix it with a dollop of yak butter and a heavy dash of salt.

Tenpa Woser was making his own preparations for the evening when a member of Tenzin's group wandered into camp. He was a lookout who had climbed a rise that lay slightly to the south of the two camps. From this vantage point he could see Tenpa's party and decided to descend and chat with his friends. He was warmly received and invited to tea. If the lookout had remained atop the mountain, he might have seen Chinese soldiers stealthily moving toward Tenzin's camp.

The troops were armed with machine guns, mortars, and Chinese copies of Soviet submachine guns and semiautomatic rifles. As the soldiers crept into position, most of those in the Tibetan camp were drinking tea, making preparations for the evening meal, or feeding the animals.

The sudden chatter of machine-gun fire and exploding mortar shells rent the peaceful evening, hurling the camp into confusion as monks and nomads ran to save themselves or to yank their families out of their tents. A few charged the soldiers with drawn swords and were shot dead.

Instinctively, Tenzin began running. As he ran, he heard the whish of bullets passing close. The sand nearby exploded in a line of small puffs in rapid succession. A few yards away, bullets ripped into three close friends, monks Gelong Gyasho Lhazo, Gyasho Rinchen Phuntshog, and Menyag Yungdrung Tenzin, slamming their lifeless bodies to the ground. Moments later he felt a blow to his leg, pitching him heavily to the earth.

In a few minutes only the dead and wounded remained among the yak-hair tents pitched on the treeless plain, their multicolored prayer flags fluttering in the breeze.

The Chinese caught Tenpa Woser's advance party by surprise as well. They were drinking tea and chatting with the lookout from Tenzin's group when they heard a volley of gunfire. The camp fell silent for a moment as everyone listened. Within minutes, Chinese soldiers appeared near the point on the slope where the lookout had been stationed and poured toward their encampment.[2]

The camp dissolved as men, women, and children ran, with the Chinese giving chase and firing at their backs. Horses that had broken their tethers in Tenzin's camp ran ahead of the soldiers. The panicked horses overtook Tenpa and his fleeing companions and scattered with them across the landscape of broken boulders and gullies.

The hardy Tibetans, bred to the thin air of the high plateau, easily outdistanced the pursuing Chinese. Once a safe distance ahead of their pursuers, a half-dozen members of Tenpa's party regrouped. The rest were dead, captured, or scattered in all directions. The strategy of separating the monks into two parties had failed. Chinese troops had attacked Tenzin and Tenpa's camp nearly simultaneously. As Tenpa and his group of survivors discussed what to do next, they came upon several of the wayward horses. They approached the horses, but the animals spooked and disappeared at a gallop. Determined to retrieve their mounts, they began tracking them.

Tenzin lay in pain, unable to move, his blood darkening the earth. He heard the chattering of Chinese soldiers punctuated by gunfire as they finished off the wounded. A soldier, the furry flaps of his Russian-style cap covering his ears, examined the bodies close to Tenzin. Tenzin lay still. Then the soldier turned to him. "Shoot him," he heard a voice say.

Tenzin waited for the bullet, calming his mind in preparation for death. He heard another soldier say, "Don't shoot." He understood only a few words of Mandarin but enough to grasp that they didn't want to waste a bullet on a monk who was going to die anyway.

Tenzin lay motionless, accepting his fate. He was sure the Chinese soldier was right. He would die alone on this desolate plain. He heard the banter of Chinese soldiers and the clatter of their equipment slowly fade as they departed the scene of carnage, leaving him in the solitude of the wild vastness.

Stillness settled over the demolished camp as the setting sun cast long shadows over the mangled bodies and scattered belongings. As Tenzin silently chanted, preparing himself for death, a peculiar movement drew his attention. The sand a few dozen feet away began to move. At first he thought he must be hallucinating. Then a figure emerged from the moving sand, rising to sitting position as it brushed away the grit. To his astonishment, Tenzin recognized his assistant, Sherab Tsultrim. Devoted to Tenzin, Sherab Tsultrim had refused to flee. Amid the confusion he had escaped detection by covering himself in sand and placing a stone over his face. The Chinese had nearly stepped on him as they walked through camp finishing off the wounded. When he was sure the soldiers had gone, Sherab Tsultrim wriggled free, then stood and looked around to get his bearings. He saw Tenzin and ran to his side. A few minutes later he was joined by their abbot, Sherab Lodrö, who had managed to remain concealed behind a pile of rocks.[3]

The bullet had broken the thigh bone in Tenzin's right leg. He was bleeding and suffering from thirst. The monks tore strips from their clothing to bind his wounds, using a short piece of wood as a splint. Fearing the Chinese would return, the two monks put Tenzin's arms over their shoulders and carried him away from the remains of the encampment in search of a place to hide.

They found an overhanging rock where Tenzin could shelter for the night and remain hidden from Chinese patrols. The monks pulled green clumps of stepa grass, with their feathery white tops, to form a makeshift bed for their wounded master. After placing him on the bed of grass, they returned to the abandoned camp to look for food, water, the sacred reliquary, and other religious objects. There, to their relief, they found two wounded survivors who had escaped and returned to the desolate camp to scrounge for food: Tsewang and Machen, who was lucky to survive but unlucky to be wounded for the second time since fleeing Menri Monastery. The four monks retrieved the reliquary and other sacred objects, gathered as much food and water as they could carry, and returned to Tenzin. The rock overhang was too small for all five, so they left Tenzin after making him as comfortable as possible and moved to small caves farther up the mountain. They shivered through the night without a fire for fear it would be spotted by the Chinese.

For three days they cared for Tenzin, who hovered near death. They chanted prayers for healing and protection, tended his wound as best they could, and watched for Chinese patrols. When their food and water ran out, Sherab Tsultrim and the abbot returned to the ambush site to search for food among the piles of strewn gear. At the abandoned campsite they discovered a nomad scavenging through the scattered baggage, all that remained to attest to the lives taken in the ambush. They confronted the nomad, who was loading his booty onto yaks. The two monks described the attack to him and how a high lama was seriously wounded and near death. The nomad was so moved by their story that he took nothing from the camp, gave the monks one of his three yaks, and accompanied them to where Tenzin lay. The nomad mentioned that the Chinese had established a concentration camp for captured Tibetans, prompting Machen and Tsewang to decide to surrender to the Chinese camp in order to get medical treatment and food. They discussed taking Tenzin, but the abbot and Sherab Tsultrim worried that the camp was too distant for Tenzin to survive the journey. The nomad, meanwhile, offered the hospitality of his nearby encampment, and the monks gladly accepted. Machen and Tsewang set off for the concentration camp as Tenzin was loaded onto the yak for the trip to the nomad camp.

Tenzin's survival became even more doubtful as he bumped painfully along atop the yak. The yak stumbled, throwing Tenzin forcefully to the ground. The impact injured his hip and caused so much pain to his damaged leg that he lapsed into unconsciousness. The alarmed monks worried that the second injury would further narrow Tenzin's chances of survival. Without herbs or traditional healing implements, they could do nothing but mutter prayers. After Tenzin revived, they loaded him back onto the yak and continued to the nomad encampment. At the camp, the nomads welcomed Tenzin and placed him in a black yak-hair tent that was home to an elderly couple.

Soon after Tenzin was made comfortable, the sound of voices pierced the evening stillness. A Chinese patrol had arrived at the nomad camp and was searching tents. They soon discovered the monks. The soldiers arrested Sherab Tsultrim and the abbot, but Tenzin appeared too close to death to bother. For the second time Tenzin was left to die. The soldiers ignored the sacred Nyame Kundung reliquary and other religious artifacts, considering them useless religious trinkets. They kicked the reliquary to show their contempt.

Spooked by the unwelcome visit, the next day the nomads began breaking camp. Tenzin's elderly hosts prepared to leave and told him they could not take him with them. They were poor and had no food to spare. Tenzin asked to be taken with the religious objects to a stream so that he could quench his thirst and die near the soothing sound of running water. A young man who had come to help the elderly couple dismantle their tent put Tenzin on a yak and guided him to the creek, burying the precious objects. He tenderly lay Tenzin where he could hear the soothing burble of water over rocks. Again, Tenzin composed himself for death.

As Tenzin lay dying, Tenpa Woser and his companions were intent on finding him. First they had to recapture the horses panicked during the attack that wounded Tenzin. They followed hoofprints through a series of ravines. After awhile they heard voices speaking Tibetan. They cautiously approached the sound and found that a group of survivors from Nagtshang Powo's militia had caught some of the escaped horses. Tenpa greeted the small group and they exchanged escape stories. The militiamen told them Nagtshang Powo had survived and was on the run.

While Tenpa engaged the Nagtshang Powo survivors, the ex-Menri monks examined the horses and identified all of them as belonging to Tenzin and the other lamas. They asked politely for the militiamen to release the horses to their rightful owners. They refused. Tenpa approached one of the Nagtshang Powo men who was mounted on a white horse. He again asked the man to return the horse. The man answered with an insult. Tenpa grabbed the bridle. He explained that the horse belonged to a revered holy man and that it must be returned to him.[4]

The mounted man sneered his refusal. Tenpa said nothing. His right hand grasped the hilt of his sword, his left hand still gripping the bridle.

He locked eyes with the mounted man. The man tensed but began to wilt under Tenpa's hard stare. It radiated deadly intensity. The militiaman could see that Tenpa would not relent until he had the horse or one of them was dead. Without a word he slid from the saddle and walked away.

Encouraged by Tenpa's success, the four other Menri men demanded their horses as well. Seeing that keeping the horses would mean a fight, Nagtshang Powo's men relented.

Now mounted again, the five survivors rode to the site of Tenzin's ambush. They found only bodies and abandoned supplies. Uncertain whether Tenzin and the abbot were dead, captured, or on the run, the monks mulled their options and decided they should find a place to hide.

They spent the next seventeen days hiding in an area near a glacier, above the plain where they had been ambushed. Piles of jumbled rocks stretched for miles and made concealment easy.

Careful to stay hidden, they watched the movements of Chinese patrols searching for survivors. As soon as the number of patrols diminished, the Menri men set course for Nepal, riding across a relatively flat landscape broken by ravines, washes, and rocky formations that rose hundreds of feet. They reasoned that if Tenzin or any of the other lamas survived, they might be heading in the same direction. They hoped their paths would cross.

14
Prisoners

Soothed by the sound of the gurgling stream, Tenzin put himself into a meditative trance and awaited death. He was alone under a black sky studded with bright points of light, listening to eagle owls *woo-hooing* their territorial calls. About midnight, the night sounds of the plateau were interrupted by the clatter of yaks carrying baggage. The sound, at first faint, gradually grew louder. The yak train remained invisible in the black night, even though the sounds told Tenzin that it had stopped near him. With all the strength he could muster he shouted, "Who are you?" hoping that his weak voice would carry.[1] Although faint, his cry cut through the night to the ears of Lhanor, a sixty-one-year-old farmer from Kham who was intent on escaping Tibet with his thirty yaks. Lhanor followed the sound and found Tenzin, who could barely talk. The farmer could see that Tenzin was near death. He set up his tent around the monk, built a fire, and brought him food and tea.

The next morning Tenzin learned that Lhanor was a Nyingmapa, a member of the oldest school of Buddhism, similar to Bön in its beliefs and practices. Lhanor had begun his escape with his son, a Buddhist monk, but they stumbled into a Chinese ambush and a bullet ended his son's life. Lhanor escaped, forced to leave his son's body behind. As he headed toward the border he discovered a survivor of another attack, a man crippled by a Chinese bullet. Lhanor treated the man's wound, lashed him to a yak, and brought him along. The man, although unable to walk, was in much better condition than Tenzin. Lhanor set up a separate tent for himself and the other wounded man.

Lhanor cleaned and bandaged Tenzin's wounds, applying a poultice of traditional Tibetan healing herbs and blowing chants onto the wounds. He was a devout Buddhist, and every day he recited prayers and healing mantras. He delayed his escape for sixteen days, risking discovery by the Chinese to nurse Tenzin by the stream. Under Lhanor's care, Tenzin slowly began to recover.

Menri abbot Sherab Lodrö, and Tenzin's assistant, Sherab Tsultrim, were being marched under Chinese guard. As they traveled across the plateau, discipline appeared to disintegrate among their guards. The soldiers seemed to lack leadership. They began bickering among themselves and soon lost interest in their captives. To the monk's surprise, the soldiers left one night as their captives slept. In the morning, they each made a different choice about how to use their unexpected freedom. The abbot, Sherab Lodrö, decided to hide in the mountains. As the most important figure in the Bön religion, Bön practitioners in the area were sure to keep him provisioned. As a mere monk, however, Sherab Tsultrim was unlikely to fare as well. He probably would be welcomed for only a few nights. As much as he distrusted the Chinese, Sherab Tsultrim decided to find a concentration camp where he could surrender and be assured food and shelter. After saying goodby to the abbot, he joined a group of Tibetans captured while trying to escape who were being escorted to a camp near Lake Teri Namtso, less than a day's walk from where the Chinese had ambushed their party a few days earlier.

The camp was run by nomads in the pay of the Chinese. The nomad guards and many of their prisoners owned hundreds of sheep, yaks, and horses that grazed nearby. The concentration camp moved as necessary to keep pace with the animals as they grazed their way across the plain. There were no fences and no uniformed Chinese guards, although Chinese soldiers from the nearest military base occasionally visited. Camp security relied on armed nomads. The Chinese had put a man known as Tok, selected by the nomads to be their leader, in charge of the camp. Tok treated the prisoners brutally to prove to the Chinese that he deserved their confidence. Prisoners were beaten and killed at his whim. Many of the able-bodied prisoners were forced to become personal servants to Tok, his lieutenants, and his family members.

The camp grew as the Chinese brought in groups of new prisoners. Sherab Tsultrim recognized one of the new faces—the same young man who had helped take down the tent of the old nomad couple who had temporarily cared for Tenzin. He told Sherab Tsultrim that he had taken Tenzin to the mountain creek to die and described its location. Sherab Tsultrim felt a surge of hope. Perhaps his master still lived! He ran to the few other Bön monks in the camp with the news, overjoyed to learn of Tenzin's whereabouts but worried about his fate. He resolved to find his master, alive or dead.

Sherab Tsultrim told camp officials he knew where to find a high-ranking lama and volunteered to bring him to the camp. Like all lay Tibetans, Tok and the other nomads working for the Chinese still revered their lamas. Arguing that it was unthinkable to leave such an important lama languishing in the wilderness, Sherab Tsultrim easily convinced Tok that he should be allowed to fetch Tenzin. Camp officials allowed another monk to accompany Sherab Tsultrim and gave him seven yaks loaded with provisions and an eighth specially trained for riding to bear Tenzin back to the camp.

As he neared the location described by the nomad, Sherab Tsultrim came upon two tents and a cluster of grazing yaks. Remembering Tenzin's poor condition when he had last seen him, Sherab Tsultrim expected to find a corpse or a man clinging to life. He was surprised, then overjoyed, to find a lively Tenzin in one of the tents, able to sit and welcome him with a smile as an older man hovered over him attentively.

They could hardly believe their good fortune at being reunited. Each had despaired of ever seeing the other again. Jubilant at finding Tenzin alive and recovering, Sherab Tsultrim thanked Lhanor profusely. Tenzin was well enough to travel, so Sherab Tsultrim tied him to the riding yak and headed back to the wandering prison camp. Before leaving, Tenzin blessed Lhanor, thanking him for his gentleness and compassion and praying for his safe escape. The monks were certain that the Bön protector gods had brought Lhanor to save the dying Tenzin.

Upon their return to the prison camp, Sherab Tsultrim convinced Tok that Tenzin needed special care because of his severe injuries and his status as a high lama. Tenzin was taken to the tent of a local nomad, Dhachoe Lama, whom Tenzin had befriended on a previous visit to the area. Dhachoe and his family were honored to have such a high lama in their care. They made every effort to provide for Tenzin's comfort, giving him his own tent and even making woolen chubas for him and his assistant.[2]

Tenzin immediately began considering the best way to escape. The bullet had shattered his thigh bone and it would be months before he could walk, if ever. Tenzin's plans included the abbot, well-provided-for in his mountain hideout by the faithful. The abbot and Tenzin remained in contact through messages passed by trusted nomads. Tenzin urged the abbot to escape now and not wait for Tenzin's leg to heal. The abbot refused, arguing that he was needed in Tibet. Tenzin replied that it was likely that the Chinese would kill or imprison him. Moreover, he argued, the Chinese persecution of monks and destruction of monasteries and texts made it clear that the future of Bön lay outside Tibet. The abbot finally agreed. A few days later, Sherab Lodrö, the thirty-second abbot of Menri, was on his way to the border with Nepal.

The abbot left without the reliquary. Tenzin had increasingly felt that the Nyame Kundung, holding the ashes of Menri's founder, should not be removed from Tibet. Two carriers of the reliquary had been wounded—first Manchen, then Tenzin. He regarded these difficulties as divine signs. A dream confirmed his suspicions. The protector deity, Sipe Gyalmo, had come to Tenzin as he slept and told him that the reliquary should not leave Tibet.

Unaware that Tenzin was not far away, Tenpa Woser and his party abandoned their hiding place in the rocks and headed for Nepal. Over the next few days refugees from a monastery in Kham joined them, as well as stragglers from other groups. The refugees were among the thousands following the Dalai Lama into exile. They were hunted by Chinese soldiers patrolling the routes to Nepal and military aircraft scouting the terrain for lines of refugees heading south. Soldiers often made no attempt to order the refugees they encountered to halt or surrender; they simply fired as soon as they saw them.

The Menri men found that some of their new companions were more concerned about their own welfare and less willing to cooperate for the benefit of all. They gathered firewood only for their own fires, although they readily accepted firewood gathered by the Menri group. They were reluctant to share food. When a task needed to be done, like digging a fire pit or standing lookout, the former Menri monks sprang to it without asking while the others seldom offered assistance. The Menri group made no complaint and attended to the duties at hand. They had been taught to accept the foibles of others and show them compassion instead of allowing themselves to be aroused to anger or resentment. They remained helpful and cheerful, even when food was scarce and the terrain difficult.

After about fourteen days of travel, the Menri men found a spot near a village to make camp at dusk. They were too tired to make a fire right away. They sat resting and chatting, weary from travel.

Shouts from another group of refugees nearby brought them to their feet. They had bumped into a Chinese foot patrol that was herding captured refugees to an internment camp. The Menri men sprang to their still-loaded mounts and galloped away. The soldiers fired as soon as they saw them. A bullet toppled one of the group from his horse. Another grazed a second Menri man's neck, but he remained in the saddle and kept riding. The gunfire brought down one of the horses, throwing a third rider to the ground. The unhorsed rider leapt to his feet and ran, but a bullet struck his foot and sent him tumbling. Another Menri man pulled him onto the back of his horse and they quickly outpaced their attackers.

After a hard ride to put distance between them and the Chinese troops, the Menri group halted to rest. Only five remained. As they resumed their flight, they bumped into twelve monks from Drepung Monastery. The two parties joined and traveled all night, not knowing if they were being pursued. From then on they rested during the day and traveled at night. After about two days the man wounded in the foot was in too much pain to travel. They left him with a nomad family that agreed to nurse him until he could walk again.

The three remaining Menri men forged on over the harsh landscape, begging for food from nomads and isolated hamlets they encountered. They often went days without seeing another human. At one point they shot a blue sheep, but meals were few and meager. Hunger tormented them. They once went two days without food and resorted to chewing on the reins of their horses. The horses fared better than their riders, feeding on alpine grasses along the way. One morning, Tenpa, exhausted after riding all night and weak from hunger, slid off his horse and lay on the ground at their campsite. His horse wandered away because Tenpa was too spent to tether it. Without his horse, his chances of survival in his weakened state would have narrowed. Luckily, there was plenty of succulent grass nearby to keep the horse from wandering far.

As they climbed the Himalayas, the terrain became more difficult until they crossed Lalung Pass at about 16,600 feet. From there it took them nearly two days to descend through deep gorges as they followed a river into Nepal. As they descended, the cold, rocky landscape gave way to a lush, tropical forest. The territory was unknown to them and they often had to ask directions from villagers and shepherds they encountered.

They crossed an unguarded border into Nepal. The Chinese were aggressively trying to prevent Tibetans from crossing into Nepal, so it's unclear why the well-used crossing wasn't guarded. Tenpa believed the protector deities were looking out for him. Safely across the border, the former monks agreed to look for their abbot in Nepal's Dolpo region, an area populated largely by ethnic Tibetans with a heavy Bönpo presence. Traveling through a strange country where few people spoke Tibetan made getting directions and begging for food difficult. They journeyed for several weeks with no food and no money, uncertain if they would find anyone they knew.

From Dolpo they traveled to Mustang, another region of Nepal heavily populated by Bönpos. In a village where they stopped to beg for food, they met a cobbler who told them that abbots from several Bönpo monasteries in Tibet had passed through on their way to Mustang and one had stopped at his shop to have shoes made. Uncertain as to whether their abbot, Sherab Lodrö, had escaped or was even alive, they allowed themselves to believe that one of those abbots might be their own and set out in the direction the lamas had taken. They questioned every traveler they met. Several said that a group of Bönpo lamas had newly arrived at a nearby monastery. The news buoyed their spirits.

Arriving at the monastery they rushed up the steps and into a wide hall. There they saw Sherab Lodrö. They prostrated at the abbot's feet as tears of joy streamed down their faces. They had finally reunited with the abbot after weeks of grueling travel, narrow escapes, and near starvation.

Later Tenpa would learn that his brother, Tenpa Wangal, had been captured while trying to defend his master. Tenpa Wangal would spend two months in a Chinese prison and then be forced to spend a year herding sheep before being allowed to return to Menri, where he found to his sorrow that the seat of the Bön religion had been looted, its buildings destroyed and gutted.[3]

15
Tenzin's Escape

The site of the concentration camp drifted as the nomads followed their herds of sheep, yaks and ponies grazing from one area to the next until it was was more than a day's walk from Tenzin's tent. Tenzin remained in place, making a show of being too weak to move or escape. At night he exercised in his tent to strengthen himself for the escape he secretly planned to make when the opportunity arose. Sherab Tsultrim was allowed to visit Tenzin and regularly traveled from the camp to bring news, plot, and sip tea.

Sherab Tsultrim became friendly with camp commander Tok and some of the Chinese officials who regularly checked on the camp. The Bönpos had been prisoners for about ten months when those good relations proved their worth. Sherab Tsultrim learned that the Chinese were moving all the prisoners to prisons controlled by the Chinese military. He was ordered to fetch Tenzin to the main camp so that he could be taken to one of those prisons. The news was expected but unsettling all the same. In a Chinese prison they would face brutal thamzings, torture, or execution. If they survived they would likely be returned to their home province and assigned a menial job unrelated to religion and calculated to humiliate them.

The news convinced Tenzin to seize an unexpected opportunity to escape. Sherab Tsultrim had befriended a woman in the camp from Kham who had two small children. Like Tenzin's mother, she was married to two brothers. The brothers had survived a long and difficult escape to Nepal. In Nepal they learned from other refugees where their wife and children were being held by the Chinese. Without hesitation they trekked back through the snowy Himalayas to retrieve their wife and children. Making the journey the first time took courage and grit, but making the equally difficult trip back into Tibet, only to escape again within a matter of days, required a will and fortitude that can only be imagined. The brothers had found their wife and children and were preparing to help them escape when Sherab Tsultrim asked for their help.

The men were honored to be asked to assist a high lama like Tenzin. The encounter was fortunate for Tenzin and his party, who needed a guide. Chinese soldiers were guarding all the usual passes, and many fleeing Tibetans were dying in the unforgiving cold of the Himalayas as they tried to find new routes through the mountains. Although walking was still difficult for Tenzin after ten months of recovery, his leg was healed enough to travel.

As he finalized his escape plans, Tenzin's concern turned to the sacred Nyame Kundung reliquary. A dream had convinced him that it could not leave the country, but must be kept safe from Chinese troops or looters. He decided to conceal it in a cave the abbot had discovered while hiding in the mountains. The cave had a small entrance on the south face of a mountain that opened into a large chamber. Although Tenzin had never visited the cave, after discussing the potential hiding place he realized it was one he had seen repeatedly in his dreams. Tenzin became convinced that the Bön deities were telling him that this was the place to hide the reliquary.

Tenzin asked Dhachoe to place the Nyame Kundung, three gilded copper statues, a set of gold ceremonial musical instruments, three large gold butterlamps, rare pieces of agate and coral, and other sacred objects in this well-disguised cave chamber. Only one other person was entrusted with knowledge of the secret location: Tsewang, a Menri monk. Tenzin drew a map showing the location of the reliquary and hid the scrap of paper in his clothing. He would hold on to this map for twenty-five years, until the Nyame Kundung was returned to its original home at Menri Monastery.

The drift of the main camp away from where Tenzin rested in Dhachoe's camp complicated the escape plan. By this time the main internment camp was several days' journey away. Although Sherab Tsultrim was permitted to travel freely between the camp and Tenzin's tent, the Chinese were suspicious of high lamas like Tenzin. Camp officials restricted him to his tent. Moreover, many of the local nomads were informers and were certain to report any suspicious movements. Worried that any movement by Tenzin would be reported, Sherab Tsultrim decided to get a travel authorization letter they could show to locals. Using his friendly relationship with camp commander Tok, he persuaded officials that no soldiers were needed to escort the lama when it was time to move him to the main camp in preparation for a final move to a Chinese prison. Sherab Tsultrim assured camp officials that he would make sure Tenzin arrived at the main camp. All he needed was a letter showing that the movement was authorized. Tok duly issued a letter allowing Tenzin to travel with four monks to the main camp without an escort. Letter in hand, Sherab Tsultrim slipped away from the main camp at night with the brothers, their wife, and children. Evading the guards at night was relatively easy, and they headed for Tenzin's tent.

At Dhachoe's campsite, Sherab Tsultrim introduced Tenzin to the brothers and their family. Dhachoe donated seven yaks and helped load them with tsampa and other provisions as well as a number of sacred texts Tenzin had kept with him. Tenzin thanked and blessed Dhachoe for his hospitality and devotion. The nomad and the lama had formed a strong bond. As Tenzin prepared to face the dangers of escape, Dhachoe prepared to face the Chinese interrogation he knew would be coming. Each prayed for the other's safety. The escape party set out, traveling fast to put as much distance as possible between them and the pursuers they knew would come.

As daylight broke, they found themselves near a frozen lake. At first there seemed to be no place to hide from Chinese patrols during the day on the treeless plain, but as they approached the shore of the lake they saw huge slabs of ice piled high on the shore by the fierce winds that arise on the Changthang. The tumbled slabs were so large they formed cavelike spaces where they could hide. They knew it was dangerous because ice can shift, causing a massive ice slab to come crashing down. There was nowhere else to hide. They unloaded the animals and turned them out to graze. Yaks were ubiquitous on the Changthang and would raise no suspicion. They spent the day under the ice slabs without mishap and set out again at dusk.

Tenzin and his party continued to travel only at night, hiding among rocks on mountainsides, ravines, or in caves just before dawn, unloading their yaks and releasing them to graze during the day. From their daytime hiding places they sometimes watched Chinese patrols pass.

They ate once a day to conserve their food, washing down cold tsampa with a mouthful of water. Most days they refrained from building a fire for fear the smoke would betray their position. On rare occasions they found a cave or a sheltered spot that masked flames and smoke, enabling them to brew tea to mix with their tsampa. To light the fire they used a gunpowder-like mixture that they could spark with two pieces of flint.

Tenzin and his party avoided everyone, even Tibetans, fearing they would be reported to the Chinese. Many Tibetans, especially the poorest, had been won over by Chinese propaganda. Others might try to curry favor with their new masters. When Tenzin and his party occasionally blundered into a shepherd, they passed themselves off as pilgrims.

Avoiding capture wasn't their only worry. Two major geological obstacles lay ahead. One was the Yarlung Tsangpo, the river that lay between the Changthang Plateau and the Himalayas. The highest major river in the world, known as the Everest of rivers, the Yarlung Tsangpo has an average elevation of 13,000 feet. Eighteen thousand miles long, the river originates from the Angsi Glacier southwest of Mount Kailash. As it leaves the Changthang, it carves a gorge through the Himalayas so large it's known as the Yarlung Tsangpo Grand Canyon. The river winds all the way to India, where it becomes the Yarlung Tsangpo, then into Bangladesh, until finally spilling into the Bay of Bengal. The monks were uncertain about how they would cross the mighty river, which often flowed even in the heart of winter. They "worried days, days, days," Tenzin said many years later. "How could we manage something to cross the river?"[1]

South of the Yarlung Tsangpo lay the even deadlier Himalayas, standing like a wall between them and freedom in Nepal. They would climb into Earth's highest mountain range, with more than a hundred peaks exceeding 23,650 feet. They would enter a landscape of avalanches, violent weather, subzero temperatures, and precarious paths along dizzying drop-offs. Facing this daunting mountain range was the only way out for fleeing Tibetans like Tenzin.

About ten days into their escape, they began their descent from the Changthang Plateau into the river valley. They thought they must be getting close to the river when they came to what appeared to be a frozen lake. They made their way carefully across the frozen surface, fearful of plunging through a thin spot in the ice. After crossing the lake they looked back, enchanted by the sight of stars reflected from the surface of the black ice. They walked on, expecting to find the river, but instead began climbing. Eventually it dawned on them that the frozen lake was actually the Yarlung Tsangpo! "Oh my goodness . . . unbelievable," Tenzin said. "That is really special. Just the right place where we come, and there is ice!" Tenzin chanted a prayer to the divine protectors he was sure had interceded to ease their way.[2]

As they climbed into the Himalayas, they were forced to clamber over rocks that the yaks could not negotiate. The animals were set free, and each member of the group shouldered a portion of what remained of the tsampa and the sacred texts, their guides carrying their children on their backs along with their food.

The journey was difficult for everyone, especially Tenzin. Despite his months of recovery he was able to walk only with the aid of a walking stick, and each step brought a jab of pain from his injured leg. To cope, he visualized his pain as something separate. He was able to observe it as if it were displayed in a glass case, white hot and pulsating. Even with his mental ability to isolate the pain, every day was a test of will. Like everyone in the group, he was hungry, tired, and cold. As they climbed higher, the cold intensified, seeping beneath their thick woolen chubas. Snow dampened their clothing, increasing their misery. Several members of the party suffered frostbite. Frozen ears, fingers, and toes were quickly lopped off with a knife to prevent gangrene. Each morning they rose to another day of suffering.

As they climbed higher into the snow country they rested inside snow caves burrowed into immense, white drifts. They labored along the precarious edges of cliffs that fell thousands of feet into a seemingly bottomless void. The frozen ground made their footing treacherous. A slip could mean a plunge into oblivion.

As Tenzin took each painful step toward Nepal, he reminded himself that monks who had fallen into Chinese hands were suffering much worse than he was.

They finally topped the highest point in their journey, a crest unremarkable in the seemingly endless string of mountains. The downward climb was no easier. One day the party stopped for a short rest, and Tenzin lay down his walking stick. Distracted by conversation, he unintentionally left it on a rock when they moved on. Climbing over boulders was easier without the stick and he didn't miss it until he reached a place where he could walk upright. Tenzin looked back and could see it. One of the monks offered to go back for it but Tenzin refused. "No, it is finished now."[3] They were so far above the tree line that there was no chance of finding a replacement stick. One of the younger monks put Tenzin's arm over his shoulder and they moved on together.

They ran out of food just as they reached a village after crossing into Nepal in early 1961. The journey had taken twenty-two days.

Even their hunger and pain could not dim the joy they felt at finally reaching freedom. Now they could travel during the day without fear and could greet strangers without mistrust. Tenzin looked back across the border into Tibet. The realization of all that was lost—many of his friends, his country, and his religion—swept over him. He was filled with an immense sadness.

The two brothers who had guided Tenzin through the Himalayas returned to their extended family in Nepal, and Tenzin and his fellow monks made their way to Pokhara, one of Nepal's larger cities, where they were reunited with their abbot, Sherab Lodrö.

Tenzin was comforted to be in a Bön monastery again, surrounded by sacred paintings and familiar images and texts, each oblong bundle of text tucked away in its own square shelf. That night, Tenzin took one of the texts from its silk wrapping and carefully placed it on a small table. He was overcome with emotion as he read the sacred writings for the first time since they began their journey from Sezhig nearly a year earlier.

Safe in the monastery, he had time to reflect on the destruction that had befallen his religion. Tenzin had paid a terrible price to save what he could of the Bön texts and sacred objects, but Bön monasteries were sacked, monks imprisoned, and Bönpo refugees scattered throughout India, Nepal, and Bhutan. As one of the leaders of his religion he felt a tremendous responsibility for Bön and Bönpos. He had to do something, but he was unsure of his next move. The outlines would begin to emerge after he made his way to Kathmandu, where he would encounter Samten Karmay, Sangye Tenzin, and an Englishman bearing an unusual offer.

16
Refugees in a Foreign Land

Samten Karmay, his brother Soko, and their mother Zinmo, arrived in Nepal in mid-1959 and headed to the ethnic jumble that is Kathmandu.

Kathmandu was the seat of government for King Mahendra Bir Bikram Shah Dev, a ruler sympathetic to Tibetan refugees but also sensitive to the threat of a powerful Chinese army menacing Nepal's borders. That fear had caused the nearby kingdom of Bhutan to initially bar refugees before finally relenting and allowing them to stay temporarily on condition they move on to India. King Mahendra courageously allowed refugees to enter his kingdom despite Chinese threats. Many Tibetan refugees settled in Nepal, but for most it was a stop on the way to India, where the Dalai Lama now resided.

Kathmandu sits in a semitropical valley at 4,200 feet, surrounded by four mountains, with the snowcapped Himalayas towering at the north end of the valley. The city's historical status as a trading hub drew people from every religion in the region. Tibetans easily fit into the cosmopolitan city of mostly Hindus and Buddhists. Kathmandu became a hub for the Tibetan exile community in Nepal. Monasteries and neighborhoods representing each of the three Tibetan provinces, Kham, Amdo, and U-tsang, sprang up to accommodate the growing Tibetan diaspora.

Soon after arriving in the capital, Samten learned that the Dalai Lama had fled Tibet. "It was sad because it showed that there was no hope," Samten recalled decades later. "Until we heard that, we always believed that somewhere, somehow—we always believed in our hearts that there was a way back, in one way or another. So when we heard that he had left we knew the situation was terribly bad, bad."[1]

The Dalai Lama's flight from Tibet unleashed a torrent of refugees who hoped to be reunited with their spiritual leader. By late 1959, nearly twenty thousand Tibetans were living in Nepal, eighty-five thousand in India, and ten thousand in Bhutan.[2] King Mahendra created temporary refugee camps near the mountain passes that were the gateways from Tibet to Nepal and built permanent settlements in Kathmandu, Solokhumbu, and Pokhara, where Tibetan communities continue to thrive decades later. The king also allowed the Dalai Lama to send a representative to Nepal to coordinate relief efforts with the International Red Cross and United Nations High Commission on Refugees.

Most of the refugees ended up in Indian camps, where they endured polluted water, disease, and an oppressive heat. In Delhi, the Tibetan refugee camp was built next to the city dump. One of the largest transit camps in India was about a thousand miles east of Delhi, near the village of Missamari, in Assam state, where the U.S. Army had built an airstrip during World War II. Missamari is in a far eastern section of India that snakes between Bangladesh to the south and Bhutan and Tibet to the north. Missamari Transit Camp was one of two large centers where refugees were brought initially, then funneled into other Indian camps. The experience of Tsering Wyangal, a merchant from Kham, was typical of Bönpos who landed in Missamari.

Tsering Wyangal was a once-prosperous merchant forced into poverty by Chinese policies. He and his wife, Dawa Ransom, and their three-year-old daughter, Tsering Dolma, fled their home in Chungbol, Kham, in 1960. They decided to flee after the Chinese confiscated their property and elevated their servants and employees to positions of authority. Reveling in their new power, they lorded over Tsering Wyangal and his family, making their lives miserable. The abuse became intolerable, and Tsering Wyangal and his wife and daughter joined a seventeen-member group on a twenty-eight-day trek across the Himalayas. Like many of those fleeing Tibet, they had no more than a notional sense of geography. Without a guide, they struck out in the general direction of the border, avoiding areas that would be patrolled. They crossed the Yarlung Tsangpo in coracles made of hides, paddling furiously to avoid being swept away by fierce currents. On reaching the far bank they struck off cross-country over unfamiliar mountainous terrain, Tsering carrying his daughter. Heading in the proper direction without a compass proved challenging in the strange landscape. Several times they found themselves walking for hours only to arrive near the place they had started. They camped on mountains so steep that they had to lash themselves to trees at night to keep from falling down the mountainside. Four times they felled trees to bridge impassable chasms. Everyone in Tsering Wyangal's party survived, but as they slogged through snowy passes, they passed the bodies of those in other parties who hadn't.

Near starvation, their food supplies having run out days earlier, they were slowly making their way down the southern side of the Himalayas when a group of soldiers appeared out of the mist. At first they thought the Chinese army had found them. The soldiers spoke an unfamiliar language that one of the party recognized as Hindi. Once they realized the soldiers were Indian, they shouted "Iha ghyal lo!" or "May the gods be victorious!" and wept.

The soldiers escorted them to a military base where they ate for the first time in days, devouring the unfamiliar Indian food. Their names were recorded and their baggage inspected. They were asked to undress for a medical examination but refused, in keeping with the Tibetan custom of never appearing naked in front of anyone, especially strangers. They were given lodging in a barracks, where the simple cots seemed luxurious after sleeping on the ground for so long. The next day they were ushered onto a strange looking metal contraption. The Tibetans had never seen a helicopter before and were frightened by the roar of the engines. They were astounded to see the ground fall away outside the window as the helicopter soared into the air. They were deposited in the Missamari Transit Camp, where 150 bamboo barracks had been erected in only two weeks on a sandy area by a river.

In hours they had come from the cool mountains to the humid tropics. Their only clothes were thick woolen chubas, unsuitable for the intense tropical heat. The Tibetans suffered miserably. Camp officials gave the family potatoes, curry, lentils, rice, sugar, and oil. Tsering Wyangal's wife, Dawa, had never seen lentils before and didn't know how to cook them. Initially the family subsisted on the rice, a dish only occasionally eaten by Tibetans.

Unlike the clear water that flowed from Tibetan streams, the water in the camp was cloudy with pollutants. Dysentery and scabies swept through the camp. Tsering Wyangal's daughter, suffering from scabies, became nauseated and soon had diarrhea so severe she passed only blood. Helpless, he watched as she became increasingly weak. After several agonizing days, she died. Tsering Wyangal, who had carried his daughter on his back over the Himalayas, now carried her tiny body to a funeral pyre that smoldered near the river. The pyre burned constantly, consuming the bodies of refugees as they died by the scores. A grieving Tsering Wyangal and his wife prayed for their child for the traditional forty-nine days to assure her consciousness made a peaceful transition through reincarnation.[3]

Samten Karmay also suffered the miseries of Missamari, although he would not meet Tsering Wyangal there. Samten had been living in Kathmandu for about seven months when he heard that many of his friends from Drepung were at the Missamari Transit Camp. After arranging to send for his mother if India proved to have better prospects, Samten set out for Raxaul, a railhead on the Indian side of the border, traveling with a monk he knew from Drepung who had escaped with another party. The two had become reacquainted in

Kathmandu and decided to travel together, having been advised to board a train in Raxaul. They had never seen a train before, much less traveled on one. No one had mentioned that tickets needed to be purchased before boarding. The monks saw people boarding the passenger cars and followed their example. They were penniless and would have been unable to purchase tickets in any case. The train was well underway when the Indian conductor entered their car and began asking for tickets. They watched in puzzlement as the conductor worked his way down the isle, examining tickets and squeezing a handheld punch to place a hole in each one. As they watched, it dawned on them that they, too, would be asked for a ticket to be punched. The conductor, who spoke no Tibetan, asked for their tickets in Hindi, which neither could speak. Through gestures they made him understand that they had no tickets. The conductor began shouting at them and they were in danger of being tossed off the train at the next stop. Finally Samten spoke the words that even Hindi speakers knew: "Dalai Lama." He repeated the name several times and the conductor's visage calmed. He looked at them for a moment and then shook his head as if to say, "Never mind, it's alright."[4]

They rode the train for three days and nights before arriving at the Missamari Transit Camp. Nearly 15,000 refugees crowded the camp, most of them Khampa rebels who had surrendered their guns before being allowed to cross the border. Samten found a spot in a bamboo barracks with sixty people living in two rooms. Most of them had dysentery, and Samten soon had it as well. Like Tsering Wyangal, he subsisted on the monotonous diet of rice and lentils provided by the Indian government. The intense tropical heat doubled his misery.

Unaware of Samten's whereabouts, his close friend and fellow monk Sangye Tenzin began searching for him after returning his nephew, Khedup, to his father in Kalimpong, India. While visiting a Buddhist monastery in Kalimpong, he heard that Samten was in Missamari and hastened to join his friend.

Now reunited, the two friends worried more about the survival of their religion than their own pitiful living conditions. Sangye had hauled out of Tibet as many of the Bön texts containing the teachings of the ancient Bön masters as he could carry, but it was only a tiny fraction of the body of written learning. They worried that they would be unable to replace the texts destroyed by the Chinese. There was a chance, however, that a complete set of Bön texts could be cobbled together from manuscripts in monasteries in Nepal. The two monks decided that they would scrounge for texts and copy as many as they could find.

They had no money and no access to printing equipment, so could do nothing until they found other Bönpos willing to finance their proposal. Sangye returned to Kalimpong, where there were Bönpos who had escaped Tibet with their wealth intact. Meanwhile, Samten joined a group of friendly Buddhist monks heading for the refugee camp at Buxa, a town on the Indian-Bhutan frontier. At Buxa he found thirty concrete barracks surrounded by a barbed-wire fence. Refugees filled the camp and spilled outside its gates. Samten spent three months in Buxa studying with the Buddhist monks before his learning was interrupted by another bout of dysentery. Barely able to travel, he rejoined his mother, who had moved from Kathmandu to Kalimpong. His condition worsened and his mother feared he would die. Luckily for Samten, there were Western doctors serving the city's large foreign population of businessmen, diplomats, and spies. He recovered after spending two months under the care of a Western doctor.

17
Snellgrove

Once Samten regained his health he joined Sangye, and they set about organizing their printing project. Sangye already had raised some money from Bönpo refugees in Kalimpong. Not all refugees were poor. Many wealthy Tibetans escaped before their fortunes were confiscated and were able to take most of their wealth with them. The two monks raised enough money to set up their first Bön printing operation outside Tibet. The enterprise got under way with the blessings of some of the most influential lamas in the Bönpo refugee community, including Sherab Tenpai Gyaltsen, the abbot of Tibet's prestigious Yungdrungling Monastery.

Samten and Sangye at first paid a Kalimpong printer, who laboriously set blocks inscribed with characters into a press. They soon realized that they could run the operation faster and cheaper in Delhi using a more modern lithographic press. With the assistance of friends who knew the city, they relocated to Delhi and rented a room above a bakery for their printing operation. The printing operation employed Bönpo monks from Majnu Katilla, the Tibetan refugee camp in Delhi. The monks used ink to copy texts onto special grease-treated paper sheets, a method known as lithography, based on the inability of water and ink to mix. The sheets were sent to the printer, who pressed each sheet against a metal plate, the ink and grease adhering to the metal surface. An acid and water rinse was applied, the solution adhering to the grease and etching the metal. The ink repelled the solution, avoiding etching and thereby creating raised letters. The plate was then locked onto a press for printing.

Sangye and Samten cooked and slept in the copying shop, where they reproduced the ancient texts. Within three months they had printed copies of all the texts in their possession. Sangye began traveling throughout the region looking for more texts. He made long, arduous trips, traveling hundreds of miles through unfamiliar and mostly mountainous terrain to gather texts from Bhutan, Sikkim, and the Dolpo region of northern Nepal. Meanwhile, Samten kept the print shop running.

One of those trips turned out to be life-changing. Sangye had traveled with Yungdrungling abbot Sherab Tenpai Gyaltsen to the Bön monastery near Samling, in Dolpo, a long and difficult journey from Delhi to the roadless mountains of the remote Nepalese province. The monastery's library proved to hold a trove of sacred manuscripts, its walls lined with hundreds of wooden cubbyholes, each holding a *pecha,* a stack of oblong pages wrapped in silk. They spent a month there choosing manuscripts for transfer to Delhi before moving on to the Shipchhok Monastery, also in Dolpo. They were preparing to leave Shipchhok when they received a strange request. A man on horseback arrived with a message from a Westerner begging them to delay their departure by a day so he could meet with them. The abbot, who wanted to reach the foot of a difficult pass before nightfall, replied with a message asking him to come immediately. Soon, a man of average height with kind eyes framed by bushy eyebrows appeared at the monastery door. Exuding an air of command, renowned Britsh scholar David Snellgrove introduced himself to the abbot and Sangye.

Snellgrove was a product of the British public school system (the name given in England and Wales to exclusive private schools) that had supplied administrators for the British Empire's colonies. He enlisted in the British Army during World War II and was trained as an intelligence officer before being posted to India. His top-secret assignment involved breaking Japanese code. Most British soldiers stationed in India found life there unpleasant or at best tolerable and dreamed of the day they could return home. Not Snellgrove. He was entranced by the exotic sights and customs of the East, spending nearly all his leisure hours learning about his new environment.

In 1943, while recovering from an illness in a British hospital in the rugged Himalayan foothills near Darjeeling, Snellgrove began exploring the countryside on a small white horse. His wanderings led him past Buddhist monasteries that fascinated him, particularly one in the village of Aloobari. He described his experience in a letter home:

> The building is of pagoda shape three stories high. A Buddha sits on each, and on either side are Bodhisattvas (superior beings of divine status), chief of whom seems to be a "Lord of Mercy" (Avalokitesvara) with eleven heads and one thousand arms. The ceiling and wall paintings are vivid with blue and red and gold, depicting more Buddhas and gods as well as scenes of the heavens and hells. There is still so much that I do not understand.[1]

To his surprise he discovered that the monks at the Aloobari Monastery spoke Tibetan rather than Hindi and looked to Tibet for spiritual guidance. Snellgrove's curiosity soon developed into a keen interest in all things Tibetan, and he began to voraciously absorb books on the subject, including a Tibetan dictionary and grammar manual.

Snellgrove's rehabilitation leave expired and he returned to his base sixteen miles north of Calcutta (since renamed Kolkata), where he was promoted to head of naval air intelligence. In Calcutta he contracted malaria, a disease that ravaged the country, afflicting a quarter of the 330 million Indian population in the 1940s. Snellgrove spent five weeks in a hospital, where he passed his time "mastering the intricacies of

Tibetan spelling and grammar."[2] A few weeks later, as he was on his way to convalesce in a military sanitarium in Darjeeling, he found himself sitting next to an Asian man wearing a British army uniform. He asked the man if he spoke Tibetan, to which the man replied, "But I am a Tibetan." La Tsering, a captain in the British Intelligence Corps, convinced Snellgrove to accompany him to Kalimpong instead of Darjeeling because it was a better place to study Tibetan. "This proved to be one of the most fortunate encounters in my life,"[3] Snellgrove later wrote.

The railway ended at Darjeeling, and Snellgrove and his new acquaintance drove about thirty-two miles northeast to Kalimpong, a city astride a key trade route linking central Tibet and India. In this town known for its flower markets as well as residences for British military and colonial bureaucrats, Snellgrove embarked on a study of Tibetan that would lead him to become one of the world's renowned authorities on Tibetan Buddhism and culture.

His studies continued until his discharge at the end of the war. Casting about for a job that would allow him to pursue his interest in Tibetan religion, Snellgrove decided to take the civil service examination in hopes of landing a position with the Indian Civil Service. He wanted a posting to a remote Indian outpost where he could continue his scholarly pursuits in his off-time. His hopes were dashed by Britain's decision to grant India independence in 1947. "Thus by force of circumstance, an imagined life of practical good works in the Indian subcontinent, interspersed with local scholarly researches, as typical of the lives of the more worthy members of the (Indian Civil Service), was destined to become a life of scholarly research for its own sake, which proved to be only tolerable when combined with new ventures in foreign lands."[4]

His insatiable curiosity about Buddhism led Snellgrove to spend three years studying Sanskrit, Tibetan, and classical Chinese, and about a year studying under eminent Tibetologist Giuseppe Tucci in Rome, where he became enchanted with Italian culture, telling friends, "If there is a next life, I would like to be born in Italy."[5] He then spent two years at the School of Oriental and African Studies at the University of London. During the next decade of study and travel he would learn to speak Hindi as well.

By the time Snellgrove set out for the remote northern Nepalese frontier in September 1960, he had seven years of scholarly research to his credit, most of it in the field. The British scholar had first visited the area in 1956, learning then that it was called Dolpo. There he encountered practitioners of Bön and grew increasingly interested in Tibet's oldest religion. Nearly everything scholars knew about Bön came from Buddhist sources, many of whom viewed Bön similarly to the way Catholics viewed Islam during the Crusades. The sources falsely portrayed Bön as a barbaric religion with strange, sometimes bloody ceremonies. The more he learned about Bön from its practitioners, the more he came to realize that Bön and Buddhism are similar.

Dolpo, although part of Nepal, was ethnically Tibetan. Nepal annexed the region after invading Tibet in 1768. The Chinese occupation of Tibet prevented Snellgrove from studying Tibetan religion there, but the Dolpo region was so dominated by Tibetan culture that it was a good substitute. Most of the inhabitants spoke Tibetan, and those who were literate wrote Tibetan. Snellgrove encountered only a handful of people in Dolpo who knew a few words of Nepalese.

While preparing for his yearlong trek through Dolpo, Snellgrove became involved in a plan to bring twenty-four Tibetan refugees to Western universities with Tibetan studies programs. The exodus of an estimated 115,000 Tibetans by 1960 presented an opportunity for learning more about the culture of a country that for so long had remained inaccessible and mysterious to the rest of the world. The Rockefeller Foundation made $325,000 (about $3.25 million in 2022 dollars adjusted for inflation) available to universities in Germany, Italy, France, Japan, the Netherlands, Great Britain, and the United States to select refugees as guests and glean information about Tibet. The foundation hoped its seed money would lead to the establishment of permanent schools of Tibetan studies at the universities. Snellgrove received $57,000 (about $570,000 in 2022 dollars) to bring several refugees to the University of London's School of Oriental and African Studies.[6]

Snellgrove wanted to choose four or five Bönpos so he could learn more about Bön, which he had come to believe was more closely related to Buddhism than either Buddhists or Bönpos would admit. His plan horrified the Dalai Lama and his advisors, who were members of the dominant Gelug sect of Tibetan Buddhism. Although the young Dalai Lama's attitude toward Bön would eventually change to acceptance, at the time he viewed Bönpos as heretics. The Tibetan leader in exile relented only after Snellgrove convinced him that he was interested in studying Tibetan culture and civilization rather than converting to either Buddhism or Bön. Having secured the Dalai Lama's permission, he set off on his second trip to Dolpo, this time searching for Bön candidates. He was accompanied by his Sherpa assistant, Pasang Khambache, and French anthropologist Corneille Jest.

As he traveled through Dolpo, Snellgrove searched for Tibetans steeped in the Bön tradition, literate and with an acute intellect. His interest was piqued when he heard that a learned lama was nearby at Shipchhok Monastery. He rushed to the monastery after receiving a reply to his request for an interview. The learned lama was Sangye Tenzin, who was at the monastery collecting manuscripts.

Sangye impressed Snellgrove. In their brief meeting, Sangye showed himself to be extraordinarily bright and deeply knowledgeable about Bön. Snellgrove decided that Sangye was the perfect candidate for the group of Tibetans he was assembling under the Rockefeller grant. Sangye mentioned that he was working with another monk in Delhi to reproduce Bön texts. Snellgrove agreed to meet Sangye in a few months in Kathmandu.

On his return to Kathmandu six months later, Snellgrove set out for the meeting place he had arranged with Sangye—Nagi Gompa, a small

Buddhist community of monks and nuns high on a forested mountain that offered a panoramic view of Kathmandu Valley.

Tenzin Namdak, still hobbling from his bullet wound, had arrived at Nagi Gompa two weeks earlier, along with his entourage. He had come from Pokhara, making the twelve-day journey to Kathmandu to visit Menri abbot Sherab Lodrö, who was being treated in the capital for a serious illness. After visiting Sherab Lodrö, Tenzin and his cortege walked to the famed Boudhanath Stupa, a gigantic religious monument that dominates central Kathmandu. One of the largest stupas in the world, Boudhanath is 328 feet in diameter and nearly 120 feet high. Among the hundreds of faithful circumambulating the base of the stupa was a Buddhist monk from the Nagi Gompa. Tenzin struck up a conversation with the Buddhist monk, who looked with compassion at the shabbily clothed Bönpos; it was apparent that they were poor, ill-fed, and lacked shelter. Without hesitation he invited them to stay at his monastery. Abbot Sherab Lodrö joined Tenzin at the monastery after being treated for his illness. Monastery officials gave the abbot quarters on the floor above the assembly hall where he could recover. Tenzin was assigned to a much smaller space on the ground floor.

During his stay at Nagi Gompa, Tenzin wrote *A Short History of the Bön Religion,* which was later used to teach children at a refugee camp. He also had time to contemplate all that was lost: the ruined monasteries, the monks imprisoned and scattered in foreign lands, the sacred texts destroyed. He despaired for his religion and way of life. Taking meaningful action to defend and protect Bön culture seemed a Sisyphean task. He could barely feed and clothe himself, much less take on such a daunting project. Yet he was certain that an answer would come. He was not wrong.

At the Nagi Gompa, Tenzin received a visit from the monk he had met five years earlier at Menri Monastery, Sangye Tenzin. Sangye stopped briefly at the Nagi Gompa on his return from his text-hunting expedition; this short encounter would grow into a lifelong friendship.

Sangye had left Nagi Gompa by the time Snellgrove arrived for their rendezvous, but the British scholar struck up a conversation with Tenzin and was impressed by his vast knowledge. He made a copy of *A Short History of the Bön Religion* to use in his research. He was so taken by Tenzin that he returned a few days later and invited him to come to London—an opportunity for Tenzin, who found himself temporarily without a monastic post or purpose. Although tempted, he refused Snellgrove's offer, telling him that he could not leave his assistants. Snellgrove countered with an offer to bring his assistants later and Tenzin accepted.

Tenzin and his fellow monks looked disheveled and poorly fed, prompting Snellgrove to ask about their welfare. Tenzin told him that they had little to eat, and the small monastery was straining to provide what little food they had. The starving monks were grateful to learn from Snellgrove that the Swiss Red Cross, an organization they had never heard of, had set up a relief center in the valley that would give them food.

Tenzin told Snellgrove that he could find Sangye at a printshop in Delhi. Snellgrove returned to Kathmandu and booked an early morning flight to Delhi. Eager to reconnect with Sangye, he took a taxi straight from the airport to the printshop.

Sangye had not yet returned to the printshop, and Samten was fast asleep on a long work table that he used as a bed when he was awakened at 5:00 a.m. by a strange Westerner spouting Tibetan in a dialect that was nearly unintelligible to him. Snellgrove was speaking Sherpa, a Tibetan dialect far different from the eastern Tibetan dialect spoken by Samten. With only a modicum of introduction, the stranger launched into an interrogation of the bewildered monk. Snellgrove fired questions at Samten as if rousting a stranger at 5:00 a.m. and grilling him about his religion was an ordinary occurrence. The strange apparition initially frightened Samten, but eventually he was able to decipher fragments of the unfamiliar dialect. He began to answer the questions the imperious Westerner hurled at him. Snellgrove asked Samten about his background but was particularly interested in his knowledge of Bön. The grilling continued until Snellgrove, satisfied with Samten's answers, announced that he would leave and return to the printshop later. He disappeared, leaving a dumbfounded monk in his wake.

Unbeknownst to Samten and Sangye, Snellgrove had decided they were perfect candidates to join Tenzin in the Rockefeller Foundation program. Now he needed the Dalai Lama's approval of his candidates before he could ask them to come to London. If all went well, he would begin threading his way through the Indian bureaucracy to secure their travel documents. Having chosen three Bönpo monks, Snellgrove added a Buddhist layman from an aristocratic family, Sonam Panden, whom he invited as a concession to the Dalai Lama.

Snellgrove expected to see the Dalai Lama seated on a low throne as he was ushered into his presence, but instead found him standing in the middle of a room outfitted with furniture he might have seen in a London drawing room. Snellgrove and his assistant, Pasang, knelt in front of the Dalai Lama, and each in turn presented a white silk khata, which the Tibetan leader then draped over their shoulders.

After the Dalai Lama approved the list of candidates Snellgrove gave him, the two engaged in a ninety-minute discussion on the "seeming conflict of the tantric idea of vertical psychic channels in the human body and current knowledge of human physiology."[7] The Dalai Lama became so absorbed in this arcane discussion that he ignored the anxious glances of his chamberlain as the conversation extended past the time scheduled for other appointments.

The next morning the chamberlain sent a Jeep for Snellgrove's use. The British scholar set off with Pasang and Sonam Panden for Dalhousie, the summer retreat for British officials during the colonial era that had been turned into a refugee camp for Tibetans by the Indian government.

Three abandoned stone Christian churches—of the Church of England, Church of Scotland, and the Catholic faith—loomed over Dalhousie, vestiges of the British Raj. Once filled on Sundays with the families of British soldiers, diplomats, bureaucrats, and businessmen, they had become way stations for travelers. Tibetan refugees crammed the abandoned villas scattered on surrounding hillsides where British colonial officials once took their leisure.

After depositing their gear in a shabby hotel, Snellgrove and his companions took a walk through the town. They encountered a young Tibetan monk with a missing right leg hobbling toward them with the aid of a cane fashioned from a branch. This was Tashi Lhakpa Khedrup, who had helped the Sharpa Lama escape from Sera Monastery during the 1959 revolt in Lhasa. Tashi Lhakpa had ended up in the Missamari refugee camp in Assam, India. While in a working party cutting down a tree, a heavy branch broke off and crushed his leg. Camp officials refused to allow him to be treated at a nearby American hospital. Gangrene developed. His condition worsened until finally officials allowed him to be flown to a hospital in Dalhousie, where doctors had no choice but to amputate.

Tashi Lhakpa was surprised when the foreigner addressed him in Tibetan, asking him what had happened to his leg. After giving his explanation, Tashi Lhakpa put his hands together in the Indian fashion of greeting, his good leg trembling, and asked in Tibetan, "Sir, I beg you to help me obtain an artificial leg." Snellgrove could have easily dismissed the request as a single voice in a sea of misery that he could not hope to assuage. Instead he replied, "You shall have one." Snellgrove arranged with Indian refugee officials for Tashi Lhakpa to be sent to a hospital in Delhi to be fitted for a prosthetic leg.[8]

After a brief stay in Dalhousie, Snellgrove took the train back to Delhi, arriving in April 1961. There he met Sangye and Samten to broach the possibility of their coming to England. The idea seemed fantastical to the Tibetans. They had no idea where England was or even that it was an island. He met several times with them before they finally agreed. Now Snellgrove had to collect Tenzin, who had consented to go to England on the condition that his two most loyal assistants follow him at a later date. Snellgrove sent Pasang on a flight to Kathmandu to retrieve him. Still limping, Tenzin was at Nagi Gompa, where he and two assistants boarded a Jeep for the bumpy ride over a rutted track to Kathmandu. Tenzin had seen trucks and cars, but this was his first ride in one. He remembered it as rough and unpleasant. On arrival, the assistants returned to the monastery with the understanding that they would take a later flight, while Tenzin and Pasang boarded an aircraft for Delhi. Flying was a new and frightening experience for Tenzin. He gripped his seat tightly as the airplane lifted off the ground. During the flight he suffered a severe case of motion sickness, a condition that would plague him all his life.

One problem facing Snellgrove was Tenzin's lack of documents or identification of any kind to allow him to clear security at Safdarjung Airport, the only airport serving Delhi at the time. (The airport moved to a military base at Palam in 1962 and was renamed Indira Gandhi International Airport in 1986.) Snellgrove had obtained an audience for the three Bönpo monks with the Dalai Lama, who issued a letter saying he wanted to meet with Tenzin. The letter, along with some haggling by Snellgrove, got Tenzin out of the airport. At the airport, it was made clear to Tenzin that despite his vigorous protests the companions he had left in Kathmandu would not be coming. Tenzin felt betrayed and almost returned to Kathmandu. After a moment of consideration, clear-headed reason triumphed over indignation and disappointment. To return would throw away a rare opportunity. Snellgrove might have made a false promise to entice him to London, but the scholar could open doors for the Tibetans. Besides, it was the only promising opportunity for a high lama stripped of his normal duties and without a monastery to preside over. Tenzin would never forget Snellgrove's broken promise.

His new charges in hand, Snellgrove needed to present them to the Dalai Lama. The Dalai Lama was visiting Delhi, staying at the Indian government's lushly appointed guesthouse, Chowmahalla Palace, a dazzling complex of sumptuous buildings and wide pools built by the Nizam of Hyderabad before the independent kingdom was absorbed by India in 1948. This was the monks' first meeting with the most powerful and sacred figure in Tibet. The mere thought of being allowed to be in his presence filled them with awe. The three monks dropped to the floor in prostration as soon as they were ushered into his presence. The Dalai Lama barked questions at the monks, who remained with faces to the floor. A retainer put his head close to the monks to hear answers whispered to avoid speaking directly to a divinity, then repeated them to the Dalai Lama. Tenzin presented the Dalai Lama with a copy of *A Short History of the Bön Religion* and briefed him on his own education and the state of monasteries in Tibet.

The Dalai Lama asked Tenzin, "We who have left our land have the responsibility to preserve our respective religions and think about sowing the seeds for the future. Times have changed in Tibet, and this is the best we can hope for. You followers of Bön especially must secure your own religion. I will do what I can to help you, but I don't know anything about Bön. Wouldn't it be better for you to stay here instead of going abroad?"

Tenzin answered, "I've agreed to go for three years. What should I do?"

The Dalai Lama replied, "Well, you should come back after three years and consolidate your religion. I will help you."[9] His questions answered, they backed away from him, careful to never look him in the face or turn their backs to him.

As Snellgrove navigated the labyrinthine Indian bureaucracy to obtain the necessary travel documents for his refugee charges, none of whom had a shred of identification, he began preparing them as best he could for the trip to England. He rented them an apartment in Delhi, then took them to a tailor and had them fitted for lightweight shirts and trousers suitable for the hot Indian plain. The monks had never before worn pants. Tenzin looked at the zippered fly and decided it should probably be worn facing the rear. He accordingly wore his first pair of trousers in this fashion, much to Snellgrove's amusement.

Snellgrove found a surgeon at the Lady Irwin Hospital in Delhi who agreed to operate on Tashi Lhakpa's leg at no charge so that he could be fitted for a wooden leg. He placed the monk, along with a sum of money, in the surgeon's care, then set off for Dolpo. Returning from Dolpo two months later he found that the money had run out, and that the doctor had left Tashi Lhakpa with a community of Buddhist monks. Snellgrove found Tashi Lhakpa and examined his new leg. He didn't like what he saw. "The artificial limb which had been made for him was impossibly heavy and cumbersome, having been made of hinged wood with leather supports."[10] Snellgrove resolved to take him to England with the other Tibetans to obtain a proper prosthetic.

Snellgrove had tried to convince the officials running the Rockefeller program to allow his recruits to spend a year in Kathmandu learning English and familiarizing themselves with the alien culture they would encounter in the West, but he was overruled. As a result, the Tibetans were about to crash headlong into a world they never knew existed. When Snellgrove announced that their final destination was London, they asked, "Where is London?" Even Snellgrove, with his deep experience in Asia, was astounded that these men whose intellect impressed him so much had so little knowledge of world geography. It was the monks' turn to be astonished when Snellgrove showed them a globe. They had no idea until that moment that the world was round like a ball.

Snellgrove moved the monks to the cooler climate of Darjeeling in the Himalayan foothills while he continued to deal with the Indian bureaucracy. He wanted the first stop of their journey to be the island nation of Sri Lanka, then known as Ceylon, off the southern tip of

India, where they could become acquainted with Theravada, a school of Buddhism unfamiliar to them. Convincing the Ceylonese high commissioner in Delhi to issue the necessary visas for the Tibetans turned out to be unexpectedly difficult. The commissioner saw the Tibetans as troublemakers who should have remained in Tibet and cooperated with the Chinese. He worried that they would make statements to the press that could damage his country's relationship with China. The commissioner relented only after Snellgrove promised to keep the Tibetans away from the media in Ceylon.

In Darjeeling, tailors fashioned warmer clothes more suitable for London, both Western outfits and traditional robes, and Snellgrove tutored them each day in English. In August 1961, they loaded their baggage onto a train for Calcutta, where they took up temporary residence in an apartment owned by an American acquaintance of Snellgrove's while he made final preparations for their journey to Ceylon.

Snellgrove decided Tenzin should remain in Calcutta during the jaunt to Ceylon because of his motion sickness when traveling by car, train, or air. Tashi Lhakpa also remained in Calcutta because his heavy wooden leg made travel difficult. They would be put on a flight to Rome timed to connect with Snellgrove and the rest of the party after their tour of Ceylon.

Samten, Sangye, the Buddhist Sonam Panden, and Pasang, Snellgrove's assistant, accompanied Snellgrove on a flight from Calcutta to Colombo, Ceylon, that had a long layover in Madras, India. Snellgrove took the opportunity during the layover to show his charges a rock carving near the ocean depicting a scene from the life of the Buddha. He hired a car and they headed for the coast. When the ocean came into view, the monks were startled by the sight of water extending to the horizon. The Tibetans had seen lakes miles wide, but they could always see mountains on the other side. For the first time they gazed at a body of water seemingly as limitless as the sky. They were awed and even a bit frightened by its vastness. That first walk along a beach so profoundly impressed Samten that it was forever stamped in his memory.

In Colombo, Snellgrove hired a van and four local guides for a two-week tour of Buddhist sites. They visited the ancient Buddhist city of Tissamaharama on the southeast coast, swam in the Tissawewa reservoir, and toured temples and shrines in the restored royal Buddhist city of Polonnaruwa. Although enchanted by the historical Buddhist sites, the monks found more interest in the working monasteries they encountered. "For my three Tibetan companions, the places of most interest were the present-day Buddhist monasteries, though communication was difficult between them and the local monks," Snellgrove wrote.[11] From Ceylon they flew to Lebanon for their first visit to a Muslim country, one of many firsts. They learned almost nothing about Islam, but had their first tour of Roman ruins. They were far more impressed by the recreation on the Mediterranean, amazed to see people being pulled by ropes behind speedboats.

They next stopped in Rome, where they were joined by Tenzin and Tashi Lhakpa, setting foot for the first time in a Christian country. They were impressed by what they saw on a tour of the Vatican and the Coliseum, their first view of Renaissance art and architecture. Their next stop was London.

18
London

The aircraft carrying the monks touched down in London on September 21, 1961. Their introduction to Europe came at the height of the Cold War, as the world grappled with social and cultural changes. That year East Germany erected the Berlin Wall, the United States backed the ill-fated Bay of Pigs invasion of Cuba, Russian cosmonaut Yuri Gagarin became the first human to orbit the earth, astronaut Alan Shepard made the first U.S. space flight, John F. Kennedy was the U.S. president, antisegregation freedom riders were pulled from integrated buses and beaten in the U.S. South, the United Kingdom applied for admittance to the European Common Market, and the Beatles debuted at the Cavern Club in Liverpool. The changes shaking the world echoed the changes swirling in the lives of the three Bönpos.

From the airport, the Tibetans were driven about twenty-six miles north to Snellgrove's house in Berkhamsted, a small rural town outside London. Snellgrove, a bachelor, lived alone in a two-story, four-bedroom house on Cross Oak Road, on the northwest valley slope. All four bedrooms were on the top floor. The three Bönpo monks shared the largest bedroom, and Sonam Panden and Tashi Lhakpa each were assigned one of two small bedrooms, leaving the middle-sized bedroom for Snellgrove.

Neighbors at first looked askance at the Asian strangers walking past their houses to the city center or the train station, but they were soon won over by the Tibetans' unfailing pleasantness and ready smiles. The three Bönpos became friends with Snellgrove's neighbor, Peter Cuming. Cuming designed a brick fence topped with arched-shaped sections after learning that the monks wanted to master the Western method of building with bricks and mortar. Cement was virtually unknown in Tibet, where construction was done with rammed earth, stone, clay, and wood. To learn masonry they used Cuming's design to build a fence between his backyard and Snellgrove's. The wall still stands.

The three monks undertook a second construction project at Snellgrove's urging: an eight-foot tall stupa in his backyard that also still stands. Stupas are of immense religious importance to both Buddhists and Bönpos. The construction of a stupa earns spiritual merit and provides a place of meditation. Bönpos and Buddhists circumambulate stupas as another way of earning merit. Architecture rather than religion, however, provided the impetus behind the construction: Tenzin was intensely interested in stupa architecture and talked incessantly about the metric proportion of different architectural styles. Snellgrove finally suggested, "Why don't you try to build one, just a small one, here?" Tenzin accepted the challenge and with the help of the other two Bönpos built a slim structure at the rear of Snellgrove's property, painting it a brilliant white.[1]

Snellgrove used nearly every moment he spent with the monks to improve their general knowledge. He had begun their training in the Claridges Hotel garden in New Delhi, handing each of his charges an exercise book and a pencil for their first lesson in the Roman alphabet. Their education continued in Berkhamsted, where he lectured them during meals on geography, history, religion, and science. The lessons resumed on afternoon walks through the nearby woods.

Their instruction included Western etiquette and the use of eating utensils. Tibetans typically eat tsampa from a bowl with their fingers, rotating the bowl with their left hand and using their right hand to mix the tsampa with salted butter tea. The mixed tsampa is rolled into small lumps and squeezed into the mouth with fingers. Certain that Tibetan eating habits would be frowned upon in an English dining room, he drilled the Tibetans daily in Western eating customs, including the use of knives, forks, and spoons, turning them into models of European deportment.

Every day brought new discoveries and astonishments for the monks, who marveled at the London Underground, Big Ben, and women wearing revealing bathing suits on the English seashore. Initially their English was too poor for them to engage in conversation with anyone other than scholars who spoke Tibetan, so they depended on Snellgrove during their first few months at Berkhamsted.

Tenzin was amazed at the material abundance in Europe but less impressed by other aspects of Western society. In an October 31, 1963, letter to monks in Nepal, he wrote,

> In these countries the people have good food and clothing, but I haven't seen anyone who has the time to concentrate on spiritual practice. . . . Here, in a single city there are millions of people, but it's very rare to see someone who is dedicated to virtuous action or is truly free. Even though there are a few monasteries and monks, they are busy looking after their cattle and selling their sheep, pigs, and eggs for a livelihood; they take care of their animals, and from time to time they sit quietly for a little while in their temple, a great empty building filled with chairs. Then during their festivals they sing beautiful songs for the community.[2]

Pasang watched over the Tibetans as Snellgrove spent much of his time at the School of Oriental and African Studies. Before the British scholar began studying Bön, other scholars had relied on information supplied by Buddhists, much of which was skewed by prejudice and myth. Snellgrove wanted to learn about Bön directly from Bönpos and their texts, especially those describing Bön before Buddhism arrived in Tibet in the seventh century. The three Bönpos were the keys to unlocking the secrets of their largely misunderstood religion. Sangye began working closely with Tibetologist and Snellgrove associate John Driver, while Snellgrove worked with Samten and Tenzin. Cooperation was at first hampered by the Tibetans' lack of experience with modern methods of critical reading and explanation. All three eventually acquainted themselves with Western scholarly methods, especially Samten, whose fascination with the scientific method would later lead to a life-altering decision.

Tenzin and Snellgrove worked closely on translating excerpts from a fourteenth-century Bön text known as *The Glorious One,* containing key Bön precepts. Sangye had borrowed the twelve-volume work during one of his trips to Dolpo in order to reproduce it in the printing operation he ran with Samten in Delhi. He brought the texts with him to London, where Tenzin and Snellgrove, aided by Samten, began their laborious translation. Tenzin and Snellgrove spent hours working at the same desk together. Both were strong-willed and occasionally irritated one another as they labored to translate key ideas into English. Nevertheless, they persevered and coauthored the first Western scholarly work on Bön, *Nine Ways of Bön,* published in 1967. The book brought Bön out of the academic shadows and countered misinformation from non-Bön sources. When he wasn't working with Snellgrove, Tenzin remained at home, copying and editing manuscripts. All three Bönpos taught Tibetan at the University of London.

As the monks immersed themselves in study and learning Western culture, Sonam Panden became increasingly mistrustful, refusing to assist in any way or make new friends. Snellgrove wrote in a letter to a friend that, although personable, Sonam had trouble adapting to Western ways and distanced himself from the other Tibetans. Snellgrove was primarily interested in the Bönpos and had brought Sonam along only to placate the Dalai Lama. Sonam may have felt resentful once his position became clear. "Such nonsense upsets our life together here in London, where there are already subtle Amdo/Khampa/central Tibetan differences,"[3] Snellgrove wrote. Sonam, a Buddhist, would be the first to return to India.

Tashi Lhakpa was fitted with an aluminum leg that dramatically improved his life. He was so proficient with his new leg that he soon assumed duties such as shopping and cooking. Snellgrove sent him to a special driving school for the disabled where Tashi Lhakpa obtained a driver's license, making him so useful that he was made a full-time assistant.

The other monks charmed nearly everyone they met with their civility and humility. Sangye struck up a friendship with a Catholic priest at Oxford, Michael Hollings, who invited him to spend time at the university. Samten would occasionally visit, joining Sangye in long theological conversations over lunch with a dozen or more students. Hollings could not resist the temptation to try to convert Samten to Catholicism. Samten took no offense and politely declined.

After six months, their English skills had improved sufficiently for Sangye and Samten to rent their own flat in West London in 1962. There they received an unexpected visit by a scholar named E. Gene Smith, who asked questions about the locations of Bön texts. Years later they would learn that the information they gave Smith contributed to his monumental fifty-year effort to save Tibetan texts, both Buddhist and Bönpo. Smith began his quest to find and copy Tibetan religious texts while earning a doctorate in Far Eastern studies at the University of Washington. He began studying Tibetan with a visiting lama, Deshung Rinpoche, but was hampered by a scarcity of available texts. The Chinese had destroyed thousands of texts during their military campaigns and the Cultural Revolution. "We had no Tibetan books," Smith recalled in an interview with the *New York Times*. "Deshung said: 'Go and find them. Find the important books and get them published.'"[4] Smith took up the challenge and began an effort that would far outstrip Samten and Sangye's efforts in Delhi. He was able to marshal the resources of the U.S. government for his project after joining the Library of Congress field office in New Delhi in 1968, eventually becoming field director. He began amassing an unrivaled collection of Tibetan manuscripts, hunting them down by questioning refugees in India, Nepal, and Bhutan. Some of the books were the only known copies in the world. Smith eventually saved and reprinted 12,000 volumes, cataloged them, and set up an organization to digitize and translate some into English.[5]

In addition to teaching Tibetan twice a week, Tenzin taught history and explained Bön to university students. When he wasn't teaching, he transcribed Tibetan texts and studied English and Western religions. He was fascinated by Christianity's traditions and philosophies. He wrote often to lamas in India and Nepal about his experiences, but mainly he queried his correspondents about the future of Bön. As he pondered the future of his religion, he began considering for the first time the possibility of creating a Bön community and a monastery in exile.

In his many letters, Tenzin asked about refugees' living conditions and gave instructions and advice. In a November 11, 1963, letter asking about the need for food and clothing in refugee communities, he wrote, "To all you lamas and monks dwelling over there, whom I constantly embrace with my enduring affection: I know that we have been beset by circumstances, things that we thought could never happen to us and the like of which we have never experienced; however, we, the remaining survivors, should try to avoid dispersing for as long as possible, and remain united as before."[6]

A letter dated April 25, 1963, told how he had written the Dalai Lama:

> Because of my strong feeling of happiness toward you, on 2 April I wrote the Dalai Lama, telling him generally about how things were

> over here, and especially because he knows that our Eternal Bön religion is a part of the pure doctrine of the Enlightened Ones. I asked that he look with loving kindness on us, the surviving lamas and monks of Menri, who are, as he knows, the holders of the doctrine of this tradition in Nepal, and especially that he should not abandon his support for the unimpaired preservation of the transmission of the teachings of this spiritual tradition of Eternal Bön. On the 18th of this month I received a reply in which he promised that he would never cease to look on us with loving kindness.[7]

The monks accompanied Snellgrove to Catholic services on Sunday. Snellgrove, a former Anglican, recorded religious stories for them to listen to in order to learn English and become familiar with Christian ideas. The Tibetans were insatiably curious and devoured information about this strange Western religion, although their interest was purely academic. The monks, especially Sangye, were particularly interested in Western monastic organization. Their first taste of Christian monastic life came during a visit to the Mount Saint Bernard Monastery in Charmwood Forest, Leicestershire. Like the Tibetans, the Cistercian monks who founded the monastery in 1833 were refugees, having fled oppression following the second French Revolution in 1830.

Sangye became the first Tibetan monk to make a detailed study of Christian monastic organization by visiting numerous monasteries, at times accompanied by Samten and Tenzin. One of the monasteries he studied was Saint Benedict's Abbey at Fort Augustus, by Loch Ness, Scotland. Another was Quarr Abbey on the Isle of Wight, where one of the Benedictine monks surprised him with his knowledge of Tibet, having read the biography of the eleventh-century Buddhist yogi Milarepa. Sangye even journeyed to Greece to visit one of the twenty Greek Orthodox monasteries on Mount Athos.

Monks at the monasteries were as curious about the Tibetans as the Tibetans were about the monasteries. Inevitably charmed by their visitors, monastery officials invited them for extended visits, with the understanding that the Tibetans would need papal approval. Samten and Sangye decided they should meet the pope to ask his permission. They could see no reason why the pope wouldn't grant an audience to two unknown Tibetan monks representing an obscure religion that in all likelihood he had no idea even existed. Without telling Snellgrove, the two monks arranged a meeting with Pope Paul VI through an English archbishop. Samten and Sangye crossed the English Channel, then visited Tibetan friends in Switzerland before taking a train to Rome. Upon arrival at the Vatican they were informed by papal officials that they were a day late. "We kept waiting the most important person in the West!" Samten recalled.[8]

The Tibetans had somehow misunderstood the date of their audience. Their tardiness was forgiven, and they were brought before Pope Paul VI for a brief conversation through an interpreter. The Tibetans spoke broken English, making the translation into Italian sometimes challenging and the conversation difficult. The pope, dressed in a white cassock, skullcap, and red shoes, asked questions about Tibet but had trouble understanding that the monks were from eastern Tibet, an area culturally different from central Tibet and Lhasa. As in their audience with the Dalai Lama, the pope did most of the talking, giving the monks little opportunity to ask questions. He gave them each a souvenir medallion and they posed for photos by the official Vatican photographer.

The visit to the pope exasperated Snellgrove, who was responsible for the Tibetans' well-being. Their impromptu wanderings thwarted his efforts to organize a schedule for them in keeping with his own priorities and those of the Rockefeller grant. The monks had no conception of Snellgrove's responsibilities. The idea that they might be causing him problems by charting their own paths never crossed their minds. It never occurred to them that they shouldn't satisfy their curiosity in whatever way they saw fit. Snellgrove accepted the inevitable: "After one year, they traveled around England free and Scotland free. I couldn't hold them."[9]

Having obtained the necessary papal permission, the monks made the most of their invitations to visit Catholic monasteries. Those visits influenced the way Sangye would organize his own monastery when he returned to India. Traditionally, monks were served food and tea in the temple, but Sangye would adopt the Western tradition of a separate dining hall. He also adopted the Christian customs of having a monk read during meals and using a strict schedule for study and work.

One of the European connections the monks made during their stay was Dr. Hans Kepfer in Zurich, Switzerland. Kepfer and his wife had made donations through the Swiss Red Cross to a Tibetan Bön settlement in Nepal. Tenzin believed it was so important to enlist his help that he endured another bout of motion sickness to fly to Zurich in August 1964 to meet with Kepfer and discuss plans for a Bön settlement. Kepfer strongly supported the idea and was willing to help finance it.[10]

Of the twenty-four Tibetan monks invited to the West under the Rockefeller grant, only Sangye, Samten, and Tenzin were members of a religion in danger of extinction. Some of the Rockefeller monks would remain in the West and marry Western women. Won over by the Western scientific approach to research, Samten would shed his monk's robes to remain in Europe and devote his life to scholarship, furthering the world's knowledge of Bön and Tibet. Equipped with connections and a broader knowledge of the world gained during their stay in Europe, Sangye and Tenzin would return to India, where they would have an enormous impact on the fate of their religion and the Bönpo culture.

19
Return

While the monks in the Rockefeller Foundation program thrived in their various host countries, the Chinese were bombing and razing monasteries throughout Tibet. The repression worsened in 1966 when Mao instigated the Cultural Revolution in China, tasking the Red Guard with destroying the "four olds": ideas, culture, customs, and habits. In Tibet, zealous Red Guards ransacked and heavily damaged Menri, Bön's mother monastery. The Guards left in ruins nearby Yungdrungling Monastery, where Tenzin had once adorned the walls with murals.

Descriptions of the desecrations and human-rights violations seeped from behind the sealed border in the published accounts of refugees. A 1967 *Los Angeles Times* report detailed how difficult it was to get information from Tibet:

> With the sealing of the border, the flow of scraps of news needed for an understanding of events in Tibet was virtually cut off. . . . There are few hard facts. One of them is that in August of last year the Great Proletarian Cultural Revolution hit Lhasa in full force. Red Guards sabotaged the oldest cathedral in the ancient capital. Two badly damaged heads of divine images from the cathedral were smuggled out to India by Buddhist faithful. When proof of developments like these becomes available, it is usually late by weeks or even months.[1]

The Dalai Lama tried to call the abuses to the attention of the United Nations but got only sympathy. "Like evil spirits, excited hordes swept through Tibet and destroyed cultural monuments in our cities," the Dalai Lama said in a February 1967 interview. "Old Tibet is dying slowly. Our girls are forced to marry Chinese, our children are being deported to China, and our young men are being killed or tortured in prisons."[2] The U.N. General Assembly issued resolutions in 1959, 1961, and 1965 condemning Chinese human rights violations,[3] but could do little else. To date, no government has defied China by recognizing the Dalai Lama's government-in-exile.

Monks who escaped execution were imprisoned, tortured, reeducated, and sent back to their home villages, often to be assigned to menial jobs such as tending hogs. Bön sacred texts were destroyed, and Bönpos experienced a new round of persecution. Although the Chinese were indiscriminate in their persecution of religion in the wave of oppression that followed the 1959 Lhasa uprising and the later Cultural Revolution, Bön was more vulnerable than Buddhism because there were fewer Bön monasteries, and most of them were severely damaged or destroyed.

Sangye and Tenzin were among the few surviving lamas knowledgeable enough to carry the religion forward. Sherab Lodrö, the thirty-second abbot of Menri, was the figurehead of Bön, but in 1963 he succumbed to disease in an Indian refugee camp. Before his death, the abbot of Yungdrungling Monastery visited him, lamenting that the head of the Bön religion was forced to live in such poverty.[4]

After three years in London, Sangye returned to India in 1964 to assist in the founding of a school for refugee children in Dharwar, about 340 miles south of Mumbai, in Karnataka State. He landed the job with help from Snellgrove, who had contacts with the organization funding the school, Ockenden Venture, a United Kingdom–based charity. Sangye was made Tibetan headmaster, administering the school along with a British headmaster. Content to subsist on the food and modest quarters provided by the school, Sangye sent his monthly salary of 300 rupees to a group of destitute Bön monks in a refugee camp. Sangye was the only Bönpo among about twenty teachers; the others were Buddhists, some of them hostile to Sangye because of his religion.

The hostility toward Sangye alarmed Per Kvaerne, a graduate student from the University of Oslo who arrived in India in February 1966 to work as a volunteer teacher at the school. Kvaerne became entranced with Sangye. Here was a living, breathing member of the mysterious religion he had read about. "In my imagination, the Bönpos were the custodians of an ancient and enigmatic tradition, surviving in out-of-the-way parts of Tibet, now doubly inaccessible through the Chinese occupation," Kvaerne wrote in a research journal. "And yet, here was a Bön monk, not only willing to share his knowledge with me, but also speaking excellent English, having spent several years in England as the assistant of Professor David Snellgrove before taking up a teaching assignment in India."[5]

Snellgrove and Tenzin's book, *The Nine Ways of Bön,* would not be published until 1967, so there was very little scholarly literature on Bön available for avid students like Kvaerne. Sangye began teaching the Norwegian academic about Bön during lunch hour every day after a meal of rice and dal. They started by reading the biography of Tonpa Shenrab in Tibetan. Kvaerne had taught himself to read some Tibetan but he was eager to become proficient. "The Bön religion, I realized, was a living, complex and sophisticated spiritual and cultural tradition," Kvaerne wrote.[6]

The school closed, and Kvaerne returned to Norway after visiting Bönpos in refugee camps, gaining their confidence with a written introduction from Sangye. In Norway, Kvaerne secured permission from the University of Oslo to offer Sangye a teaching position for a couple of years. Sangye accepted and boarded a Norwegian cargo ship for a three-week voyage to Hamburg, Germany, then on to Oslo. For the next two years he lived in Oslo while teaching history, religion, and Tibetan at the university. Sangye's presence was a breakthrough for Tibetan studies at the university. For example, Kvaerne's professor could read Tibetan but had to guess at the correct pronunciation. "He would read it the way it was spelt," Kvaerne said. "But he had never heard a Tibetan speak or even seen or met a Tibetan before."[7]

Sangye's stay in London had accustomed him to European ways, and he quickly eased into university life. His warm and expansive charm won him a place in academic society. He frequented parties where he occasionally cooked Tibetan delicacies such as *momos,* a type of Tibetan dumpling. Sangye spent the first six months living with Kvaerne's family, cheerfully washing dishes after meals. He sang a melodious Bön chant while running water over each dish and piece of cutlery, rubbing them clean with his hands. He ignored dish soap. Most of his time was spent in his upstairs room studying Tibetan texts or Western books that interested him.

Each day Sangye would rise at about 4:30 a.m. to pray for several hours. After breakfast, wearing his traditional monk's robes, he would take the subway to the university, changing trains once or walking part of the way. At the university he took an elevator to the eleventh floor of the building housing the Indo-Iranian Institute. He had no office and taught a small class in the institute's library. From the library he had a magnificent view of the city curling around both sides of the Oslofjord. After class he would return home or visit the friars at Saint Olav's Prior, a local Dominican monastery where he had made friends.

After about six months, Sangye's small salary allowed him to rent a room in a nearby house owned by friends of the Kvaerne family. Kvaerne visited Sangye at his apartment nearly every day to study Tibetan and Bön. Sangye was comfortable in Oslo and expected to remain indefinitely.

No similar opportunity awaited Tenzin on his return to India. Tenzin, senior to Sangye in the Bön hierarchy, would find the responsibility for the future of Bön thrust upon him.

In London, the University of London awarded Tenzin a diploma and asked him to extend his stay. He cordially declined, telling his hosts that he was needed in India where his people were suffering. In September 1964, Tenzin returned to India on a passenger ship to Bombay, a twelve-day voyage. His trunks contained clothing and Western goods he thought would be useful for the Bönpo settlement he envisaged. Never losing sight of that vision, he first went to Delhi, where he began searching for Bönpo texts that would be needed to ensure the religion's survival in India. On one of his journeys in search of sacred texts he visited a refugee camp administered by the Swiss Red Cross. What he found amplified his conviction that a Bön community was urgently needed.

The heat and unsanitary conditions in the camp were killing Tibetans at a ferocious rate. Indian authorities did not recognize Bönpos as a separate group and scattered them among Buddhist-dominated refugee camps. Hampered by language differences and discrimination by the Buddhist majority in the camps, Bönpos rarely found employment other than backbreaking work building roads for the Indian government. In the evenings the Bönpo road crews were forced to recite a Buddhist prayer before their meal. Increasingly, Bönpos were leaving the camps to find employment, further dispersing their community. Fearing discrimination, Bön job seekers dared not admit their religion. Bön elders saw that conditions were eroding Bönpos' connection to their native culture and religion.[8]

The Indian government leased land to Buddhists to build monasteries in India but made no such offers to Bönpos. The Bön refugees were bereft of the monasteries that traditionally formed the heart of their communities. The small number of monks steeped in the ways of Bön were succumbing to persecution, climate, disease, and despair. Tenzin feared that the Bön way of life was on the verge of extinction. He believed that if his people were to survive, they needed a community as well as the spiritual strength that only their religion could supply.

Tenzin traveled to Kalimpong to seek the advice of important members of the Bönpo community who had sent him letters while he was in London, urging him to help the struggling and scattered community. In Kalimpong, the message was the same: do something.

Among the Bön lamas remaining in India, Tenzin alone had mastery of English and useful contacts made during his stay in London. He also had the authority and respect needed to take action because of his former position as Menri lopon and his deep knowledge of Bön teachings. The community in exile looked to him for rescue.

Tenzin's vision of a Bön community with its own land was the obvious solution. If he failed to find a place where Bönpos could erect their own temple and practice their religion safely, they would likely be absorbed into the larger Buddhist and Indian communities. Bön culture would be unrecognizably diluted at best, or forever lost, certainly in India if not in Nepal and Tibet.

To make his vision a reality, Tenzin had no compunction about turning to a Buddhist for advice. He knew a Buddhist monk who had purchased land to form a Tibetan Buddhist community in Dehradun, an Indian city in the Himalayan foothills. Tenzin questioned him about how he went about acquiring the land, and the old monk advised him on how to obtain the permits necessary for purchasing land and founding a community in India. Tenzin also visited Dharamshala several times to seek advice from the Dalai Lama, who was sympathetic to the Bönpos' plight.

In 1965 he received a letter of approval from the Indian government for his plan to establish a settlement for Tibetan Bön refugees, and began searching for a suitable property. He traveled all over northern India seeking a plot that was affordable, had clear title, and a climate suitable for Tibetans. Finding land for his people proved to be difficult, but Tenzin was certain that patience and perseverance would prevail.

While Tenzin searched from his base in Delhi, he received a visit in 1966 from David Snellgrove. Snellgrove was appalled to see one of the luminaries of Bön living in poverty in a ramshackle garage. He found the monk gathering sufficient resources to purchase property and build a settlement, but using none of it to improve his personal living conditions.

Under Tenzin's guidance, the Tibetan Bönpo Foundation was formed as the legal vehicle for acquiring land. Tenzin took his search to one of India's northernmost states, Himachal Pradesh, bordering far western Tibet. The state offered the advantage of being near Dharamshala, where the Dalai Lama had established his government-in-exile in 1960, and being on the southern slope of the Himalayas, with terrain and weather resembling the mountainous Tibetan homeland.

He found a suitable site near Dehradun, a city with a small population of Bönpo refugees in a neighboring state near the Himachal Pradesh border, and began negotiating a purchase. His Swiss friend, Dr. Hans Kepfer, donated about $23,660 in U.S. dollars through Catholic Relief Services to make the purchase. The deal was on the verge of closing when Tenzin received a phone call from Catholic Relief Services telling him to halt the final payment and immediately come to Delhi. Arriving from Dehradun, he learned that the Indian government opposed the sale. He later discovered that unnamed high-ranking Tibetan officials had interceded with the government to halt the transaction. Exactly who had blocked the sale and why remains obscure.

Unfazed, Tenzin moved his base to Dehradun and examined nine other potential sites in Himachal Pradesh, but none that were suitable or had a willing seller. The search seemed to be going nowhere when Tenzin got a tip from the principal at a Catholic school who described an attractive tract for sale near Solan, a city in central Himachal Pradesh. The description seemed so promising that Tenzin decided to send an emissary fluent in Hindi to inspect the property and conduct negotiations. For this he would rely on Jadur Sonam Sangpo, a Bönpo refugee living in the Manali refugee camp in northern Himachal Pradesh. Jadur's language skills had landed him a well-paid job as a translator for the Tibetan government-in-exile. The Manali camp was not far from the Tibetan border, and several hundred Bönpo refugees had collected there under the leadership of the abbot of Yungdrungling Monastery.

In late 1966, Jadur received a letter from his mother in Dehradun, saying that Tenzin was asking him to come there to assist him. Upon learning that Tenzin intended to found a Bönpo community, Jadur called it the "greatest joy in my life." Although elated to hear of plans for a Bönpo community, he was conflicted about leaving for Dehradun. Heeding Tenzin's call would mean the loss of a salary that made him one of the highest paid Bön refugees. There would be no salary from Tenzin. To work for Tenzin would also mean losing the status and connections that came with working with officials close to the Dalai Lama. The decision was difficult, but ultimately Jadur's sense of responsibility to his people and religion outweighed his personal gain. Besides, how could he reject a request from his mother or from Tenzin, one of Bön's most renowned holy men?

The Tibetan government-in-exile valued Jadur's services so highly that they doubled his salary to lure him into staying. The salary boost convinced him to stay another month, but he finally resigned after receiving a second letter from his mother urging him to immediately come to Dehradun. He accepted the assignment with the understanding that his only remuneration would be for transportation costs.

In January 1967, Tenzin conferred with top Bön figures, including Sangye, by way of a phone call to him in Oslo, detailing his challenges finding a suitable property and the tip he had received about the availability of land near Solan. After conferring, Tenzin directed Jadur to find the owner near Solan and assess the suitability of the property. At Solan, Jadur found a tall, dark-complexioned priest in white robes sitting behind the principal's desk at the Catholic school. The principal told him the property was owned by a retired Indian railroad executive named Sardar Mohan Singh. The priest gave Jadur directions to Singh's home in the tiny village of Dolanji.

There were no roads to Dolanji, so Jadur took a bus as far as he could. Taking a path he thought would lead him to Dolanji, he soon became lost in a thick forest. He wandered for hours before encountering a local woman who set him on the right course. Eventually he arrived at the cluster of houses called Dolanji and followed the principal's directions to a small house with flowers growing on either side of an iron door. Before he could knock, a large, intimidating man with a beard as white as the turban on his head rushed out of the house and challenged him menacingly in English: "What do you want?" Jadur stood his ground, asking, "Is this Sardar Mohan Singh's house? Are you Mohan Singh?"[9] Jadur explained that a priest from a Catholic school in Solan had sent him there to inquire about the property. Mohan Singh's mood changed instantly. He smiled, opened the iron door, and invited Jadur in for tea. Jadur explained that one of the most important lamas in Tibet wanted to purchase land for a settlement and would pay cash. Learning that the purchase was for the benefit of a religious community and not for personal enrichment, Mohan Singh appeared sympathetic. He assured Jadur that he was willing to sell for a reasonable price. The next day Jadur toured the property with the owner. He returned to Solan and phoned Tenzin to describe a lush, verdant piece of land with access to water. His report so impressed Tenzin that he decided to travel to Solan to negotiate the purchase.

Tenzin arrived in Solan five days later and met with Mohan Singh and his son, a general in the Indian army. He toured the real estate and was pleased with what he saw. A creek split the property, a steep-sloped valley that included the village of Dolanji. The property had been used for farming and its hillsides were terraced. With Jadur translating they agreed on a price of 1,000 rupees for about 150 acres. Allowing for inflation, the price would be about 50,000 in 2022 rupees, or about $628 in 2022 U.S. dollars. The acreage was conveniently located about nine miles from Solan, and its wooded hills and 4,900-foot altitude made it feel almost like home. An Indian land grant added an additional six acres, making the Bönpos one of the few Tibetan refugee groups with title to their own property. In contrast, the major Buddhists sects built monasteries on property leased from the Indian government.[10]

Tenzin named the new land Thobgyal, after the valley below Menri Monastery in Tibet. He added the Tibetan word *sarpa,* for "new," calling it Thobgyal Sarpa. The land secured, Tenzin needed to lead Bönpo families to the promised land.

20

Promised Land

The first eighty Bönpo families who arrived at Thobgyal Sarpa in the summer of 1967 camped in tents. There was no road, no housing, no electricity, and no running water. Their Hindu neighbors in Dolanji viewed them with suspicion and hostility. The promised land would have its challenges.

The newly arrived refugees were supervised by Romila Kapoor, a twenty-year-old Catholic Relief Services employee who had recently earned her B.A. in history from Delhi University. She had been drafted to replace her boss after his death in an automobile accident. Kapoor had only one previous job: nine months at the Sterling Castle Children's Home in Simla, where she worked reuniting Tibetan refugee children with their families.

Kapoor met the Bönpo families for the first time in Clement Town, in neighboring Uttarakhand State, where they lived in a road-work camp.[1] Tenzin had sought out the families against the advice of other prominent monks, who argued that it would be impossible to form a Bön community with refugees hailing from different regions of Tibet who spoke different dialects and came from different walks of life. How could merchants from Amdo live in harmony with nomads from Kham? Tenzin answered that the old Menri Monastery in Tibet was open to monks from every region of Tibet. He was certain that the binding power of their religion would be stronger than their regional differences.

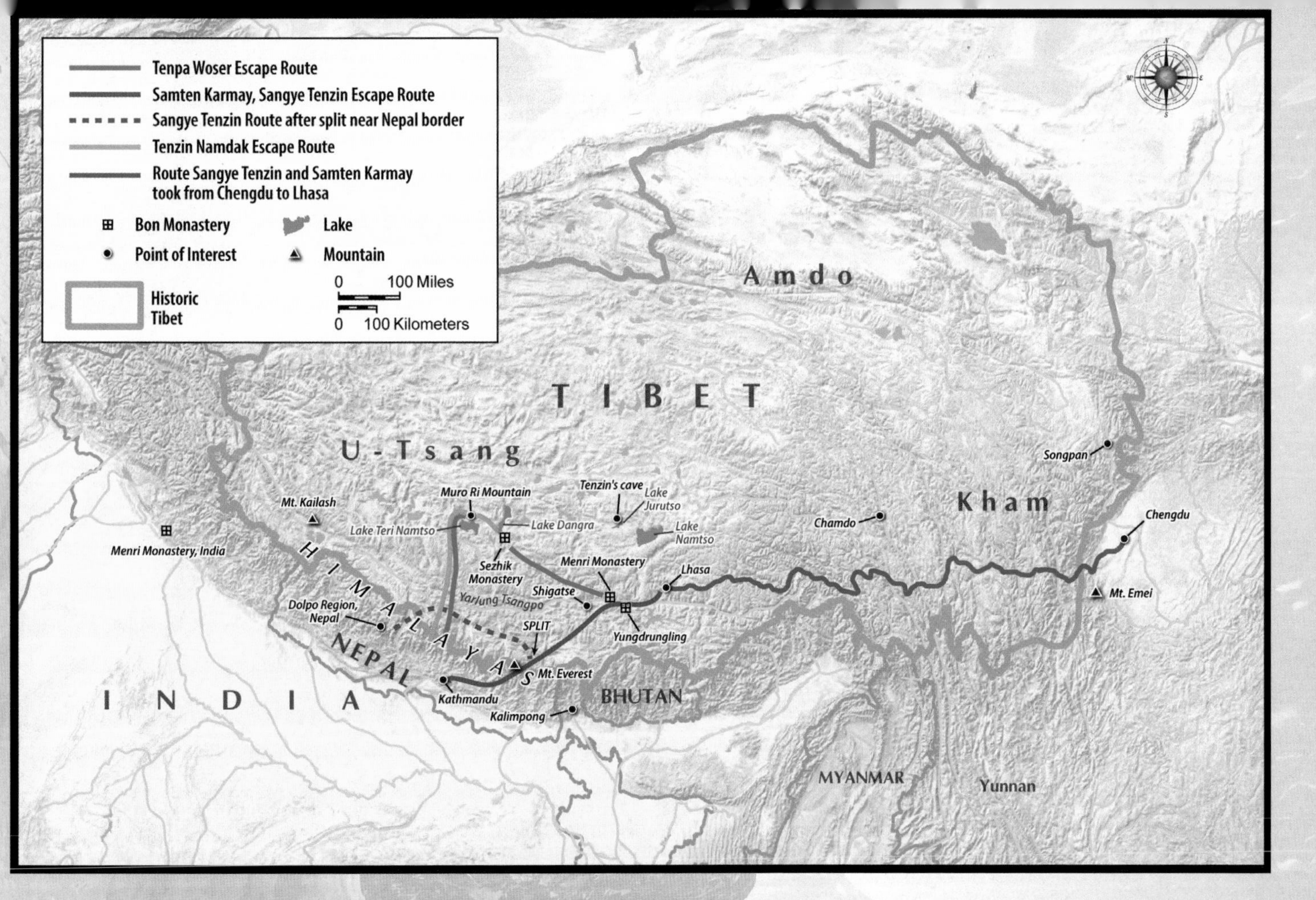

Escape routes. Map by Topographics.

From left, Sangye Tenzin and Samten Karmay at Dreprung Monastery, Lhasa, 1957. Photo courtesy of Samten Karmay.

Tenzin Namdak in Nepal after his escape from Tibe
Photo courtesy of David L. Snellgrove.

The sacred Nyame Kundung, removed by escaping monks from Menri Monastery, hidden in a cave by Tenzin Namdak and returned to Menri Monastery in Tibet decades later. Photo courtesy of Khenpo Tenpa Yungdrung.

Sherab Lodrö, the thirty-second abbot of Menri, in Nepal following his escape from Tibet. Photo courtesy of Menri Monastery.

Sherab Tsultrim, Tenzin Namdak's
levoted assistant, who escaped with
him to Nepal.
hoto courtesy of Menri Monastery.

From left, Samten Karmay, Sangye Tenzin, Tenzin Namdak, and Sonam Panden. They were surprised to learn that the Earth was round after David Snellgrove gave them this globe.
Photo courtesy of David L. Snellgrove.

Group photo in London. Standing, from left, David Snellgrove, Pasang Khambache, Samten Karmay. Seated, from left, Tashi Lhakpa, Sangye Tenzin, Tenzin Namdak.
Photo courtesy of David L. Snellgrove.

rom left, Sangye Tenzin, Samten Karmay, Vatican official, Pope Paul VI.
The two visited the pope in 1964.
Photo courtesy of Samten Karmay.

Menri Monastery in Tibet, rebuilt after being severely damaged during the Cultural Revolution. Photo by authors.

Yungdrungling Monastery, where as a young man Tenzin Namdak helped adorn the walls with religious art. The monastery was rebuilt after Tenzin's work was destroyed during the Cultural Revolution. Photo by authors.

Sezhig Monastery on the Changthang Plateau, where Tenzin planned his escape to Nepal.
Sezhig was spared Chinese depredation because of its remoteness.
Photo courtesy Khenpo Tenpa Yungdrung.

The remote cave where Tenzin Namdak studied for four years with his master.
Photo by authors.

Tenpa Woser, center, in Nepal after surviving an arduous escape from Tibet. The names of his two companions are unknown.
Photo courtesy of Tenpa Woser.

From left, Tenzin Namdak and Tenpa Woser at Triten Norbutse Monastery in Kathmandu, Nepal, 2012, fifty years after their escape from Tibet.
Photo by authors.

Cremation ceremony of His Holiness Lungtok Tenpai Nyima (aka Sangye Tenzin) at Menri Monastery in India, October 2, 2017. Photo by authors.

Muro Ri Mountain, where Chinese troops ambushed Tenzin Namdak and Tenpa Woser. Photo courtesy of John Bellezza.

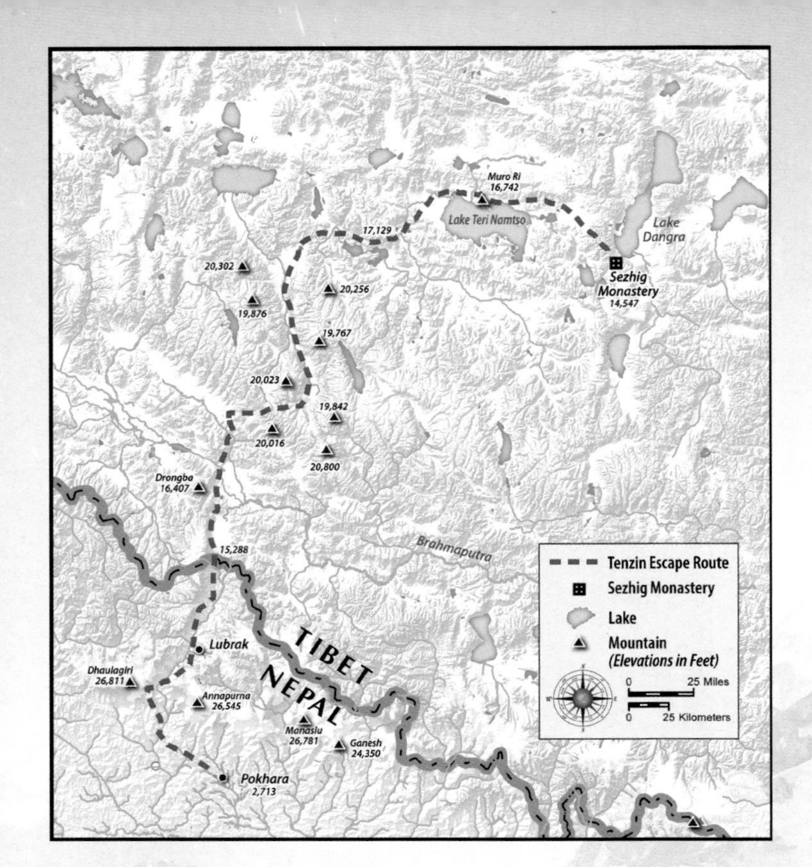

Tenzin Namdak's escape route to Nepal, based on map in Tenzin's autobiography, *The Life of a Great Bonpo Master*. Map by Topographics.

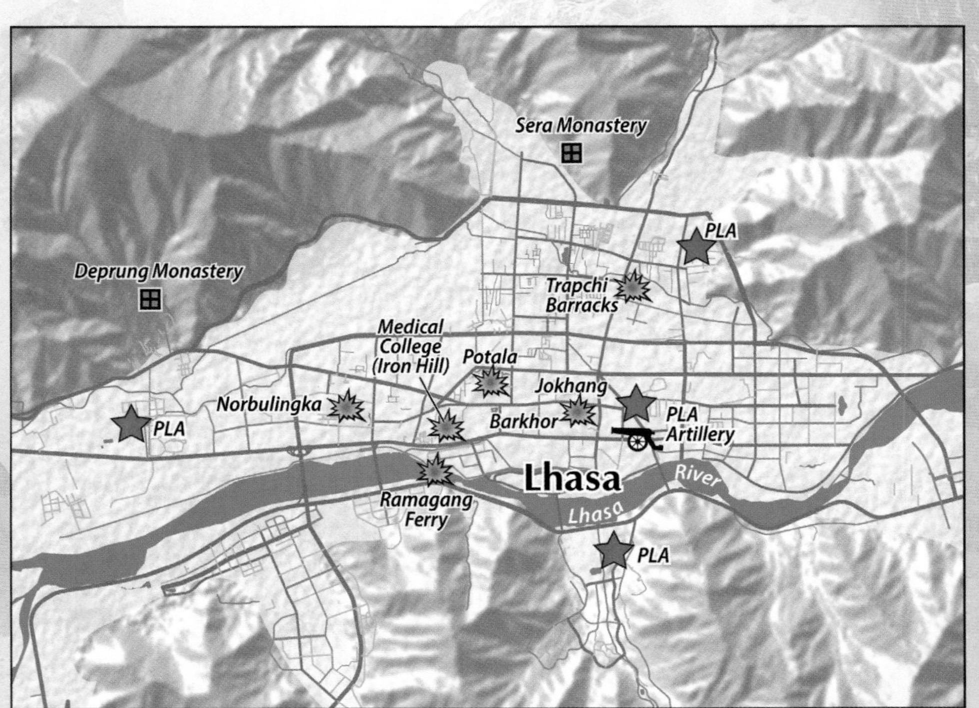

Lhasa uprising, based on map by M10 Memorial website (m10memorial.org). Map by Topographics.

Kapoor found her new charges fearful and timid. Scorned by Buddhists, distrusted by Hindus, and ignored by the Indian government, they usually hid their identity as Bönpos. They were strangers in a foreign land with mystifying customs, living among people who spoke an alien language. Feeling like outcasts wherever they went, they came to Clement Town because Tenzin had promised them a place where they could form a community and be free to practice Bön. They now put their fate in the hands of a young Indian woman who exuded a confidence they lacked.

Kapoor began issuing directives through a Tibetan translator. The Bönpos followed her directions without question, boarding buses for the hundred-mile ride over dirt roads to the Kalka train station. In Kalka they embarked on a special train provided by the state government to haul the families up the mountain to Solan. They then boarded a collection of buses and trucks that took them to a point where the road passed closest to the newly acquired property.

They arrived in the late afternoon and pitched tents close to the road. The temporary encampment was blessed by Sherab Tsultrim, Tenzin's assistant who had accompanied him during his escape and who resumed his duties after Tenzin's return from London. The primitive conditions of the makeshift camp did little to dampen their soaring spirits. Their mood had changed from expectation to elation at having arrived at last at a place they could call home.

The next morning the new arrivals packed up their tents and meager belongings and walked more than two miles along a trail through tall cedars, pines, and rhododendrons. Monkeys scolded them from the trees, and startled Muntjac deer bolted from the undergrowth. The trail took them to the top of a wooded hill overlooking their new home. Before them lay a steep-sided valley divided by a small creek. They saw the abandoned farmland on narrow terraces set into the hillside like a giant staircase, a place where they could plant their future. The few springs scattered through the valley ensured a supply of fresh, clean water.

Kapoor also was seeing the valley for the first time. She became the de facto mayor of the fledgling Bönpo community, arranging for distribution of powdered milk and meat provided by the Indian government and negotiating with local officials. She took up residence in the only structure on the property, a one-room shack used by the previous owner near the creek. Khedup, Sangye Tenzin's nephew, joined Sherab Tsultrim and Kapoor in overseeing the refugees, including measuring plots of land to be distributed to the families. Kapoor helped design simple one-bedroom houses to replace their government-issued tents and arranged for building materials. The Indian government gave each family 1,400 rupees (about 70,000 in 2022 rupees, $880 in 2022 U.S. dollars) to make a start, and provided the community with a nurse and an agricultural advisor. The Dalai Lama made a contribution of 4,000 rupees (about 200,370 in 2022 rupees, $2,500 in 2022 U.S. dollars).

Although all the new settlers were Tibetan Bönpos, the differences among them became apparent when Kapoor began helping Tenzin distribute plots. Rather than causing conflict, the differences helped ease the distribution of land. The nomads, who had been herders in Tibet, were willing recruits for farming. Merchant families had no interest in farming and were happy to have a much smaller plot. The merchant families purchased goods, such as sweaters, in bulk and traveled to Delhi and other cities to sell them.

Kapoor and Tenzin would sit together in front of Kapoor's shack and dip scoops into bags of government-supplied wheat to measure portions for each family. As the community blossomed, the Bönpos gradually shed their timidity. They were no longer afraid to tell the world they practiced Bön. With a home base and the support of a community, they grew confident in their dealings with outsiders.

The Hindu residents of Dolanji initially viewed their new neighbors with distrust. Kapoor and Tenzin sensed the unease and quickly moved to improve relations by frequent visits to the village elders to educate them about the strangers from the other side of the Himalayas. The villagers gradually warmed to their new neighbors and granted a right-of-way for a road to the new settlement. A few villagers even volunteered to help build the new road. The village was completely won over when residents learned that their neighbors could bring them the prized electricity that they had been unable to get on their own. Dolanji was just one of innumerable tiny villages throughout a state that lacked the resources to extend power to every poor community. The Tibetan immigrants, however, benefited from an Indian government resettlement program that made resources available. Electrical power was one of those benefits. The new power lines had to run through Dolanji to reach the new community, electrifying the village and earning the gratitude of villagers.

Despite her youth and gender, Romila Kapoor never wavered as the responsibilities mounted. She found herself negotiating regularly with the governor and other state officials, all of them men. She was often seen driving a Jeep making trips to Shimla, the state capital, to ask for food and supplies. Kapoor discovered that she could negotiate as well as any of the men she dealt with. Through her efforts and Tenzin's, the Bön community gathered the resources it needed to thrive.

A Bön community was coming together, but the the death of the thirty-second abbot of Menri five years earlier had left the religion without a titular head. Tenzin was the de facto leader, but he knew that for the community to thrive his people needed their traditional figurehead—a Menri abbot carrying the traditional title of Menri Trizin, meaning "throne holder of medicine mountain." The vacant abbotship needed to be filled according to tradition.

The choice would be crucial for the survival of Bön. The new abbot needed to have the vision and organizational skills to sustain the expatriate Bön community and keep its adherents from drifting away. To find this rare leader, Tenzin and the other monks did what they had always done: they appealed to the gods.

Bön lamas living in India, Nepal, and Bhutan, including the fifteen highest-ranking, gathered in 1968 at the Dolanji settlement to choose a new abbot in the traditional way. The names of ten qualified monks with geshe degrees were written on slips of paper. The slips were encased in balls of tsampa and holy medicine. The balls were placed in a vase, then Tenzin and a dozen Bön monks prayed for fourteen days in a recently constructed protector's temple. After the prayers and rituals, the abbot of Yungdrungling shook the vase. The ten balls bounced inside until three fell from the vase. The room was silent as the monks watched with tense anticipation, each knowing that the future of Bön would be determined by a ball of tsampa. One by one, the three balls fell onto a specially created sand mandala, each disturbing the lines of colored sand carefully laid in an intricate pattern. The vase was emptied and the three balls returned to it. The Yungdrungling abbot then shook the three balls until two popped out, one after the other. The first of the two would contain the name of the thirty-third abbot of Menri, head of the Bön religion. The ball was opened and on the paper inside was written the name Sangye Tenzin.

On March 14, 1968, Sangye lay in his bed in Norway and dreamed that he and another monk sat atop a temple in a high wind, each with a conch shell like those blown like a trumpet during religious ceremonies. The fierce wind blew the conch shell from the hand of the other monk, dashing it to pieces on the ground below. Sangye held on to his conch and sounded it from the temple top.

The next day Sangye received a telegram informing him that the protectors of Bön had selected him as the Menri Trizen. He would later learn that the name of the monk in his dream was in the second ball.

Sangye's instinct was to decline. He sent a cable saying that he was too young and inexperienced to assume such a heavy mantle. Tenzin's cabled reply said that the lamas had not chosen him. He was chosen by the gods. Unable to refuse the gods, Sangye made his way back to India. From that point on his name would be Menri Trizin Lungtok

Tenpai Nyima, and he would be addressed as His Holiness.

The gods had chosen well. Sangye had learned much about the need for modern education during his stay in Europe and about organization from his visits to European monasteries. He was more steeped in the intricacies of the Bön religion than most of his contemporaries. He had led the effort to regather and print Bön scriptures lost to Chinese depredations in Tibet. His travels in Europe had given him language skills and a grasp of the world that would enable him to negotiate successfully outside the Bön community. His charisma, kindness, and his physically imposing presence compelled others to look to him for leadership. During his first year in Dolanji the most learned Bön lamas flocked to the settlement to tutor him, as tradition dictated.

Sangye and Tenzin set out to build a new future for Bön by building a Menri Monastery in India and making it a spiritual beacon. Menri in India would supplant the old, severely damaged Menri Monastery in Tibet that could never fulfill its traditional role as long as it was under the control of the Chinese.

Together they transformed a few roughly constructed buildings and a handful of monks into the heart of the Bön religion. The monastery would provide a place for the training of Bön monks, ensuring that the religion would endure. From its founding onward, the Menri Monastery in India would be a lure for those seeking freedom or religious instruction without Chinese interference. Many would risk their lives crossing the Himalayas to get to Menri.

Tenzin founded a dialectic curriculum within Menri in 1978. Under the guidance of Tenzin and Sangye, the monastery would institute a rigorous training regimen that would produce Bön's most learned monks. The first six students graduated with geshe degrees in 1986. Since then more than 140 monks have earned their geshe degrees there.

A school for Bönpo and village children, now run by the Tibetan government-in-exile, was established on the slope below the monastery, and a nunnery was completed in 2003 near where Kapoor's shack once stood on a slope overlooking the river. The new children's school departed from the traditional emphasis on religious training by using a modern curriculum that prepared its graduates for the fast-changing world outside Dolanji. In addition, a combination orphanage and boarding school, the Bön Children's Welfare Center, was built at the monastery.

As Bön grew, so did financial support for Menri. In the early years, Sangye and Tenzin struggled to keep the Bön settlement and monastery afloat. Food was often scarce. Tenzin on occasion would forego his meals, saving them for the youngest monks at the monastery. As late as 1995, Menri was a collection of crude concrete buildings. The main temple lacked the artwork that typically covers every paintable surface in monasteries. Menri's fortunes began to change after geshes educated at Menri traveled abroad in the 1980s, where they found a receptive audience to Bön teachings in Europe and North America. Bön teaching centers began to spring up in the West, and contributions from new adherents began flowing into Menri by the late 1990s. The contributions led to a construction boom at the monastery, allowing it to grow into a complex of dormitories, temples, a hospital where traditional Tibetan medicine is practiced, a building for housing the many foreign guests, and subsidiary buildings.

Tonpa Shenrab may have founded Bön, but Tenzin kept it alive. The rebirth of Bön at the settlement near Dolanji might never have become a reality if a Chinese soldier had decided to finish off a badly wounded monk at Muro Ri Mountain.

Tenzin, whose only desire was to remain in a cave and meditate, was forced by circumstances into leading his people out of the wilderness. Through his efforts, together with those of Sangye, Bön was rescued and is flourishing. Romila Kapoor would recall a half century later: Sangye and Tenzin's efforts "revived the Bön religion, otherwise there would be no Bön. . . . If it hadn't been for them, at least in India, it would have been finished, and whatever religion was left, even in Tibet, would not have survived."[2]

Epilogue
Where They Are Now

Tenzin Namdak (His Eminence Yongdzin Tenzin Namdak Rinpoche)

Six decades after Tenzin was left for dead at Muro Ri in the desolation of the Changthang Plateau, he lives tranquilly in a monastery he founded in Kathmandu.

Tenzin, who is now known as His Eminence Yongdzin Tenzin Namdak Rinpoche, began searching in 1977 for a site near Kathmandu to serve the large population of Bönpos in Nepal. Although there were about twenty existing Bön monasteries in Nepal at the time, most were remote and had little influence beyond their immediate communities. They were not up to the task of bestowing geshe degrees and educating the younger generation of Bönpos, a void Tenzin intended to fill. He finally selected a patch of jungle on a hillside in an unpopulated area in the outskirts of the city that could be reached only by walking. He purchased the land and founded the monastery in 1987. Work began on a simple four-room building on the slope. The modest building served as a monastery for about four years. Tenzin named it Triten Norbutse, after a monastery established in the fourteenth century in Tsang, central Tibet, demolished by the Red Guards during the Cultural Revolution. He had studied under a master educated at the old Triten Norbutse and wanted to honor the connection.

In 1991, Tenzin supervised the construction of a new temple, and artists from Bhutan were contracted to build a giant statue of Tonpa Shenrab, Bön's founder.

Like Menri, Triten Norbutse has grown, adding a library, halls for retreats, a large kitchen, an herbal pharmacy, dormitories, and housing for teachers, all spread across the slope. The monastery is reached from the base of the hill by a long stone staircase. A 7.3 magnitude earthquake shook Nepal in 2015, killing at least 153 people. The temblor damaged Triten Norbutse, although no one at the monastery was injured. Engineers pronounced the monastery structurally safe afterward, and work began to reinforce the foundation against future earthquakes. In 2019, construction began on a new temple with seating for five hundred and a new residence for Tenzin.

By the twenty-first century, geshes from Menri Monastery in India had gained followings in Europe, prompting Tenzin to found Shenten Dargye Ling Center in France in 2005.

In 1986, twenty-six years after escaping from Tibet, Tenzin returned to tour Bön monasteries. His visit was made possible by a softening of the hard line toward religion by the Chinese during the 1980s and his abstention from politics. Tenzin was in the good graces of Chinese officials because of his efforts to raise money for Tibetan schools. His trip was intended to inspire and encourage the monks laboring under Chinese oppression who had rebuilt monasteries damaged or destroyed during the occupation.

One of his stops was at in Ngawa, Amdo, at the Nangzhig Monastery, the largest Bön monastery, with over a thousand monks. He was keeping a promise he had made to an old friend who had perished during the Cultural Revolution, Lama Tenpa Woger. Tenpa Woger was one of the most learned monks at the Menri Monastery in Tibet. Under orders from Tenzin, Tenpa Woger (not to be confused with Tenpa Woser, the monk who renounced his vows and was wounded by Chinese soldiers) returned to the Nangzhig Monastery in the mid-1950s, amid savage fighting between Tibetans and Chinese occupiers. Tenpa Woger had been content with his duties at Menri and was reluctant to return to Amdo, but Tenzin insisted. Tenzin believed the Nangzhig Monastery needed a wise leader to guide Bönpos through those treacherous times. Eventually Tenpa Woger acceded to Tenzin's request but exacted a promise that Tenzin would visit Nangzhig at his earliest opportunity. Tenzin's escape from Tibet forced him to postpone his promise for decades. Tenzin would never see his friend again, but he would keep his promise to visit the monastery.

During his trip to Tibet he traveled to his birthplace, where he was reunited with his mother, then 82, for the first time in forty-five years.

In 1999, after overcoming initial reluctance from Chinese officials, Tenzin sponsored a four-year residential school that taught traditional Tibetan medicine in his hometown in Kham. The school was so successful that the Chinese government took over its sponsorship in 2007.

Until 2018 he occasionally traveled to the United States and other countries to teach, spending his summers at Shenten Center in France and his winters in Nepal. His wounded leg became increasingly painful as he aged, causing him to end travel in 2019 and remain at Triten Norbutse Monastery in Kathmandu.

Tenzin's devoted assistant, Sherab Tsultrim, who saved Tenzin's life and crossed the Himalayas with him during his escape, was living in Kham in 2021. He was not interviewed for this book.

His Eminence Yongdzin Tenzin Namdak Rinpoche, who turned ninety-eight in 2023, has turned administration of Triten Norbutse Monastery over to a younger generation, but still is consulted on major decisions. He remains the éminence grise of the Bön religion, and his advice is sought in consequential matters by the highest Bön officials. Of all living lamas, he is the most beloved and admired figure in the Bönpo community because of his compassion and his role in saving Bön culture. Many consider him a living Buddha.

Tenzin still mourns the friends who died in the ambush at Muro Ri mountain. He says he knows two Chinese words: the word for "shoot" and the word for "don't shoot." For many years Tenzin thought the local gods and spirits of Muro Ri where he was shot had cursed him, but now believes they saved his life.

Sangye Tenzin (Thirty-third Menri Trizin, His Holiness Lungtok Tenpai Nyima)

As Menri India flourished, an unresolved question lingered about the ultimate seat of the Bön religion. There were now two Menri monasteries, and the abbot of Menri traditionally headed the Bön religion. Which abbot, the one in India or the one in Tibet, should be recognized as the leader of Bön?

Although the Dalai Lama cannot safely travel to Tibet, the head of the Bön religion can. Bönpos, historically excluded from Tibet's political life, looked inward to their own affairs. Sangye, now called His Holiness, continued that tradition in exile. Bönpos' avoidance of politics and Sangye's status allowed him and other high Bön officials to travel in Tibet at the whim of Chinese officials. He visited Menri and Yungdrungling monasteries on a trip to Tibet in 1994. To reach Menri, His Holiness and the monks accompanying him rode horses up a steep trail to Gang Yak Pass because there were no roads at the time. As he topped the pass, the monastery came into his view for the first time in thirty-five years. His Holiness dismounted and prostrated himself on the ground. As he did, three thunderclaps boomed out of a cloudless blue sky, according to Geshe Nyima Dakpa, then a member of the abbot's staff. After topping the pass, His Holiness stopped to perform ceremonies at a rock known as the Golden Throne, where the Menri abbot traditionally would sit to minister to laymen and women. He stopped again at a nearby shrine where all Menri abbots are said to "receive a transmission" of knowledge and authority from Menri's founder, Nyame Sherab Gyaltsen.

Geshe Nyima Dakpa, responsible for planning the trip, worried about how His Holiness would be received by the head of the monastery, then an eighty-year-old lama. Would the abbot of Menri Tibet see the abbot of Menri India as a rival? Because no monastery could operate without Chinese permission and supervision, he feared His Holiness would receive a cold reception by politicized monks. Would His Holiness be accepted as head of the Bön religion? When they reached the monastery grounds, Nyima Dakpa sought out the head of the monastery. Before Nyima Dakpa could ask, the old monk invited His Holiness to be officially enthroned as abbot at the monastery in accordance with tradition. The elderly lama brought out the sacred Nyame Kudam, a fragile, tattered, six-hundred-year-old silk cloth worn by the founder of Menri, and gave it to His Holiness to wear during the ceremony. The ceremony erased all doubt about the seat of the Bön religion. All Bönpos now would accept Menri in India as the headquarters for their faith, and His Holiness as their uncontested leader.[1]

For the rest of his life, His Holiness remained at Menri India, traveling occasionally to one of Bön's fledgling outposts around the world to teach. He visited the United States several times, including travel to New York, Charlottesville, Houston, Los Angeles, and San Francisco to give religious instruction. Under his guidance, Bön spread throughout the world.

By 2014 His Holiness's health began to fail. As he neared death three years later, His Holiness began making preparations. He asked that Tibetan children from the nearby school be brought to his bedside. He gave each a piece of candy as a goodbye gift. The next day he blessed all those from the Bönpo settlement, calling the elderly his old friends and wishing them farewell. They stood in single file chanting his blessing prayer, waiting to spend a few moments with the revered holy man. The third day he held an audience with all the Menri monks. Later that day, as death approached, he placed himself in meditative posture. As he sat in meditation, his breathing ceased and his head dropped, according to monks who witnessed his last breath. After forty-nine years as abbot, His Holiness died while in meditative pose at the age of eighty-nine on September 14, 2017.

After a doctor pronounced him dead, a monk made the traditional call to meditation with three notes from a conch shell as others in the room chanted prayers. As the conch sounded, witnesses said His Holiness raised his head.[2] By their account, his head remained erect for five days before finally drooping down to his chest. The unusual circumstances surrounding his death are found in traditional accounts of the deaths of Bön masters who have achieved enlightenment. Because His Holiness was deemed to have realized that state of liberation, the traditional rituals to speed his spirit on its journey were not needed and were replaced by elaborate ceremonies and special rituals celebrating his life. Thousands of Bönpos, many from Europe and North America, traveled to Dolanji, waiting in long lines to view the body of His Holiness in the room where he died. Monks built a special oven, or *chorten,* next to the temple for his cremation. On October 2, 2017, his body was placed on a litter and taken to the chorten in a procession led by monks blowing sacred horns. The body was placed in a sitting position inside the chorten and fires lit. After fire consumed the body, thousands of offerings that had filled the temple were tossed into the fire, including platers laden with fruit, sculptures of molded tsampa tormas, and long wooden boards bearing prayers written in pure gold and silver.

Later, monks tore down the chorten and in its place erected an eighteen-foot stupa carved from five blocks of snow-white Makrana marble, as flawless and pure as the marble used to build the Taj Majal. The room where he died was turned into a museum displaying the few artifacts from his life. A wax statue of His Holiness sitting in perpetual meditation crowns the exhibit.

Samten Karmay

At the end of his three-year Rockefeller scholarship, Samten Karmay remained in London to learn Sanskrit and began writing a history of the Bön religion. His efforts would make him the first Tibetan to achieve international academic fame.

He earned a master's in philosophy in 1966 from the School of Oriental and African Studies, University of London. He mastered French and in 1981 entered the Centre National de la Recherche Scientifique (CNRS), Paris. Samten Karmay earned a doctorate in 1985 from the University of London. He eventually married an Englishwoman, Heather Stoddard, a Tibetologist. They have a son, Ozer Rowan Karmay. Samten and Stoddard are divorced.

In 1990 he was awarded the Centre National de la Recherche Scientifique silver medal for his Tibetan research. Samten was elected president of the International Association of Tibetan Studies in 1996, the first Tibetan chairman, a post he held until 2002. The entire October 2008 edition of the French scientific journal *Revue d'études Tibétaines* was dedicated to him. He has authored numerous scholarly works on Tibetan history, writing in English and in French, and travels around the world giving lectures.

As he embraced the scientific method he became increasingly distanced from the religious view of the world held by his friend Sangye (His Holiness). He increasingly viewed Bön from the viewpoint of anthropologists and historians, a view that sometimes clashed with the worldview of traditional Bön. Despite their differences, His Holiness and Samten Karmay remained lifelong friends. After His Holiness died, Samten Karmay wrote a tribute to his friend on his Facebook page dated October 16, 2017:

> [His Holiness Lungtok Tenpai Nyima] encouraged many of his students after the completion their studies to go back to Tibet when it

> was open at the beginning of 1980s to help rebuild monasteries that were destroyed during the Cultural Revolution. In my view, this had a far-reaching beneficial influence in restoring what was lost not just for the Bönpo people but for the Tibetan people as a whole. To enhance this initiative he undertook visits to Tibet to guide his students who were there on mission. Personally, he was my closest friend since childhood and his passing away, although expected, is a tremendous loss for me. Life took us on different paths but we remain close and respectful of each other's engagements.

Samten's brother, Soko, and his mother Zinmo, immigrated to London. Zinmo died in 1979 in Chichester, United Kingdom. Samten's father, Tsega, died during the Cultural Revolution. The date and circumstances of his death are unknown to his family.

Tenpa Woser

After escaping Tibet, Tenpa Woser lived in a Red Cross camp for Tibetan refugees in Dorpatan, a city near the Tibetan ethnic region in the mountains of northern Nepal. He never returned to monastic life. He married Nyima Choedon, a widow with a child. Together they had five children. His stepson, Khenpo Tenpa Yungdrung Rinpoche, became abbot of Triten Norbutse Monastery in Kathmandu, making him Yongdzin Tenzin Namdak Rinpoche's closest associate.

Tenpa Woser earned a living growing potatoes, the only crop he could grow at 11,500 feet. He hauled the potatoes to the valley for sale, then used the proceeds to buy salt. Tenpa traded the salt for butter, barley, corn, and other essentials. The farming and trading were difficult and barely earned enough to sustain his family. His children, who obtained a Western education in public schools, left the cold remoteness of Dorpatan as soon as they could and found jobs in Kathmandu, the United States, and France. Tenpa and his wife moved to Kathmandu, where they lived in a modern apartment until Tenpa's death on July 4, 2020, at the age of eighty-four. His brother, Tenpa Wangal, remained at Menri Monastery in Tibet for the rest of his life.

Robert Ford

After his capture in 1950, British radio operator Robert Ford was charged with espionage, spreading anti-Communist propaganda and the murder of Geda Lama, a Chinese envoy assigned with submitting a ten-point peace plan to the Dalai Lama. Prior to the invasion, Tibetan officials had refused to allow Geda Lama to proceed to Lhasa so he stayed in Chamdo, where he met Ford. The Chinese emissary became deathly ill and asked Ford for medical care based on an erroneous impression. Ford had no medical training, but he had some bandages and drugs he had used to help other Tibetans. Those few good-will gestures gave him an undeserved reputation among Tibetans in Chamdo as a healer. Ford refused the emissary's request because he feared he would be blamed if Geda Lama died. Ford believed there was a chance that Geda Lama was poisoned because there were many Tibetan officials who would have wanted him dead. The Chinese blamed Ford anyway. Ford spent five years in prisons in Kandze and Chungking, in constant fear of being put to death. The Chinese interrogated him constantly and tried to break his will. He was not allowed to send a letter to his parents until 1954. He was tried that year and sentenced to ten years imprisonment. The next year he was released and expelled.

In 1957, Ford published *Captured in Tibet* in the United Kingdom, a book about his experiences in Chamdo and in captivity. It was released in the United States under the title, *Wind between the Worlds*. The book was reissued in 1990 with a preface by the Dalai Lama. Ford was appointed to Her Majesty's Diplomatic Service in 1956 and over his career assigned to Foreign Office postings in London, Vietnam, Indonesia, the United States, Morocco, Angola, Sweden,

France, and served as Britain's consul general in Geneva, Switzerland. On his retirement in 1983 he was awarded Commander of the Order of the British Empire. In 1956, he married Monica Tebbett, whom he had known since childhood. They were married for fifty-five years and had two sons.

Ford became an active supporter of the Tibetan government-in-exile after his retirement. In 1992 the Indian government put him under house arrest, bringing to a halt a lecture tour throughout the country, because his lectures coincided with an official visit of then Chinese premier Li Peng. The Indian government feared Ford's lectures would offend the Chinese.

At the time he was arrested and imprisoned by the Chinese in 1950, Ford was still owed his salary from the Tibetan government. On his ninetieth birthday March 27, 2013, the Tibetan government-in-exile finally handed him his long overdue paycheck: a note for a hundred *tam srang,* the Tibetan currency at the time of his capture, or about $90, at a ceremony in London. The next month the Dalai Lama presented Ford with the International Campaign for Tibet's Light of Truth Award in Fribourg, Switzerland.

Ford died September 20, 2013, in London.[3]

David Snellgrove

British scholar and Tibetologist David Snellgrove went on to write numerous books and scholarly articles about Tibetan religion and culture after the three-year Rockefeller grant expired for his Tibetan guests. In 1966 he helped found the Institute of Tibetan Studies in Tring, Hertfordshire, north of London, better known as Tibet House. In 1968, Snellgrove, a Catholic, was made consultant for Buddhism at the Vatican.

In 1975 he visited Menri Monastery in Dolanji, where he was pleased and impressed to find a thriving Bön community where His

Holiness, aided by Yongdzin Tenzin Namdak Rinpoche, oversaw about thirty monks. During his visit, Snellgrove spent most of his time reading Bönpo historical texts with his old friend Sangye, who was now His Holiness, the abbot of Menri.

By 1985, Snellgrove had fulfilled his wish to move to Italy and taken up permanent residence on his property in Torre Pellice, near Turin. He never stopped traveling, making repeated visits to India, Nepal, Bhutan, Indonesia, Malaysia, Thailand, Cambodia, and the United States. Eventually, age made travel and independent living increasingly difficult, and he moved in with an English friend, Carl Stacy, in the nearby village of Pinerolo. There he enjoyed cigars, fine wine, and his cats Chi 1 and Chi 2. He never married.

In 2014, the Department of Art and Archaeology at the School of Oriental and African Studies, University of London, created a new senior lectureship in Tibetan and Buddhist art named after David Snellgrove.

Ever the devout Catholic, Snellgrove died in Pinerolo on Good Friday, March 25, 2016. His ashes were interred next to a Buddhist monastery near Angkor, Cambodia.

Dhachoe Lama

Dhachoe Lama, the man whose family cared for Tenzin while he was in the Chinese concentration camp, helped hide the Bön reliquary, and assisted in Tenzin's escape, spent years in a Chinese prison. Once Chinese officials discovered that Tenzin had escaped, Dhachoe was immediately suspected of assisting him. Informants among the nomads told the Chinese about the powerful symbolism of the reliquary and its great value to Bönpos. Chinese officials wanted to know where the reliquary was and how Tenzin had escaped. Dhachoe refused to talk and was imprisoned and tortured. He never divulged the hiding place. After his release from prison he was constantly harassed by local authorities. The harassment became unbearable, and he moved to an area near Mount Kailash. Along the way he encountered Tsewang, the Menri monk who also had been entrusted with the whereabouts of the hidden reliquary. Tsewang joined Dhachoe and became part of his family. Dhachoe pitched his tent near a Chinese military camp, where he survived by doing odd jobs for soldiers. Dhachoe's reliability won him the respect and confidence of Chinese officers, who had learned of his difficulties with officials in the Lake Teri Namtso area. Before they broke camp, they gave Dhachoe a letter giving him permission to return to the Lake Teri Namtso area. He moved back to the lake region and showed the letter to local authorities. He was never harassed again.

Menri in Tibet lay in ruins, but several surviving monks from the monastery began looking for the reliquary. They came to Dhachoe in the early 1980s and asked him about its whereabouts. Dhachoe refused to tell them. By 1985, the Chinese had eased their persecution of religion. An official from the Tibetan Communist Party approached Dhachoe and told him about the new policy. Dhachoe was suspicious that the government was trying to lull him into revealing his secret. His suspicion made him worry about the safety of the reliquary, left in a cave he had not visited in two decades. He asked Tsewang to go to the cave and make sure the sacred object was safe. Tsewang reported that he could not find the reliquary. Someone must have taken it, he thought.

Alarmed, Dhachoe decided to visit the the cave himself. If the reliquary had been found, he reasoned, gossip about the find would have quickly spread, but there had been no such gossip. He entered the cave and found a carpet of animal dung but no sign of the sacred relic. He began digging and finally discovered the reliquary, hidden from potential looters by the droppings of animals that had inhabited the cave.

Finally convinced that Chinese government policy now tolerated religion, Dhachoe retrieved the reliquary from the cave and took it to Nagchuka, the regional capital. The government promised to ensure that the reliquary was given to the proper religious authorities and gave Dhachoe a historical preservation award. Once it became known that the Nyame Kundung had been found, all the surviving Bön monasteries in Tibet clamored for its possession. The Chinese government decided it should be restored to Menri, which would be rebuilt to house the sacred reliquary.

Tenzin was reunited with the reliquary when he visited Tibet in 1986. It remains at Menri Tibet on display in a glass case with the three gold butterlamps in a locked room reserved for sacred objects.

Nagtshang Powo

Nagtshang Powo, the powerful tribal leader who took up arms against the Chinese and promised to give CIA-supplied weapons to escaping monks, was never seen again by anyone interviewed for this book. Several interviewees said that they believed he was killed in an ambush about three months after his troops were routed by the Chinese.

Jadur Sonam Sangpo

Jadur Sonam Sangpo, who assisted Tenzin in acquiring the land at Dolanji, eventually was chosen as one of two Bön representatives to the Tibetan government-in-exile's Assembly of Tibetan People's Deputies. He served from 1982 to 2001. He was the Dalai Lama's choice for Chief Justice Commissioner, serving from 2002 to 2004. He is retired and now lives in Dolanji.

E. Gene Smith

E. Gene Smith, the Amercian scholar who made a surprise visit to the three Bön monks in London, retired from the Library of Congress in 1997. He and Leonard van der Kuijp, professor of Tibetan and

Himalayan Studies at Harvard University, founded the Tibetan Buddhist Resource Center in 1999, since renamed the Buddhist Digital Resource Center, to digitize the 12,000 volumes of Tibetan texts Smith had been instrumental in assembling. Since then the center has digitized more than fifteen million pages of text from throughout the Buddhist world. These texts are available online at the center website, www.tbrc.org. Smith amassed the largest collection of Tibetan books outside Tibet. He died in 2010. The center's obituary read:

> For decades, Smith has been universally recognized among scholars of Tibet around the world as the dean of Tibetan Studies. This undisputed and splendid reputation in the field is due to Smith's extraordinary accomplishments in the preservation and dissemination of Tibetan literature; his unparalleled knowledge of Tibetan religious history; his dedication to making Tibetan literature universally accessible, particularly for Tibetans; and the unstintingly generous assistance that he has provided to scholars around the world for more than forty years.

Romila Kapoor

Romila Kapoor, the young Indian woman who led the first group of despairing Bönpo families to the site of the new Bön settlement at Dolanji, married Ashok Dhawan in 1971. They moved to the United States, where their daughter was born. They returned to India in 1985. Romila had lost touch with the Bönpo community, but His Holiness Lungtok Tenpai Nyima—known in this book as Sangye Tenzin—never forgot her and her crucial role in the founding of Thobgyal Sarpa. They were reunited in 2002 after a chance meeting between her daughter and an American benefactor in New York. Learning Romila's whereabouts from the benefactor, His Holiness phoned her New Delhi residence. Romila nearly dropped the receiver after hearing the voice of His Holiness. He had been searching for her for nearly fifteen years.

After the phone call to Romila, a delegation from Menri Monastery in India arrived on her doorstep with an invitation to visit Menri, which she accepted. Her first stop on the way to Dolanji was in Kalka, where His Holiness met her and her husband with a full complement of Bön officials. The next day they drove to Dolanji, where the whole village turned out to welcome her and her husband. For nearly the entire day, villagers, both Hindu and Bönpo, filed by to see the woman so many had relied on to make the Bön settlement a reality.

Romila would make at least six other trips to Thobgyal Sarpa; her final one was to attend His Holiness's funeral ceremonies in 2017. She and her husband live in New Delhi.

Drepung Monastery, Lhasa

The once imposing Drepung Monastery in Lhasa, where Samten Karmay and His Holiness studied, is greatly reduced. The Chinese destroyed 40 percent of its buildings. Even with the destruction, what remains sprawls over several acres. Most of its monks were arrested or killed. The grand monastery that once housed more than 7,000 monks is now limited to about 300. The Chinese government is interested in fostering tourism and has made a few repairs and installed running water and electricity. Most of the buildings have fallen into disrepair and many are in ruin. Despite Chinese Communist efforts to control the monastery, Drepung monks have continued to defend their religion. The Chinese shuttered the monastery in 2008 after monk-led protests in Lhasa degenerated into looting and arson. Drepung was closed again in 2013 for five months following similar disturbances.

To this day resistance to Chinese rule remains widespread in Tibet, and China has countered by increasing its repression. In monasteries the Chinese government has appointed administrators whose authority supersedes that of the abbot. Every monastery must worry about informers and is watched by police and cadres. Possession of a picture of the Dalai Lama or his writings is punishable by imprisonment and, often, torture. Police kiosks are found about every three hundred feet in some areas of Lhasa. At least 300,000 Chinese troops are stationed in Tibet, and dozens of military bases are scattered throughout Lhasa, each with a glass box at the entrance with a soldier in dress uniform inside holding a rifle at port arms. From the rooftop of the sacred Jokhang Temple, soldiers can be seen going through drills on the rooftop of a neighboring building, their shouts easily heard.

The repression is especially evident around the Jokhang, the site of several self-immolations protesting Chinese rule. At least 157 people, mostly monks and nuns, set themselves alight between 2009 and January 2021 throughout Tibet and China to protest Chinese oppression to protest Chinese oppression according to the International Campaign for Tibet. The profusion of stalls with merchants hawking everything from chubas to divinations that once crowded the Barkhor, the streets surrounding the Jokhang, are all gone, removed by Chinese decree. The government forced vendors to relocate their stalls to buildings in areas not normally frequented by tourists or Tibetans. In 2014, merchants in the new buildings said their sales had dropped drastically. The Barkhor can only be entered through police checkpoints with metal detectors. All matches and lighters are confiscated.

If the the intense control is intended to dampen Tibetan devotion to religion, there is little evidence of its success to the casual visitor. On any day in Lhasa, hundreds of the faithful can be seen circumambulating the Potala, left empty by the Dalai Lama for six decades. Pilgrims still crowd the entrance to the Jokhang. There they prostrate themselves on the stone-paved plaza to earn spiritual merit, wearing cloth and leather pads on their hands to protect them as they repeatedly slide across the hard surface. They ignore police officers writing on clipboards walking among them. No one knows what the officers are writing, making their presence even more intimidating.

The Chinese government makes little distinction in principle between Bön and Buddhism. The government says that religion must serve the state, and it views the Dalai Lama as a threat to its rule over Tibet, declaring him a "splitist" seeking to separate Tibet from China. This is despite the Dalai Lama's denial that he seeks independence and his assurance that he only wants Tibetan culture and religion preserved. The Dalai Lama's images and recordings are banned in Tibet. In December 2013, the Buddhist chant leader of the Drongna Monastery in central Tibet was sentenced to eighteen years in prison for possession of pictures of the Dalai Lama and recordings of his teachings.[4] Although Bönpos revere the Dalai Lama, they are less likely to engage in overt acts of protest. Of the four schools of Buddhism, the Gelug have been most active in the protests and self-immolations that periodically flare in Tibet.

Despite the Chinese government's overt hostility to religion in Tibet, Buddhism has a following within the Han Chinese majority in China, and some in central China have converted to Bön.

Foreign journalists are largely banned or allowed in only under tight controls. Tibetan journalists are regularly jailed. Checkpoints with police and soldiers armed with automatic weapons on major highways are plentiful. Identification is always required at checkpoints, and foreigners must show their passports. A ticket is issued at each checkpoint showing the time of arrival. The ticket is checked at the next checkpoint. Those arriving too early are cited for speeding, causing lines of cars and trucks to park alongside the road ahead of each checkpoint, waiting for enough time to elapse so that they can proceed. Arriving too late can result in an interrogation about the driver's whereabouts.

Menri Monastery, Tibet

In the 1980s, the Chinese government softened its antagonism toward religion and helped finance some of the rebuilding of surviving monasteries, including the original Menri that suffered grievously during the 1966 Cultural Revolution. Before 1959 there were an estimated 6,500 monasteries in Tibet. Now only a fraction of that number remain. A survey of Bön monasteries published in 2003 found only ninety remaining Bön monasteries and shrines in the Tibetan Autonomous Zone.[5] Many have been rebuilt in recent years, including thirty in the Kham area.

After the brief relaxation of repressive religious policies in the 1980s, the restrictions resumed as hard-line factions within the Chinese Communist Party gained ascendancy. Unauthorized rebuilding of monasteries was banned, the number of monks and nuns living in monasteries was limited, restrictions were imposed on the ability of young people to join monasteries, members of the Tibetan Communist Party were prohibited from practicing religion, and "democratic" management committees were placed in control of each monastery to ensure state control.

Menri was rebuilt and a road cut into the mountain to make it easier for Chinese officials to exert control at the remote mountaintop location. A government building, which appeared to be a police station, was under construction just below the monastery in 2014. Visitors that year were warned by their guide to avoid asking probing questions because of the presence of spies among the monks who would report to Chinese authorities. Every monk who speaks with a foreigner can be expected to be grilled by Chinese officials about his conversation.

Menri Monastery, India

The Menri Monastery in India is a thriving religious and cultural center overseeing a steady spread of Bön. Menri India has become a beacon for those who want to study under Bön's foremost scholars or desire to be of service to the Bön religion. To get to Menri, young men and women risk their lives as Tenzin did in crossing the Himalayas and evading Chinese and Nepalese border guards. Other than their desire to study under Bön masters, they are no different from the Tibetans who continue to flee their country despite some of the tightest border restrictions in the world.

More than 100,000 Tibetans followed the Dalai Lama into exile in the years following the Lhasa uprising. Most were scattered in refugee camps strung across India, Nepal, and Bhutan. Over the years Tibetans have continued to escape in small groups, and more than 150,000 were estimated to be living outside Tibet in 2020.[6] Some of those who escaped would graduate from Menri India and scatter throughout the world.

Menri India graduated its first class of geshes in 1986, each having completed thirteen years of study. The graduates brought Bön to the Americas and Europe, including Canada, the United States, Mexico, Brazil, Poland, Russia, France, the United Kingdom, and Italy. Once a tradition so obscure it was known only by scholars outside the Tibetan cultural areas, Bön is now practiced in Asia, Eastern and Western Europe, and North and South America. Despite Bön's dramatic resurgence, it remains tiny in comparison to other spiritual traditions and is still relatively unknown to the general public.

Although Bönpos eschew proselytizing their beliefs, Bön's growth has been rapid. Before the 1990s there were no Bön organizations in North America. The first was established in Houston, Texas. Since then, Bön organizations have been established in Virginia, California, Colorado, New York, Pennsylvania, Minnesota, Mexico, and Canada. Bön has been especially vibrant in Mexico, where adherents built a 3,300 square-foot, 131-foot-high temple near the southern city of Valle de Bravo, and a smaller temple in the northern city of Torreon. Other Menri graduates returned to Tibet, where they helped rekindle Bön in its home country. Their efforts were assisted by a change in Chinese policy in the 1980s. Having established control over the monasteries, Chinese officials began to see them as tourist attractions. The government made money available for rebuilding monasteries damaged or destroyed during the dark days of the Cultural Revolution. In more recent years, Chinese policies toward Tibetan monasteries have turned repressive again, and religion of any sort is viewed by Chinese Communist officials with great suspicion.

In 1977, the Tibetan government-in-exile granted a longstanding request by the Bön community for the same representation in the Tibetan Parliament accorded the four officially recognized Buddhist schools. The next year the government gave formal recognition to His Holiness Lungtok Tenpai Nyima, giving the head of Bön equal rank with the heads of the Gelug, Sakya, Kagyu, and Nyingma schools of Tibetan Buddhism.

Menri has grown to include a nunnery housing about ninety nuns, allowing nuns to also earn the geshe degree. As of 2020 there were 120 children at a monastery orphanage, 300 Bönpo children from India and Nepal attending a boarding school, and about 150 monks. The lay community over time expanded to several hundred, but in recent years has declined as children came of age and sought opportunities in the world at large. The lay population of the settlement in 2020 was 140.

The Menri Trizin

After Sangye's death in 2017, His Holiness's successor had to be chosen using the traditional methods, but those methods had not been used for a half-century. The responsibility for rediscovering those methods fell to Menri Lopon Trinley Nyima, the head teacher at the monastery. Lopon Trinley Nyima spent weeks consulting with older lamas, relying mostly on Yongdzin Tenzin Namdak Rinpoche, one of the few lamas then living who participated in the selection of the thirty-third Menri abbot. He sent emissaries to Tibet to pry information from the oldest Bönpo lamas there. Lopon Trinley Nyima pieced together the ancient procedures and sent the final draft to lamas in Tibet and Nepal for approval. He then recorded his findings so that posterity would not be forced to repeat his research.

To avoid Chinese influence, the candidates had to be from outside Tibet. That narrowed the selection to candidates from Menri Monastery in India and Triten Norbutse Monastery in Nepal. Of the geshes from those two monasteries who were still monks living outside Tibet and willing to be considered, sixty-four qualified candidates were found. A process was designed to allow the protector deities to make the selection.

In the presence of at least ten monks, Lopon Trinley Nyima wrote each name on a piece of paper and rolled it inside a ball of tsampa. Each ball was weighed to make sure all were exactly the same size. The balls were allowed to dry, placed in two crystal bowls, and each bowl covered with a multicolored silk cloth. The bowls were sealed in wax and placed inside a locked iron box, which was locked in a room inside the temple. Monks prayed continuously while the box remained locked away. A week before New Year's Day 2018, Lopon Trinley Nyima unlocked the room and carried the sealed box to the main hall, where monks and villagers waited. He placed the box in front of a statue of Tonpa Shenrab and removed both bowls. Lopon Trinley Nyima held each bowl in turn and moved his arms from side to side in a circular motion so that the balls rolled around inside the bowl until a single ball tumbled out onto a silk cloth. The process was repeated and the two balls were placed in a single bowl, resealed and returned to the locked room. The remaining balls were burned. On January 1, 2018, after another week of prayers to the protector deities, the remaining bowl was again brought to the main hall. Once again the bowl was shaken until a single ball rolled over the lip and fell onto the silk cloth. Before the ball was opened, all the monks present pledged their allegiance to the monk whose name would be revealed. Only then did Lopon Trinley Nyima open the tsampa ball and read the name: Geshe Dawa Dargyal, Menri Monastery administrator, was the thirty-fourth abbot of Menri. A great cheer filled the temple with the reading of his name. The new Menri abbot had been trained by His Holiness Lungtok Tenpai Nyima and had traveled and worked closely with him as administrator. Unlike many of the other candidates who were born in India or Nepal, the new abbot hailed from the same area of Amdo as his predecessor. The smooth leadership transition after His Holiness Lungtok Tenpai Nyima's death ensured that the religion would continue along the path he had envisioned. The Bön religion, although still one of the world's smallest and least known, was thriving in 2023.

Main Characters and Glossary

TIBETAN NAMES

Tibetan names are often translated differently into English. We used spellings from source materials or as they were spelled to us by interviewees. When sources disagreed on spellings, we chose the spelling most familiar to us. Tibetan names, especially for monks, can change throughout their lifetime, so we have chosen to use a single name throughout this book to avoid confusion. The only exception is in the epilogue, where we use the full titles of two of the central characters.

THE MAIN CHARACTERS

Tenzin Namdak: The central figure. He becomes one of the most learned scholars of the Bön religion, is wounded while trying to flee Tibet, escapes from a concentration camp, lives in London for three years, and returns to India to found the first Bön monastery and community for Tibetan refugees in that country. He is now addressed as Yongdzin Tenzin Namdak Rinpoche.

Sangye Tenzin: The monk who would eventually become His Holiness Lungtok Tenpai Nyima, the thirty-third Menri Trizen. He travels from the far eastern Tibetan province of Amdo to Lhasa to study at Tibet's most prestigious monastery, Drepung, witnesses the rebellion against Chinese rule in Lhasa, escapes to Nepal, lives in London and then Oslo, is chosen as head of the Bön religion and abbot of the first Bön monastery in exile in India.

Samten Karmay: Sangye Tenzin's lifelong friend. Together they travel to Lhasa, escape to Nepal, and live in London. Samten decides to remain in Europe, becoming a renowned scholar.

David Snellgrove: The renowned British Tibetologist who takes Tenzin Namdak, Sangye Tenzin, and Samten Karmay from India to London and introduces them to the Western world.

Tenpa Woser: A monk who renounces his vow of nonviolence to protect the lamas of Menri in Tibet trying to escape Chinese oppression. He is wounded during the escape and survives several encounters with Chinese troops.

PERSONS, PLACES, AND THINGS

amban: A Chinese official residing in a country under Chinese political control.

Amdo: Tibet's far northeastern region before the Chinese invasion.

Barkhor: Pilgrimage and commercial square in Lhasa surrounding Tibet's holiest of holies, the Jokhang Temple.

Chamdo: Tibetan administrative capital of Kham Province before the Chinese invasion.

Changthang Plateau: Tibet's highest plateau, with an average elevation of 15,000 feet, higher than the tallest mountain in the continental United States.

chuba: A traditional Tibetan garment that reaches to the ground and is tied at the waist with a cloth belt.

Chushi Gangdruk: The poetic name for Kham, meaning "Four Rivers

Six ranges," a reference to the rivers that have their source in Kham and the mountain ranges within its boundaries. The name was adopted by a Tibetan resistance group formed to fight the Chinese occupation.

Dachoe Pasang: One of Tenzin Namdak's four paternal uncles. Dachoe took over the family farm and care of Tenzin after the death of Tenzin's father. Under the Tibetan tradition of polyandry, Dachoe also was also one Tenzin's three legal fathers. When Tenzin's mother married his biological father, she also married his two brothers.

Dalai Lama: The head of Tibetan Buddhism, the Gelug school of Tibetan Buddhism, and the Tibetan government, who fled to India in 1959; he remained the head of the Tibetan government-in-exile until 2011, when he ceded his political authority to an elected parliament of exiles.

Denkok: A Tibetan town near the eastern edge of the Tibetan government's zone of control prior to the 1950 Chinese invasion; alternatively called Dengo.

dob-dob: A warrior monk.

Dolpo: An area of northwestern Nepal, where the population is ethnically Tibetan and predominantly Bönpo.

Dongdo: Tenzin Namdak's maternal ancestor several generations removed, and a renowned artist who painted the original temple at the prestigious Yungdrungling Monastery.

Dongza Gachung: Tenzin Namdak's mother, from whom he was separated at age four.

Drepo Padang: Tenzin Namdak's father, who died when Tenzin was four.

Drepung: The largest of three monasteries in Lhasa that dominated Tibetan religion and politics. Drepung, Sera, and Ganden monasteries were all run by the dominant Gelug school of Tibetan Buddhism.

dzo: Cross between a yak and an ox.

Emei Mountain: A mountain in Sichuan Province, one of four sacred Buddhist mountains in China.

Gangru Tsultrim Gyaltsan Rinpoche: Bön master who lived in a cave on the shore of Lake Jurutso, where he mentored Tenzin Namdak for four years.

Gelugpa: A practitioner of Gelug, the dominant sect of the four Tibetan Buddhist schools. The Dalai Lama is a Gelugpa.

geshe: A title bestowed on monks who earn the geshe degree, similar to a doctorate of divinity.

Geshe Dawa Dargyal: The thirty-fourth abbot of Menri, who took office in 2018 following the death of His Holiness Lungtok Tenpai Nyima (Sangye Tenzin).

Gompo Tashi Andrugtsang: A prosperous trader who united Tibetan resistance movements under the banner of the Chushi Gangdruk.

Gyalo Thondup: The second oldest of the Dalai Lama's four brothers; Gyalo helped the CIA recruit candidates for a U.S.-trained unit of Tibetans who were parachuted into Tibet.

Gyalwa Lodro: Thirty-first abbot of Menri Monastery in Tibet.

Horwa Aku: Hortsun Tenzin Lodro Gyatsho Horwa, Samten Karmay's great-uncle and head teacher at the Nateng Monastery in Amdo.

Jadur Sonam Sangpo: A Tibetan Bönpo refugee who helped Tenzin find and purchase property for a Bön community in India.

Jokhang: The first Buddhist temple in Tibet, the Jokhang sits in Barkhor square in central Lhasa. It attracts thousands of Buddhist pilgrims annually and is one of the most revered holy places in Tibet.

Kapoor, Romila: A Catholic Relief Services employee who helped organize and administer the fledgling Bönpo settlement at Dolanji, India.

kartsi: A Tibetan mathematical system derived from Indian astrology used to predict solar and lunar eclipses.

Kashag: A group of advisors to the Dalai Lama comprised of members of the aristocracy and monks from the Lhasa's three main Buddhist monasteries. Although the Dalai Lama was supreme, he relied on the Kashag for advice and depended on it to run the government.

khata: A ceremonial scarf that Tibetans traditionally offer to a lama or drape around one another's necks in greeting, celebration, and blessing.

Khedup Datsun Gyatso: Sangye Tenzin's nephew who accompanied Sangye during his escape and later was instrumental in the administration of the new Bön community founded in Dolanji, India.

Lake Jurutso: Small lake on the Changthang Plateau; Tenzin Namdak lived in a small cave on the edge of the lake for four years, studying under Bön master Gangru Tsultrim Gyaltsan.

Lake Namtso: Tibet's largest lake, near the much smaller Lake Jurutso.

Lhalu: Lhalu Shape, governor of Kham before the Chinese invasion.

Lopon: Title of the head teacher in a Bön monastery. In Bön, the title is interchangeable with *Ponlob.* Most Buddhist sects use *Lopon* to designate a degree similar to a master's degree.

Lopon Sangye Tenzin: Not to be confused with the Sangye Tenzin who became His Holiness and is a central character in this book. Lopon Sangye Tenzin was head teacher at Menri Monastery in Tibet. After his escape and the establishment of a Bön community in India, he once again took on the role of lopon at Menri Monastery in India. He was considered by many to be the greatest Bön scholar of his generation. He died in 1977 at age sixty-seven in Dolanji, India. His savings were used to found the Bön dialectic school at Menri in India.

mala: A string of 108 beads used to count each recited mantra or prayer, similar to a Catholic rosary.

Mao Tse Tung: Chinese Communist Party chairman who ruled the People's Republic of China from 1949 to 1976.

mendrup: A blessing pill made of an assortment of herbs, relics, and other sacred substances.

Menri Monastery: The mother monastery of the Bön religion. The abbot of Menri is the head of Bön. There are two Menri monasteries: the original one in central Tibet, and the one founded in northwest India under Tenzin's guidance. The seat of the Bön religion shifted from Menri Tibet to Menri India to avoid Chinese control.

Menri Trizin: The title given to the abbot of Menri Monastery, meaning "throne holder of medicine mountain."

Mimang: Lhasa resistance organization. It literally translates to "the public," or "the people." Prior to the Chinese invasion, the public—those who were neither aristocrats nor part of the religious hierarchy—were referred to as *miser.* The arrival of the Chinese Communists forced Tibetans to translate the terms "the masses" and "the people." The result was a new word, *mimang,* cobbled together from words meaning "person" and "common." The Chinese used the word in their propaganda, leading anti-Chinese Tibetans to believe that if they co-opted the word it would increase their ability to influence the Chinese to make the changes they sought. Other authors have translated *mimang* as "peoples party," a term we adopted as more accurately describing its use.

Mount Kailash: A mountain in western Tibet, the most sacred mountain in the Bön religion and the prime pilgrimage location for Bönpos as well as Buddhists, Jains, and Hindus.

Mount Ponse: The mountain overlooking Lake Jurutso, where Bön master Gangru Tsultrim Gyaltsan lived in a cave. The lake and mountain form a sacred dyad, or union, the mountain the patriarch and the lake his consort.

Nangzhig Dawa Gyaltsen: The great Bön master whose life was depicted on the walls of Yungdrungling Monastery.

Narendradeva: The exiled king of Nepal granted refuge in seventh-century Tibet; he used Nepalese artisans to build the Jokhang, Tibet's first Buddhist temple.

Ngabo Jigme Norbu: A member of the ruling Kashag who, as governor of Kham, made a series of blunders that hastened the collapse of Tibetan defenses during the Chinese invasion. He also signed, without the consent of the Dalai Lama, the infamous seventeen-point agreement on May 23, 1951, that capitulated to Chinese demands after the invasion. He aligned his interests with those of the Chinese.

Ngawang Lobsang Gyatso: The "Great Fifth" Dalai Lama (1617–1682), who studied Bön and recognized it as an official Tibetan religion.

Norbulingka: The summer residence of the Dalai Lama.

Nyame Kudam: A fragile, tattered, six-hundred-year-old silk cloth worn by Nyame Sherab Gyaltsen, the founder and first abbot of Menri.

Nyame Kundung: A six-hundred-year-old reliquary containing the bones and ashes remaining from the cremation of Nyame Sherab Gyaltsen, the founder and first abbot of Menri.

omze: A monastery chant leader.

Palchenpo: Sangye Tenzin's brother and father of Khedup Datsun Gyatso. Palchenpo fought with the Tibetan resistance and left his son, Khedup, with Sangye at Drepung Monastery.

Panchen Lama: The Panchen Lama is the head of the Tashilhunpo Monastery in Shigatse and is the second highest leader after the Dalai Lama in the Gelug school of Tibetan Buddhism. The Panchen Lama controversy is complicated. It is traditional in Tibetan Buddhism that the incarnation of the Panchen Lama is recognized by the Dalai Lama, and vice versa. When the Ninth Panchen Lama died in 1937, there were two candidates for the office, and the Dalai Lama's choice was disregarded in favor of a boy selected by the Panchen Lama's office, who was later recognized by the Chinese government. This set up a rivalry with the office of the Dalai Lama. Later, after the Communist Party came to power in China, the Panchen Lama defected to the Communists, but they imprisoned him in 1964 for his criticism of Chinese abuses, and he died in 1989 at the age of fifty-one. His successor was chosen by the Communist Chinese government and has not been recognized by the Fourteenth Dalai Lama, who chose a boy who was "disappeared" by the Communists.

pecha: A stack of oblong pages of religious text wrapped in silk and bound with a silk ribbon.

Ponlob: Title of the head of instruction at a monastery. In Bön, the title is interchangeable with *Lopon*.

Potala: The thousand-room winter residence of the Dalai Lama that overlooks Lhasa from the Red Hill.

puja: A religious ceremony of gratitude and purification involving prayer and meditation, and usually small offerings such as bits of food, smoke, or water.

ragyabpa: A Tibetan caste considered low because they were consigned to tasks forbidden to other Tibetans, such as dismembering bodies for sky burial and butchering animals.

Sezhig: A small Bön monastery on the Changthang Plateau.

Shakyamuni: The founder of Buddhism, also known as the Buddha, or Siddhartha Gautama.

shappe: A lay minister of the Tibetan government's ruling Kashag. In theory, the Dalai Lama is supreme, but he relies on the Kashag to carry out day-to-day government business.

Sherab Lodrö: The thirty-second abbot of Menri who was Tenzin's assistant before being chosen abbot; he accompanied Tenzin on his initial escape attempt.

Sherab Tsultrim: Tenzin's assistant who accompanied Tenzin during his escape and played an important part in organizing the Bön settlement at Dolanji.

sky burial: The Tibetan burial practice of dismembering bodies and leaving them on mountaintops to be devoured by vultures.

Soko Karmay: Brother of Samten Karmay who fled Lhasa with Samten and escaped with him and his mother to Nepal.

Songtsen: A seventh-century Tibetan king who allowed Buddhism to become a court religion and whose conquests greatly expanded Tibetan territory.

stupa: A religious shrine. Large stupas contain halls and rooms, while the smallest measure only a few feet tall.

Talsang Tsultrim: One of Tenzin Namdak's four paternal uncles, a monk who cared for Tenzin following the successive deaths of Tenzin's father and another of Tenzin's uncles.

Tashi Lhakpa Khedrup: A dob-dob, or warrior monk, who participated in the Lhasa rebellion against Chinese occupation, lost a leg in a refugee camp accident, and became an assistant to Tibetologist David Snellgrove.

thamzing: Tibetan for "struggle sessions," thamzings were meetings that Tibetans were forced to attend by Chinese officials that were aimed at shaping public opinion through false accusations, humiliation, and executions.

thanka: Also spelled *thangka, tangka,* or *tanka,* a painting on cotton or silk appliqué, usually depicting a Bön or Buddhist deity, scene, or mandala.

Tokden: A title meaning "realized one," given to monks who have earned the meditation degree by spending three years in meditation, usually at a remote location.

Tonpa Shenrab Miwoche: The founder of Bön.

torma: Ceremonial figures or cakes made of barley flour and dyed, often red and white.

Trisong Detsen: The Tibetan king who made Buddhism the official Tibetan religion in the 780s.

tsampa: Roasted and ground barley, a Tibetan staple food.

Tshering Yangphel: Tenzin Namdak's maternal uncle who instructed him the art of painting.

Wangdu Gyatotsang: Given the nickname "Walt" by CIA trainers who couldn't pronounce Tibetan names, he was the first of six

Tibetans recruited for the initial CIA training course for a special Tibetan covert unit.

yarsa gunbu: The Tibetan name for caterpillar fungus, also known as cordyceps. Yarsa gunbu sprouts mushroomlike from the bodies of caterpillars and is valued for its medicinal properties.

Zhang Zhung: Ancient kingdom on the Changthang Plateau where Bön originated, according to Bön texts; Bön officials and Western scholars disagree on Bön's origin.

Zinmo: Samten and Soko Karmay's mother.

Zopa Gyaltshen Rinpoche: The abbot of Yungdrung Palri Monastery who recognized Tenzin as a prodigy and encouraged him to become a monk.

Acknowledgments

This book would not have been possible without the assistance, advice, and encouragement of dozens of friends, relatives, and professionals. We are most indebted for the close cooperation of the three main characters. Yongdzin Tenzin Namdak Rinpoche warmly and patiently relived memories as he retold the story of his escape and the founding of Menri Monastery in India. Samten Karmay, with his academic insight, spent hours teaching us about life in Tibet before the Chinese invasion. We appreciate his patience with our questions and encouragement throughout the process. We are forever grateful to the late His Holiness Lungtok Tenpai Nyima Rinpoche, who kindly allowed us to tell his story.

We also are indebted to Khenchen Tenpa Yungdrung Rinpoche, Yongdzin's closest associate, who was generous with his time, invaluable in clarifying facts, and always encouraged us. Tenpa Woser met with us on our several trips to Kathmandu and generously shared his story, including charting his escape route. Romila Kapoor graciously answered questions while in Dolanji for the funeral of HH Lungtok Tenpai Nyima. Per Kvaerne gave us valuable information in interviews over coffee at an Estonian cafe. We thank Khedup for graciously meeting us for an interview while we were in New York City.

We are grateful to Tsering Wyangal for giving us the details of his escape and his decades in Dolanji.

Carl Stacey arranged for our interview at his home in Italy with David Snellgrove and permission for use of Snellgrove's photos.

We are grateful for extensive background information gained in interviews with Menri Lopon Trinley Nyima Rinpoche, Geshe Latri Nyima Dakpa Rinpoche, Geshe YongDong Losar Rinpoche, Geshe Chapur Rinpoche, and Chime Tsering Lingtsang, who also helped with information from the Menri Monastery library. Alysia Trombley shared her kora of Mount Kalaish. John Reynolds gave an afternoon at Shenten discussing the history of Bön. Linda and Martin Kitwood opened their home to us in Berkhamsted to see the stupa built by the three monks in their backyard.

Special thanks to Geshe Denma Gyaltsen Rinpoche, resident lama in Houston, who translated Tibetan sources, used his contacts to find information, and was always there to help. Geshe Tenzin Yangton guided us on our first trip to India and Nepal and translated several interviews with Tibetan speakers.

John Bellezza's books informed us on Tibetan geography, archeology, and customs. We recommend them to anyone interested in Tibet. Nick Tichawa designed our beautiful book website.

We want to thank early readers of the book for suggestions that helped make the book better. Sandy Sheehy and Julia Scheeres edited early editions. Jackie's book club gave valuable suggestions. Margaret Canavan read the book repeatedly over several iterations, and Suzanne Peloquin offered detailed edits and suggestions. Bets Anderson, Peggy Baldwin, Lori Del Bono, Terry McNearney, and Dorothy Trevino read with care. Early readers with helpful suggestions also included friends and family: Kaki Burruss, Billy Burruss, Marvine Cole, Ginger Turner, Claudia Listman, Anita Roberts, Lee Roberts, Scott McMartin, Ed Sulzberger, Ani Sherab Wangmo, and Dorothy Matthews.

We thank our agent, Wendy Keller, for having faith in our project. Gratitude to Elizabeth Perry, our editor, for her careful and meticulous editing. We thank acquisitions editor Richard Grossinger for recommending our book to Inner Traditions. We are grateful to the editing and publicity staff at Inner Traditions for their patience and expertise.

We have done our best to bring this exceptional story to life. We are solely responsible for any errors or omissions.

Ki ki so so lha gyal lo!

Notes

All interviews were conducted by the authors.

CHAPTER 1. BEGINNINGS

1. Bellezza, *Dawn of Tibet,* 29.
2. Gyaltsen, *Heart Drops,* 147.
3. Norbu, *Warriors of Tibet,* 11–33.
4. Ramble, *Life of a Great Bonpo Master,* 45.
5. Norbu, "In Defence."
6. Khenpo Tenpa Yungdrung interview, Oct. 19, 2010.
7. Ramble, *Life of a Great Bonpo Master,* 64.
8. Samten Karmay email Aug. 10, 2020.
9. Dakpa, *Opening the Door,* 24.
10. Namdak and Denma, *Ponse Lame,* dedication page.
11. Khenpo Tenpa Yungdrung interview, Oct. 19, 2010.

CHAPTER 2. AN ARTIST BECOMES A MONK

1. Khenpo Tenpa Yungdrung interview, Oct. 5, 2013.
2. Ramble, *Life of a Great Bonpo Master,* 65.
3. Ramble, *Life of a Great Bonpo Master,* 65.
4. Ramble, *Life of a Great Bonpo Master,* 72–74.
5. Ramble, *Life of a Great Bonpo Master,* 81.
6. Goldstein, *History of Modern Tibet, Vol. 1,* 22.

CHAPTER 3.
FOUR YEARS IN A CAVE

1. Khenpo Tenpa Yungdrung interview, Oct. 5, 2013.
2. Ramble, *Life of a Great Bonpo Master,* 92.
3. Khenpo Tenpa Yungdrung interview, Oct. 19, 2019.
4. Ramble, *Life of a Great Bonpo Master,* 102.
5. Khenpo Tenpa Yungdrung interview, Oct. 5, 2013.

CHAPTER 4. INVASION

1. "Robert Ford: Radio Operator."
2. Ford, *Captured in Tibet,* 9–13.
3. Ford, *Captured in Tibet,* 58.
4. Goldstein, *History of Modern Tibet, Vol. I,* 638–97.
5. Dunham, *Buddha's Warriors,* 56–57.
6. Ford, *Captured in Tibet,* 98.
7. Ford, *Captured in Tibet,* 105.
8. Morell, "China's Hengduan Mountains."
9. Goldstein, *History of Modern Tibet, Vol. I,* 690.
10. Goldstein, *History of Modern Tibet, Vol. I,* 697.
11. Ford, *Captured in Tibet*, 138–39.
12. Goldstein, *History of Modern Tibet, Vol. I,* 697.

CHAPTER 5.
RECLUSE NATION

1. Goldstein, *History of Modern Tibet, Vol. I,* 542.
2. Goldstein, *History of Modern Tibet, Vol. I,* 89–103.
3. Goldstein, *History of Modern Tibet, Vol. I,* 199–212.

CHAPTER 6. BEST FRIENDS

1. Dhondup and Diemberger, "Last Mongol Queen," 200.
2. Samten Karmay interview, July 8, 2012.
3. Sangye Tenzin interview, March 20, 2012.

CHAPTER 7. TIBET'S HARVARD

1. Conboy and Morrison, *CIA's Secret War,* 26.
2. Samten Karmay interview, July 10, 2012.
3. Barber, *From the Land,* 20–21.

CHAPTER 8. BROKEN PROMISES

1. Ramble, *Life of a Great Bonpo Master,* 115.
2. United Nations, *International Commission.*
3. United Nations, *International Commission.*
4. United Nations, *International Commission.*
5. United Nations, *International Commission.*
6. McCarthy, *Tears of the Lotus,* 122.
7. McCarthy, *Tears of the Lotus,* 122.
8. Sperling, "Matter of Mass Death."
9. United Nations, *International Commission.*
10. United Nations, *International Commission.*
11. United Nations, *International Commission.*
12. Conboy and Morrison, *CIA's Secret War,* 26.
13. Knaus, *Orphans of the Cold War,* 129.
14. John Vincent Bellezza, unpublished journal entry, Aug. 24, 1993.

CHAPTER 9. IRON HELL

1. For further information on the Battle of Lhasa, see Goldstein, *A History of Modern Tibet, Vol. 4* (2019); Khedrup, *Adventures of a Tibetan Fighting Monk* (1998); Li and Wilf, *Tibet in Agony* (2016); Dunham, *Buddha's Warriors* (2004); Barber, *From the Land of Lost Content* (1970).
2. Khedrup, *Adventures of a Tibetan Fighting Monk,* 81–82, 87–89.
3. Khedrup, *Adventures of a Tibetan Fighting Monk,* 89.
4. Dunham, *Buddha's Warriors*, 278–79.
5. Dunham, *Buddha's Warriors*, 274–75.
6. Dunham, *Buddha's Warriors*, 284–85.
7. Dunham, *Buddha's Warriors,* 280. Li, *Tibet in Agony,* 157 (has the date as March 14).
8. Dalai Lama, *My Land and My People,* 155.

9. Barber, *From the Land,* 101.
10. Goldstein, *History of Modern Tibet, Vol. 4,* 446–47.
11. Dunham, *Buddha's Warriors,* 295.
12. Khedrup, *Adventures of a Tibetan Fighting Monk,* 87–98.

CHAPTER 10. FLIGHT

1. Samten Karmay interview, July 7, 2012.
2. Samten Karmay interview, July 7, 2012.
3. Dunham, *Buddha's Warriors,* 298.
4. Samten Karmay interview, July 21, 2012.

CHAPTER 11. FORSAKEN VOWS

1. Tenpa Woser interview, translated by Geshe Tenzin Yangton, March 25, 2012.
2. Tenpa Woser interview, March 25, 2012.
3. Tenpa Woser interview, March 25, 2012.
4. Tenpa Woser interview, March 25, 2012.
5. Tenpa Woser interview, March 25, 2012.

CHAPTER 12. ENTER THE CIA

1. For further information, see Conboy and Morrison, *The CIA's Secret War in Tibet* (2002); Dunham, *Buddha's Warriors,* (2004); Goldstein, *A History of Modern Tibet, Vol. 4* (2019); Knaus, *Orphans of the Cold War* (1999); McCarthy, *Tears of the Lotus* (1997); McGranahan, *Arrested Histories* (2010).
2. Yongdzin Tenzin Namdak Rinpoche interview, March 25–26, 2012.
3. Tenpa Woser interview, translated by Geshe Tenzin Yangton, March 25, 2012.
4. Yongdzin Tenzin Namdak Rinpoche interview, March 25–26, 2012
5. Thondup and Thurston, *Noodle Maker of Kalimpong,* 69–70.
6. Thondup and Thurston, *Noodle Maker of Kalimpong,* 76.
7. Thondup and Thurston, *Noodle Maker of Kalimpong,* 167–69.
8. Knaus, *Orphans of the Cold War,* 319.

9. Dalai Lama, *Freedom in Exile,* 122, 192.
10. Conboy and Morrison, *CIA's Secret War,* 37–38.
11. Dunham, *Buddha's Warriors,* 205; Conboy and Morrison, *CIA's Secret War,* 55.
12. Goldstein, *History of Modern Tibet, Vol. 4,* 88–92.
13. Conboy and Morrison, *CIA's Secret War,* 55.
14. Dunham, *Buddha's Warriors,* 218, 221; Conboy and Morrison, *CIA's Secret War,* 59.
15. Conboy and Morrison, *CIA's Secret War,* 65.
16. Khenpo Tenpa Yungdrung interview, Oct. 5, 2013.
17. Knaus, *Orphans of the Cold War,* 222–23.
18. Knaus, *Orphans of the Cold War,* 233.
19. Goldstein, *History of Modern Tibet, Vol. 4,* 93.

CHAPTER 13. AMBUSH

1. Yongdzin Tenzin Namdak interview, May 25, 2012.
2. Tenpa Woser interview, translated by Geshe Tenzin Yangton, March 25, 2012.
3. Yongdzin Tenzin Namdak interview, May 25, 2012.
4. Tenpa Woser interview, translated by Geshe Tenzin Yangton, March 26–27, 2012.

CHAPTER 14. PRISONERS

1. Yongdzin Tenzin Namdak interview, July 29, 2015.
2. Yongdzin Tenzin Namdak interview, July 29, 2015.
3. Tenpa Woser interview, translated by Geshe Tenzin Yangton, March 25, 2012, April 14–15, 2013.

CHAPTER 15. TENZIN'S ESCAPE

1. Yongdzin Tenzin Namdak interview, March 25, 2012.
2. Yongdzin Tenzin Namdak interview, March 25, 2012.
3. Yongdzin Tenzin Namdak interview, March 25, 2012.

CHAPTER 16. REFUGEES IN A FOREIGN LAND

1. Samten Karmay interview, July 7, 2012.
2. Bernstorff and von Welk, *Exile as Challenge,* 313.
3. Tsering Wyangal interview, translated by Geshe Tenzin Yangton, March 12, 2012.
4. Samten Karmay interview, July 7, 2012.

CHAPTER 17. SNELLGROVE

1. Snellgrove, *Asian Commitment,* 14–15.
2. Snellgrove, *Asian Commitment,* 16.
3. Snellgrove, *Asian Commitment,* 17.
4. Snellgrove, *Asian Commitment,* 52.
5. Samten Karmay interview, Aug. 4, 2015.
6. Rockefeller Foundation Annual Report, 172.
7. Snellgrove, *Asian Commitment,* 192.
8. Khedrup, *Adventures of a Tibetan Fighting Monk,* 115–116, 129; Snellgrove, *Asian Commitment,* 192–93.
9. Ramble, *Life of a Great Bonpo Master,* 162–63.
10. Snellgrove, *Asian Commitment,*194.
11. Snellgrove, *Asian Commitment,*196.

CHAPTER 18. LONDON

1. Samten Karmay email, Aug. 22, 2023.
2. Ramble, *Life of a Great Bonpo Master,* 172.
3. Snellgrove, *Asian Commitment,* 197.
4. Fox, "E. Gene Smith."
5. Yachin, *Digital Dharma,* 2012 documentary.
6. Ramble, *Life of a Great Bonpo Master,* 168–69.
7. Ramble, *Life of a Great Bonpo Master,* 169–170.
8. Samten Karmay interview, Aug. 4, 2015.
9. David Snellgrove interview, July 26, 2015.
10. Ramble, *Life of a Great Bonpo Master,* 175.

CHAPTER 19. RETURN

1. "Grapevine News Service."
2. "Dalai Lama Still Hopes."
3. Xu, "United States and the Tibet Issue," 1062–77.
4. Sangpo, *Brief History,* 14.
5. Kvaerne, "Introduction," 12.
6. Kvaerne, "Introduction," 12.
7. Per Kvaerne interview, March 15, 2018.
8. Sangpo, *A Brief History,* 1–8.
9. Sangpo, *A Brief History,* 17–20.
10. Romila Kapoor interview, Oct. 2, 2017.

CHAPTER 20. PROMISED LAND

1. Romila Kapoor interview, Oct. 2, 2017.
2. Romila Kapoor interview, Oct. 2, 2017.

EPILOGUE
WHERE THEY ARE NOW

1. Geshe Nyima Dakpa interview, Dec. 9, 2013..
2. Nyima, 2019 untitled lecture.
3. "Robert Ford: Radio Operator."
4. "China Shuts Down."
5. Karmay and Nagano, *Survey of Bonpo Monasteries,* 19–21.
6. Arya, "Tibet, Tibetan Refugees and the Way Ahead."

Bibliography

Allen, Charles. *Duel in the Snows: The True Story of the Younghusband Mission to Lhasa*. London: John Murray Publishers, 2004.

Arya, Tsewang Gyalpo. "Tibet, Tibetan Refugees and the Way Ahead," June 20, 2020. Central Tibetan Administration website, www.tibet.net.

Avedon, John F. *In Exile from the Land of Snows: The First Full Account of the Dalai Lama and Tibet Since the Chinese Conquest*. New York: Alfred A. Knopf, 1984.

Barber, Noel. *From the Land of Lost Content: The Dalai Lama's Fight for Tibet*. Boston: Houghton Mifflin, 1970.

Bellezza, John Vincent. *The Dawn of Tibet: The Ancient Civilization on the Roof of the World*. London: Rowman & Littlefield, 2014.

———. *Divine Dyads: Ancient Civilization in Tibet*. Dharamshala: Library of Tibetan Works and Archives, 1997.

Bernstorff, Dagmar, and Hubertus von Welk, eds. *Exile as Challenge: The Tibetan Diaspora*. Hyderabad, India: Orient Longman Private Limited, 2004.

"China Shuts Down Drongna Monastery in Drier, Arrests Teacher," December 31, 2013, www.phayul.com.

Conboy, Kenneth, and James Morrison. *The CIA's Secret War in Tibet*. Lawrence, University Press of Kansas, 2002.

Craig, Mary. *Tears of Blood: A Cry for Tibet*. Washington, D.C.: Counterpoint, 1999.

Dakpa, Nyima Tenpa. *Opening the Door to Bön*. Ithaca, N.Y.: Snow Lion Publications, 2005.

Dalai Lama. *Freedom in Exile: The Autobiography of the Dalai Lama.* New York: Harper Perennial, 2008.

———. *My Land and My People.* New York: McGraw-Hill, 1962.

"Dalai Lama Still Hopes for Tibet Independence." *Los Angeles Times,* Feb. 15, 1967.

Dhondup, Yangdon, and Heldegard Diemberger. "The Last Mongol Queen of 'Sogpo' (Henan)" *Inner Asia* 4, no. 2 (2002): 197–224.

Dunham, Mikel. *Buddha's Warriors: The Story of the CIA-Backed Tibetan Freedom Fighters, the Chinese Invasion, and the Ultimate Fall of Tibet.* New York: Jeremy P. Tarcher/Penguin, 2004.

Ford, Robert. *Captured in Tibet.* Hong Kong: Oxford University Press, 1990.

Fox, Margalit. "E. Gene Smith, Who Helped Save Tibetan Literary Canon, Dies at 74." *New York Times,* Dec. 28, 2010.

French, Patrick. *Tibet, Tibet: A Personal History of a Lost Land.* New York: Vintage Departures, 2004.

Goldstein, Melvyn C. *A History of Modern Tibet, Volume 1: The Demise of the Lamaist State 1913–1951.* Berkeley and Los Angeles: University of California Press, 1991.

———. *A History of Modern Tibet, Volume 2: The Calm before the Storm 1951–1955.* Berkeley and Los Angeles: University of California Press, 2007.

———. *A History of Modern Tibet, Volume 3: The Storm Clouds Descend 1955–1957.* Berkeley and Los Angeles: University of California Press, 2014.

———. *A History of Modern Tibet, Volume 4: In the Eye of the Storm 1957–1959.* Berkeley and Los Angeles: University of California Press, 2019.

"Grapevine News Service Keeps an Eye on Tibet." *Los Angeles Times,* April 10, 1967.

Green, Jonathan. *Murder in the High Himalaya: Loyalty, Tragedy, and Escape from Tibet.* New York: Public Affairs, 2010.

Grunfeld, A. Tom. *The Making of Modern Tibet.* London and New York: Routledge, 1996.

Gyaltsen, Shardza Tashi, with commentary by Yongdzin Lopon Tenzi Namdak. *Heart Drops of Dharmakaya: Dzogchen Practice of the Bön Tradition.* Ithaca, N.Y.: Snow Lion Publications, 2002.

Gyatso, Janet, and Hanna Havnevik, eds. *Women in Tibet*. New York: Columbia University Press, 2005.

Hay, Jeff, and Frank Chalk, eds. *Tibet: Genocide and Persecution*. Farmington Hills, Mich.: Greenhaven Press, 2014.

Hopkirk, Peter. *Trespassers on the Roof of the World: The Secret Exploration of Tibet*. New York: Kodansha America, 1995.

International Campaign for Tibet. *A Season to Purge: Religious Repression in Tibet*. Washington, D.C.: International Campaign for Tibet, 1996.

Johnson, Tim. *Tragedy in Crimson: How the Dalai Lama Conquered the World but Lost the Battle with China*. New York: Nation Books, 2011.

Karmay, Samten Gyaltsen. *The Great Perfection rDzogs Chen: A Philosophical and Meditative Teaching in Tibetan Buddhism*. Leiden, Netherlands: Brill, 1989.

———. *The Treasury of Good Sayings: A Tibetan History of Bon*. Delhi: Motilal Banarsidass, 2001.

Karmay, Samten Gyaltsen and Yasuhiko Nagano, eds. *A Survey of Bonpo Monasteries and Temples in Tibet and the Himalaya*. Delhi: Saujanya Publications, 2008.

Karmay, Samten Gyaltsen and Jeff Watt, eds. *Bon, the Magic Word: The Indigenous Religion of Tibet*. London: Philip Wilson Publishers, 2007.

Khedrup, Tashi. *Adventures of a Tibetan Fighting Monk*. Bangkok: Orchid Press, 1998.

Khetsun, Tubten, with Matthew Akester, trans. *Memories of Life in Lhasa Under Chinese Rule*. New York: Columbia University Press, 2008.

Knaus, John Kenneth. *Orphans of the Cold War: America and the Tibetan Struggle for Survival*. New York: Public Affairs, 1999.

———. *Beyond Shangri-La: America and Tibet's Move into the Twenty-First Century*. Durham, N.C., and London: Duke University Press, 2012.

Kvaerne, Per. "Introduction." *Journal of the International Association for Bon Research* 1, no. 1 (2013): 11–17.

Laird, Thomas. *Into Tibet: The CIA's First Atomic Spy and His Secret Expedition to Lhasa*. New York: Grove Press, 2002.

Li, Jianglin, with Susan Wilf, trans. *Tibet in Agony: Lhasa 1959*. Cambridge, Mass.: Harvard University Press, 2016.

Mayhew, Bradley, and Robert Kelly. *Lonely Planet Tibet*. Lonely Planet Guide, 9th ed., 2015.

McCarthy, Roger E. *Tears of the Lotus: Accounts of Tibetan Resistance to the Chinese Invasion, 1950–1962*. Jefferson, N.C.: McFarland and Co., 1997.

McGranahan, Carole. *Arrested Histories: Tibet, the CIA, and Memories of a Forgotten War*. Durham, N.C., and London: Duke University Press, 2010.

Morell, Virginia. "China's Hengduan Mountains." *National Geographic,* April 2002.

Namdak Rinpoche, Yongdzin Tenzin, with Geshe Denma, trans. *Ponse Lame Zhel Dam Nying Gi Tek Le*. Kathmandu: Triten Norbutse, 2019.

Norbu, Dawa. *Red Star over Tibet*. Glasgow: William Collins Sons and Co., 1974.

Norbu, Jamyang. *Warriors of Tibet: The Story of Aten and the Khampas' Fight for the Freedom of their Country*. London: Wisdom Publications, 1986.

———. "In Defence and Tibetan Cooking," Feb. 7, 2011. www.jamyangnorbu.com.

Nyima, Trinley. Untitled lecture, Ligmincha Texas Center, Houston, Tx., Oct. 10, 2019, unpublished.

Osada, Yukiyasu, Gavin Allwright, and Atushi Kanamaru. *Mapping the Tibetan World*. Tokyo: Kotan Publishing, 2004.

Pachen, Ani, and Adelaide Donnelley. *Sorrow Mountain: The Journey of a Tibetan Warrior Nun*. New York: Kodansha America, 2000.

Powers, John. *The Buddha Party: How the People's Republic of China Works to Define and Control Tibetan Buddhism*. New York: Oxford University Press, 2016.

Ramble, Charles, ed. *The Life of a Great Bonpo Master: The Biography of Yongdzin Tenzin Namdak Rinpoche*. Chicago: Serindia Publications, 2021.

"Robert Ford: Radio Operator in Tibet Was Jailed by China for Being an 'Imperialist Spy.'" *London Independent,* Oct. 18, 2013. www.independent.co.uk.

Rockefeller Foundation, *1960 Annual Report*. New York.

Sangpo, Jadhur Sonam, with Geshe Denma Gyaltsen, trans. *A Brief History of Tibetan Bönpo Foundation in India*. Dolanji, India: Jadhur Publications, 2015.

Schaller, George B. *Tibet Wild: A Naturalist's Journeys on the Roof of the World*. Washington, D.C.: Island Press, 2012.

Shakya, Tsering. *The Dragon in the Land of Snows: A History of Modern Tibet Since 1947.* New York: Columbia University Press, 1999.

Snellgrove, David. *Asian Commitment: Travels and Studies in the Indian Sub-Continent and South-East Asia.* Bangkok: Orchid Press, 2000.

———. *The Nine Ways of Bon: Excerpts from gZi-brjid.* London: Orchid Press, 2010.

Snellgrove, David and Hugh Richardson. *A Cultural History of Tibet.* New York: Frederick A. Praeger, 1968.

Sperling, Elliot. "The Matter of Mass Death in Tibet: The Body Count." *Tibetan Buddhism in the West: Problems of Adoption and Cross-Cultural Confusion,* Sept. 14, 2012. www.info-buddhism.com.

Thomas, Lowell. *The Silent War in Tibet.* Garden City, New York: Doubleday, 1959.

Thondup, Gyalo, and Anne F. Thurston. *The Noodle Maker of Kalimpong: The Untold Story of My Struggle for Tibet.* New York: Public Affairs, 2015.

Trinley Nyima, Lopon. Untitled lecture, Ligmincha Texas Center, Houston, Tx., Oct. 10, 2019, unpublished.

Tsarong, Dundul Namgyal. *In the Service of His Country: The Biography of Dasang Damdul Tsarong, Commander General of Tibet.* Ithaca, N.Y.: Snow Lion Publications, 2000.

Tsukphu, Menyag Geshe Namdak. *Bön Stupa, Illustrations and Explanations.* Solan, India: Tibeto Zhang-Zhung Research Centre, 1998.

Tuttle, Gray, and Kurtis R. Schaeffer, eds. *The Tibetan History Reader.* New York: Columbia University Press, 2013.

United Nations. *Tibet and the Chinese People's Republic,* A Report to the International Commission of Jurists by its Legal Inquiry Committee on Tibet. Geneva: International Commission of Jurists, 1960.

Van de Wijer, Birgit. *Tibet's Forgotten Heroes: The Story of Tibet's Armed Resistance against China.* Stroud, Gloucestershire: Amberley Publishing, 2010.

Van Schaik, Sam. *Tibet: A History.* New Haven, Conn.: Yale University Press, 2011.

Wilson, E. H. *A Naturalist in Western China.* London: Cadogan Books, 1986.

Xu, Guangqiu. "The United States and the Tibet Issue." *Asian Survey* 37, no. 11 (1997): 1062–77.

Yachin, Dafna. *Digital Dharma: One Man's Mission to Save a Culture.* Documentary. Lunchbox Productions, 2012.

Yungdrung, Tri, and Kalsang Nor Gurung, trans. *A Short History of His Holiness the 33rd Abbot of Menri, Lungtok Tenpei Nyima Rinpoche.* Dolanji, India: Yungdrung Bön, 2017.

Index

BOOKS OF RELATED INTEREST

The Lone Ranger and Tonto Meet Buddha
Masks, Meditation, and Improvised Play to Induce Liberated States
by Peter Coyote

Zen in the Vernacular
Things As It Is
by Peter Coyote

Riding the Spirit Bus
My Journey from Satsang with Ram Dass to Lama Foundation and Dances of Universal Peace
by Ahad Cobb

When Shadow Meets the Bodhisattva
The Challenging Transformation of a Modern Guru
by Andrew Cohen

Immortality and Reincarnation
Wisdom from the Forbidden Journey
by Alexandra David-Neel

Instructions for Spiritual Living
by Paul Brunton

The Hundred Remedies of the Tao
Spiritual Wisdom for Interesting Times
by Gregory Ripley

Psychedelic Refugee
The League for Spiritual Discovery, the 1960s Cultural Revolution, and 23 Years on the Run
by Rosemary Woodruff Leary

INNER TRADITIONS • BEAR & COMPANY
P.O. Box 388
Rochester, VT 05767
1-800-246-8648
www.InnerTraditions.com